Educating the U.S. Army

T. R. BRERETON

Educating the U.S. Army

ARTHUR L. WAGNER AND REFORM,
1875–1905

University of Nebraska Press
Lincoln and London

Portions of chapter 5 were previously published as "First Lessons in Modern War: Arthur Wagner, the 1898 Santiago Campaign, and U.S. Army Lesson-Learning," *Journal of Military History* 64 (January 2000).

Library of Congress Cataloging-in-Publication Data
Brereton, T. R. (Todd R.), 1954–
Educating the U.S. Army: Arthur L. Wagner and reform, 1875–1905 / T. R. Brereton.
p. cm.
Includes bibliographical references and index.
ISBN 0-8032-1301-8 (cl.: alk. paper)
1. Wagner, Arthur L. (Arthur Lockwood), 1853–1905. 2. Generals—United States—
Biography. 3. Military education—United States—History—19th century. 4. Military
education—United States—History—20th century. 5. United States. Army—Officers—
Training of. I. Title.
U53.W24B74   2000
3555'.0071'073—dc21
[B]
99-047299

For my Mother and Father,
who encouraged me,
and
For Jodi.

CONTENTS

ILLUSTRATIONS

Following page 76
Arthur Lockwood Wagner, age fifteen
Wagner prior to his graduation from West Point
Wagner as second lieutenant, Sixth Infantry, Fort Buford
Staff of Brigadier General Henry W. Lawton
    during the Santiago Campaign
Colonel Arthur L. Wagner, Third Division General Staff
Posthumous portrait of Wagner

Acknowledgments

No work of history is the effort of a single person, and in the lengthy preparation of this book I have been fortunate to have the kind and generous help of many people. My research at the National Archives was simplified and aided by Michael D. Myers, DeAnne Blanton, and Mitch Yockelson of the Military Reference Branch. All good-naturedly attended to my many questions and requests. Their intimate familiarity with the records under their care is astonishing, and they are all a credit to the National Archives. Liz Snoke, of the Combined Arms Research Library at the U.S. Command and General Staff College, provided me with numerous copies of official records from the Infantry and Cavalry School and guided me to materials I did not know existed. Captain Thomas T. Smith, a former colleague at Texas A&M University, generously agreed to conduct research on my behalf into Arthur Wagner's days at West Point. Others who aided me along the way with advice and relevant information include Edward M. Coffman, James L. Abrahamson, Timothy Nenninger, and Robert Wooster. I could not have completed this book without their unselfish assistance.

I am especially grateful to two of Wagner's grandsons, Leet and William Shields, and their wives, both named Betty. Leet's wife provided me with many interesting and valuable anecdotes about her husband's grandfather; they are good friends and have been unswervingly devoted to my pursuit of Arthur Wagner's family history. I wish them the best of health. Bill's wife was responsible for discovering a hitherto unknown journal written in Wagner's hand during the early days of his career. It is the only sizable corpus of Wagner material outside the National Archives and is, at present, still in the hands of the Shields family. Bill and Betty sent the journal to me, with some trepidation, and afforded me a rare and wonderful opportunity few historians enjoy—to be the first researcher to view previously unknown material. Another Wagner descendent, Colonel (Ret.) Dwight L. Adams, provided me with addresses of family members, took an active interest in my research, and has encouraged me all along the way.

Members of my own family and several very generous friends provided their own special support during my frequent research trips to

Washington DC; my cousin Ellen Bachman and her family, and Bill Chapman of the Falls Church Sheriff's Department, were particularly helpful. My former spouse, M. J. Helms, put up good-naturedly with Arthur Wagner for many years, eventually calling him the "other man" in her life. Although we are no longer married, I wish to thank her with utmost sincerity for her support and patience during my project.

Finally, I must extend my thanks to the members of my graduate dissertation committee, who guided the writing of the manuscript upon which this book is based: Professors Joseph G. Dawson III, Arnold P. Krammer, my good friend and mentor Frank E. Vandiver, and Pamela R. Matthews. All were helpful and sensitive in their criticisms and are in large part responsible for its present form. I thank them from the bottom of my heart.

Introduction

Arthur Lockwood Wagner was one of the best known and most influential U.S. Army officers of his day, his name easily as familiar to his peers as that of any of the army's commanding generals. Although he had graduated near the bottom of his West Point class in 1875, he nonetheless commanded the attention of his fellow officers without ever having set foot on the field of battle. Dozens of lieutenants and captains passed under his purview, and if an officer had not actually met Arthur Wagner, it was very likely that he had read one of Wagner's many books and articles.

Undoubtedly the army's premier intellectual and educator during the late Gilded Age and early Progressive years, Wagner directed or assisted in some of the most critical reforms in army history. He was instrumental in transforming the newly created Infantry and Cavalry School at Fort Leavenworth from a place derisively called "the kindergarten" into the army's foremost institution for the tactical training of officers. He tirelessly campaigned for enacting advanced military education, adopting modern combat tactics, holding large-scale maneuvers, and developing a new doctrine of combined arms combat. Moreover, he was an early proponent of the General Staff and the Army War College. By the time of his death in 1905, Wagner's army had been transformed. Although by no means an untroubled service, it had left far behind the days when its forces were scattered in isolated garrisons across the West, when an educated officer was looked upon with derisive amusement, and when its methods of war making seemed a throwback to another era. That these changes took place at all was due, in fair measure, to the work of a slight, sickly, goateed, and bespectacled writer who had once been expelled from West Point.

Wagner was a peculiarity in his day. An unapologetic intellectual, he made his military reputation on that quality alone, despite criticism that his unorthodox talents made him an "impractical" sort of officer.[1] Wagner saw clearly the army's need to discard old ideas, abandon its frontier mentality and obsession with Civil War glories, and adopt a new professional ethic based on rigorous education and training. He took the place of the brilliant Emory Upton, going far beyond his predecessor in the application of military modernization, so much so that by 1898 he was universally regarded as the army's chief spokesman on matters of tactics and doctrine. That he is not better known to present-day military historians is because he died at the height of the army's transition from one era to another and because he did not leave a corpus of personal papers upon his death.[2]

While Wagner's intellect might not have been quite as dazzling as Emory Upton's, he was no plodder. His superiors regularly characterized him as "indefatigable," "reliable, capable and excellent," and "in a class almost by himself." It was Wagner, not Upton, who prepared the basic operational foundation upon which the army would build its twentieth-century strategic edifice. Wagner might best be described as a generalist who had the capacity to understand, explain, and apply new ideas to an extent that his peers did not. What he lacked in original thought he made up for in exhaustive research and irrefutable argument on tactical and educational matters. Wagner was not so much interested in the "why" as the "how," which was best demonstrated in his persistent ideal to make his work applicable to that world in which the army had to be its most proficient: the battlefield. He was most adept at interpreting and then applying new ideas and methods of warfare, and his aptitude in this regard was his ability to grasp their core principles and apply them to American practice. Through Wagner, military theory was turned into doctrine. At a time when some officers were arguing for a socially redeeming mission for the army—strike breaking or universal military service—Wagner insisted instead that its chief responsibility was to fight war. To that end, he busied himself with the problems of attack and defense in a dangerously technological age, while prodding the army to hasten its acquisition of the modern tools and tactics of war. Throughout, Wagner was keenly aware of the increasing need to establish a tradition of professional military leadership based on continual and sustained academic study.

Making his case provoked a collision with the entrenched belief among older officers that nothing was to be gained from an academic study of war. This view held that educated soldiers were incapable of understanding the art of war because experience could not be learned. Army anti-intellectualism had a long tradition, even in Wagner's day. Despite the prestige accorded a West Point education, for many officers it was merely a formality. Rare was the officer who actually studied his profession, and the more thoughtful among them were ridiculed as eggheads or bookworms. Prior to the Civil War, for example, Henry Halleck's scholarly pursuits earned him the contemptuous nickname "Old Brains." Once commissioned, graduates of West Point quickly learned that high academic standing was no guarantee of advancement, nor a matter of much consequence. The frequency with which West Point mediocrities like Ulysses S. Grant or George Armstrong Custer rose to prominent command clearly demonstrated that determination, personal bravery, and luck had far more to do with advancement than did academic achievement. With examples like these, the tacit argument was made that natural ability, not intellectual prowess, was the guidon for promotion.

When reformers, beginning with William T. Sherman, began pressing for postgraduate officer education, reactionaries responded with the argument that only men with genius—an artistic, innate talent for war—were able to comprehend and apply the principles of strategy and command.[3] Wagner vehemently dismissed what he considered a dangerous, foolish opinion. "It would be interesting, but hardly profitable," he wrote, "to speculate upon the probable condition of the art of war if every commander had to learn the art from his own experience."[4] Combat had become too complex and hazardous to resort to a trial-and-error approach of military leadership. Talent was necessary in war, but undisciplined talent was unpredictable. Safety and good judgment were equally necessary, and Wagner insisted that learning from the examples of past successes and failures was a better, less costly means of achieving an understanding of war. In the long run, Wagner had the better argument. As one of his colleagues at the Infantry and Cavalry School wrote, because of Wagner "the army became [his] students at once, and [his] books became as familiar as the drill books."[5]

As an educator Wagner's influence was most profound. His talents as a teacher and writer established the credibility of postgraduate military education in the army, a field in which his contemporaries deemed him a pioneer, at the Infantry and Cavalry School at Fort Leavenworth, Kansas. Using innovative techniques like staff rides, map exercises, and small-unit war games, students at the school were introduced to the principles of staff duty and combat leadership, neither of which was much understood before Wagner appeared. Wagner himself designed much of the curriculum used at Leavenworth, and wrote the school's two principal texts, *The Service of Security and Information* and *Organization and Tactics*, which combined military history, tactical theory, and directions for the conduct of battle into a systematic whole. These books served as the basis for army postgraduate education until 1910, were read by hundreds of officers, and in some ways revamped the way the army conducted the business of war. In addition, Wagner produced numerous other books and dozens articles and reviews, through which he advanced his ideas on military policy and organization, tactical modernization, the conduct of American and European campaigns, the challenge of combat against new military technologies, and the manner in which the U.S. Army should prepare its officers for war. Wagner's military expertise in these matters was the result of his comprehensive familiarity with a wide body of literature on the operational art of war, both American and European. That knowledge enabled him to extend to his students the most recent advances in military doctrine and theory, helped them understand their responsibilities before, during, and after combat, and put them early to the practice of continual study of their profession. It also enabled him to validate, through his work at the Infantry and Cavalry School and in his writing, the army's first step toward twentieth-century warfare, the 1891 *Infantry Drill Regulations*. Having assisted in their design, Wagner promoted and explained the tactical principles expounded therein and helped establish them as accepted military doctrine. The manner in which he accomplished this task, moreover, qualifies Wagner as an early American disciple of the Prussian strategist Carl von Clausewitz, and to a large extent he provided the army with an operational system that followed Clausewitzian principles long before the army "discovered" *On War* in the 1920s. More than any other individual officer of his day, Wagner reinforced and confirmed the offensive ideal of Ulysses S. Grant and backed up his conclusions with appropriate examples from European and American military history.

The focus of Wagner's literary and instructional attainments was practicality. As a historian (and an excellent one, at that), Wagner pursued a utilitarian view of the past. History was a tool to be used in the present; it was a guide for avoiding past errors. To that end, Wagner sought to demonstrate in books, articles, and lectures the "lessons" of history. He was the first American military writer to excavate methodically the histories of wars past for such lessons. (Emory Upton had done something similar in *The Military Policy of the United States*, but he had a rather narrow political axe to grind.) Rather than simply say "history proves," Wagner isolated specific examples to demonstrate a particular successful or failed tactic and then expounded upon its significance. He did not, however, resort to turning history into dogma—that is, "always do this, never do that." Context mattered. Outcomes in battle were situational and based on contingencies, facts that Wagner went to some length to ensure were understood. The broad lesson he sought to instill in his readers and students was that success in battle depended on a commander's common sense, preparation, and flexibility. Wagner saw it as his role to make the transition from academics to actual practice less bewildering and more predictable.

To that end, Wagner's zeal as an educator was to create a balanced system of instruction that cultivated an officer's understanding of the artistic side of war—the elements of leadership and command—but also the increasingly rational, technical qualities of war. In promoting that goal, he became one of the army's first "new" military educators, as opposed to the "old" type, who argued that only war could teach war and that the principles of command were innate and unteachable. For Wagner, awaiting the appearance of a military genius to save the nation in an emergency was not only absurd but a stupid waste of military resources. Wagner knew that most officers were not prodigies, and that many were only mediocre, but that it was the likes of these who would eventually lead men into battle. Because of his own knowledge of the art of war, Wagner was well aware that the combat of his day was becoming more complex and deadly. The army could ill afford the old school's wait-and-see attitude toward command. Realizing that, Wagner was intent on providing the army's officers with at least the rudiments of modern warfare, combined with practical applications of certain functions and principles, in the belief that forewarned was forearmed. This would reduce the prospect of military disasters at the hands of incompetents, since prior schooling would winnow out the bad while improving the abilities of the good. The truly qualified, meanwhile, would rise in rank and responsibility and thus ensure the formation of a cadre of what Carol Reardon calls "safe" senior officers on whom the army could confidently rely in the moment of truth.[6]

Considering his persistent focus on education, and his desire to increase the army's military effectiveness and efficiency, Wagner's actions and attitudes define him squarely as a reforming professional typical of the early Progressive Era. His entire career exemplifies the military Progressive ideal, even though he did not share the social agenda of civilian reformers. Wagner's was not a mission to improve society, but by pursuing reforms designed to advance his own service, he hoped to benefit society in the long run. Despite his separate agenda, Wagner, like other reform-oriented officers, shared a number significant characteristics with civilian progressives, particularly in his expression of professionalism.

Just as civilian professionals pursued specialized education, certification, discrete knowledge, and status, Wagner followed and advocated a similar course by engaging in many of the same professionalizing activities as his civilian counterparts, particularly those in the sciences or social sciences. He belonged to several military service organizations designed to promote the interests of his profession; he read and published in refereed journals that provided a forum for new ideas and a means of keeping up with military developments at home and abroad; he played a central role in the development of postgraduate education that turned out officers "certified" in their specialty. Allan Millett notes that progressive officers "sought professional status and worked assiduously to justify their occupation as a skill-oriented, theoretically based, socially useful, and culturally unique career."[7] Military reforms of the late nineteenth and early twentieth centuries were pursued, in part, to affirm and fortify the army's increasingly professional temper. For Wagner, the surest road to professionalism was formal, applied education and continual study. Only in this way could the army cultivate and maintain its reputation as an expert institution deserving national respect. In his insistence, moreover, on an officer corps rigorously trained in its craft, Wagner's own agenda suggests a professionalism linked to social-oriented progressive reforms: well-trained officers could be trusted not only to execute their duties in wartime in the most effective manner; they could also be trusted not to waste the lives of American soldiers needlessly, as a military amateur might. While army reforms might not directly change American society for the better, they certainly had the welfare of the general public as a broad objective. Wagner himself may thus be considered a progressive because he extolled the burgeoning ethic of modern professionalism and sought reform as a means of producing a more socially responsible armed force. In so doing, the army would regain the respect it had lost in the years following the Civil War.[8]

Wagner's advocacy of tactical modernization, officer education, practical training, and responsible command came at a time when the army, under the impetus of a small group of visionary reformers, abandoned the parochialism and limitations under which it labored during the Gilded Age and assumed a new twentieth-century identity that stressed a rational managerial philosophy. It did not come easily, for the army to which Wagner belonged was uncomfortably poised on the cusp of two eras. Its senior leadership looked back with longing to the heady days of the Civil War, when fame and rank came easily. Now in advancing years, colonels and generals seemed more intent on pursuing personal vendettas born of the war and writing memoirs that defended their achievements. A few, like William T. Sherman and Wesley Merritt, understood and embraced the need for change; but others, perhaps most notably personified by Nelson A. Miles, resisted and even feared it. Junior officers, denied promotion by the shriveled postwar officer corps, chafed under the restrictions of the seniority system and sought an outlet for their own stunted ambitions. These "young Turks," as Peter Karsten calls them, turned to the issue of reform, intent on rehabilitating the army's declining reputation and perhaps, along the way, creating new avenues for advancement. Their efforts resulted in the proliferation of service journals and societies, through which reformers trumpeted their pet projects, railed at incompetent civilian leadership, decried the deterioration of civic virtue, warned of the dangers of immigration and socialism, and suggested ways the army might intervene to turn the nation away from internal decay. In general, causes like these mirrored similar worries among civilians, but most young Turks were more interested in rejuvenating the army's military spirit and bringing the service up to the quality of the armies of Germany and France. Wagner was among these. Moreover, because of his high literary profile and his growing stature as an educator, he was more successful than most in actually getting his reforms implemented.

Just as Wagner's career spanned the army's transition from old to new, Wagner himself was an officer of both camps. He was not above pursuing petty jealousies like his superiors, and he was equally anxious about rank and personal honor. He revered the military experience of the Civil War and emphasized the lessons to be learned from it. Yet he also sought to break into a new era that promised for the army both challenges and rewards. Wagner did more than just advocate change; he acted, resolute in his belief that the army could only benefit from that change. In calling for a knowledgeable, disciplined, and dependable officer corps, Wagner put the army on the road to maturity and genuine professional status. Because he did not live long enough to see his ambitions for the army come to fruition, Wagner remains a transitional figure who provided the army with the means to grasp successfully the full meaning and application of twentieth-century warfare, rather than one who actually directed its achievement. As a result, he is not as well remembered as those who came after him, like John Pershing, Robert Bullard, or James MacAulay Palmer.

Military history is often centered around the lives of "great captains" whose achievements overshadow the mundane but important work of lesser mortals who made those achievements possible in the first place. Wagner was among the latter, yet his influence is just as enduring. Largely because of him, postgraduate military education and constant study became professional requirements; field maneuvers and war games became the chief vehicles for military readiness; new tactics were adopted and perfected to meet a new age of warfare; and performance in battle became the manner by which the army revised and promulgated doctrine. Through Arthur Wagner's single-minded vision for a new breed of officers, he taught them, and the whole army, not so much what to learn but how to learn.

Educating the U.S. Army

Chapter 1

A Mind Which Matured Slowly

On the evening of 15 June 1875, according to a West Point tradition, cadets of the class of 1876 gave the graduating class of 1875 a farewell ball. Most of the cadets took part in the festivities that night; but one absentee, under arrest for a disciplinary infraction and resentful at being forbidden to attend the dance, decided to have a celebration of his own in his quarters. A small but noisy party ensued and liquor was plentiful, the host happily consuming more than his share. Before long the event drew the attention of the tactical officer, Lieutenant John F. Stritch, who knocked on the cadet's door, entered silently, then walked through the room with reproving eyes. The revelers fell quiet except the host. Drunk, loquacious, and nervous, he followed the lieutenant about, saying, "Mr. Stritch, I am glad to have the call. We are having a little party, you see. If anything is wrong, I hope you will mention it." Stritch said nothing and ignored him. He knew the cadet well. The young man seemed always to be in some kind of trouble: he was frequently under arrest, had accumulated hundreds of demerits, and had even been suspended during his plebe year for lying to a superior officer. For this latest offense Stritch could easily dismiss the cadet from the academy. Buckets of beer were in full view, and Stritch had only to ask the cadet to walk a straight line. But it was, after all, the night before graduation. Circling the room, eyeing each cadet in turn, Stritch arrived at the door and walked out, leaving the cadet and his guests more sober than when he had arrived. Nothing came of the incident. The troublesome cadet received his diploma with his colleagues the next day, 16 June 1875, fortieth of forty-three in his class.[1]

From this unlikely beginning Arthur Lockwood Wagner, aged twenty-two, embarked on a career that would establish him as one of the most influential officers of his day. Wagner was born in the northern Illinois town of Ottawa on 16 March 1853. His father, a surveyor and Civil War veteran, died when Wagner was thirteen, leaving a wife, two sons, and three daughters practically destitute. To help support his family, Wagner sold newspapers in the streets of his home town. At seventeen, Wagner was taken to the home of Illinois Congressman Benjamin C. Cook by family friend William Thomas, who asked

Cook to give the young man an appointment at the United States Military Academy. Cook obliged, and Wagner was admitted to West Point on 1 July 1870. Wagner was one of the youngest members in his class, and it showed. Unaccustomed to the stringent discipline required of cadets, he was suspended in December for lying about his whereabouts to the officer of the day. He was allowed to return in July the next year, but he had to start again as a plebe.[2]

Although a year older upon his return, Wagner did not seem to be any wiser. Classmates remembered that his "fun-loving nature" frequently got him into trouble, and he accumulated demerits at an astonishing rate. By June 1875, he had amassed no fewer than 731 of them. The bulk of his infractions were minor and typical of most cadets, but others—like "neglecting to comply with instructions to clean his musket," or submitting a report "containing disrespectful and irrelevant matter"—were met by confinement to quarters, "light prison," and punishment marches. As noted, he was even under arrest at the time of his graduation. A classmate reflected that Wagner had "a mind which matured slowly," and his academic progress was sluggish. His marks were well below average in all subjects except French and drawing. Mostly, he was just not a serious student. The story is told that Wagner was asked to draw a bridge in a civil engineering class. He complied, sketching in a river with a small boy fishing on its bank. His professor admonished him and told him to draw the bridge again. Wagner did so, but drew a tombstone where the boy had stood.[3]

Wagner's only genuine interest at West Point was writing. He edited and wrote for two cadet tabloids, one called the "Weekly Spyglass" and the other, the newsletter of the cadet Dialectic Society, called the *Dialectic Howitzer*. Both were little more than gossip and humor columns, for which Wagner collected jokes and trivia. One of his memorable contributions to the *Dialectic Howitzer* was titled "The Leaning Tent Pole, or the Bald-Headed Maniac's Revenge: The History of a Skin." A classmate thought it was one of the funniest things he had ever read, being a satirical account of Wagner's ordeal at the hands of a captain "for not having his tent pole in alignment on Sunday morning in camp." The "Weekly Spyglass" was Wagner's creation alone. Only one copy of each number, in Wagner's elegant handwriting, was distributed. Each issue circulated from student to student, was widely appreciated, and offered, as one cadet recalled, "much amusement."[4]

Wagner's subsequent career displayed none of the frivolity that marked his days at West Point, although he never lost his sense of humor. He became a serious scholar, an eloquent spokesman for reform, even a workaholic, which killed him in the end. But then Wagner was never a robustly healthy man. Throughout his career he suffered from migraines, chronic indigestion, exhaustion, and nervous depression. He frequently applied for medical leaves, which sometimes lasted for months, and on occasion his health deteriorated so markedly that he had to have others read for him. A superior officer noted in an 1895 efficiency report that Wagner was destined to "achieve distinction," but only "if his health lasts." The officer also noted that Wagner had "a quick temper," a trait that was talked about years later by his descendants. Wagner was easily offended by any slight, real or imagined, to his reputation or character and rose instantly to his own defense. On these occasions he typically responded with biting sarcasm or the self-righteousness of the maligned.[5]

Throughout his career Wagner openly aired his disputes with others, subjecting his detractors to subtle or sometimes outright insults regarding their intelligence or ability. Even near the end of his life, and at the height of his career, he complained that he yet had adversaries who were thwarting his advancement toward high rank. In all of these contests Wagner tended to view himself as the intellectual superior of his peers. His published works were often sermonizing and condescending to those who disagreed with him, and he had no patience for obtuseness or hidebound rigidity.

A case in point took place during his assignment at the Infantry and Cavalry School at Fort Leavenworth in early 1892. Wagner, suffering from a cold, sought the aid of Dr. Charles Richard, assistant surgeon at the military prison, following a meeting at which both were in attendance. Dr. Richard refused to treat Wagner, explaining that he was not assigned to the post, and that doing so would violate professional courtesy. Wagner sought medical attention elsewhere, but the doctor had upset his sense of propriety. Pen in hand, Wagner devised a lengthy report to the adjutant general, complaining that Dr. Richard was motivated by a "monstrous conception of professional courtesy," and wondered what might happen to that soldier who needed prompt attention but could not find the appropriate physician. Wagner asked the adjutant general to require all army doctors to examine any supplicant to determine the seriousness of his illness and treat him if he needed immediate care.[6]

As Wagner's complaint went through military channels, Dr. Richard was given the opportunity to respond, and he stated that Wagner's

illness was not serious enough to require his attention. Wagner thereupon wrote another letter to the adjutant general, inquiring how Dr.
Richard could have known his illness was not serious, not having examined him. There followed an itemized list of twelve questions Wagner wanted the doctor to answer regarding how he had arrived at his di-
agnosis. Having sent this letter on its way, Wagner continued to stew
about the situation and wrote yet another to the adjutant general,
claiming that Dr. Richard's response was "both irrelevant and mislead-
ing," and suggested that the doctor's idea of professional courtesy
could have been extended even if "I had been 'sick unto death.'" While
he claimed a reluctance to make much ado about a simple "personal
controversy," Wagner's actions suggest that he thought much more
was at stake than a matter of army medical care. In Wagner's view, he
was right and Dr. Richard wrong; it was a question of personal honor,
and Wagner would not be denied. He demanded that the doctor be officially reprimanded as "evidence that a commissioned officer of the line
has a right to expect courteous and humane treatment from his more favored brethren of the Medical Corps."[7]

Wagner was ultimately unsuccessful. The medical director of the
Department of Missouri denied his request with a severe rebuke that
Wagner chose not to challenge.

As temperamental personalities sometimes are, Wagner was a su-
premely ambitious officer. He craved recognition. Soon after he
reached the rank of captain, he began campaigning for promotion to
major in the inspector general's or adjutant general's department. He
did not particularly care which, as long as he got the promotion. Wagner lobbied friends, former commanders, politicians and peers, collecting testimonials and recommendations like so many postage stamps.
He even had the record of his military career professionally printed,
with choice excerpts from the most laudatory of his endorsements, and
sent it to the promotion board. After Wagner became a full colonel, he
pulled every string he could to get promoted to brigadier general. He
collected two dozen separate endorsements from general officers alone,
including such contemporary luminaries as Nelson A. Miles, Adna R.
Chaffee, Arthur MacArthur, Wesley Merritt, J. Franklin Bell, and
Tasker H. Bliss. Endorsements from politicians, national guardsmen,
and influential private citizens (even his father-in-law, a well-connected
Pittsburgh businessman) equaled those he solicited from army men.
Wagner was not much different from other officers where his desire for
promotion was concerned, but he was certainly more systematic and

energetic about it than most. Everywhere he went, whatever his assignment, Wagner made a concerted effort to curry favor with anyone who might help his career. Considering that he rose through the ranks from captain to brigadier general in a brief thirteen years, his efforts obviously paid off.[8]

Wagner's graduation from West Point was followed by an assignment to Company G of the Sixth Infantry Regiment at Fort Buford, in what was then the Dakota Territory. Fort Buford was no garden spot; the *Army and Navy Journal* once described the country there as "exceedingly barren," its climate severe, and the landscape ruled by fierce northern winds. The regiment's commander, Major General William B. Hazen, considered an assignment to Fort Buford as "banishment" and the post itself "generally out of the world." Since only top-ranked West Point graduates were permitted to choose their first assignments, Wagner's low standing was undoubtedly responsible for his own exile to Fort Buford.[9]

Wagner's duties at the post were varied and routine, and typical of assignments given to a junior lieutenant. At one time or another he inspected rations, led parties in search of deserters, sat on courts martial, and one winter supervised a fatigue detail that cut and stored ice from the nearby Missouri River. Although Wagner participated in the fateful 1876 Centennial Campaign that cost George A. Custer his life, he was not involved in any of the actual fighting. In late August, Hazen relieved Company G's first lieutenant, leaving Wagner in charge. Wagner was then detailed to assist in the riverine supply of Brigadier General Alfred H. Terry's column from Fort Buford down the Yellowstone River to Glendive Creek. On a number of occasions he accompanied the escort or inspected the stores of a small flotilla of river boats navigating up and down the Glendive, including the steamer *Far West*. During this assignment, Terry detailed Wagner to serve as topographical officer to the supply train of Nelson A. Miles's eastward march to the Powder River. Wagner recalled the difficulties of the march, crossing "swollen streams" and "'bottomless' alkali flats." Wagner performed these tasks admirably. His reward was a transfer to Company E, Sixth Infantry, where he commanded the artillery attached Terry's headquarters until the end of the Sioux campaign.[10]

In September and October, Wagner was reassigned to his own company and again assisted the convoy of supplies from Fort Buford to Glendive Creek. In November his company traveled with General Hazen in the Sixth Infantry's pursuit of the Sioux under Long Dog, from Glendive Creek to Fort Peck, Montana Territory. Between August and December, during the Nez Percé campaign of 1877, Wagner commanded a detachment assigned to General Miles that guarded a supply depot on the Yellowstone. The conclusion of this campaign ended Wagner's involvement in the Indian wars for several years. In the fall of 1878 he oversaw the construction of a telegraph line between Fort Stevenson and White Earth River, in Dakota Territory. Upon the line's completion, in October 1878, Wagner moved to Fort Abraham Lincoln, where he remained until June 1880, when the Sixth Infantry was transferred to White River, Colorado.[11]

The move was precipitated by the Milk Creek Massacre, in which the Uncompahgre Utes attacked an army cavalry detachment and killed a number of white civilians at the White River Agency in western Colorado. Wagner was assigned to the tribe's forced resettlement to the Uintah Reservation in Utah. Wagner then moved to Fort Lyon, Colorado, until May 1881, when trouble with the Utes flared again. The Sixth Infantry was then under the command of Major General Ranald S. Mackenzie, who replaced General Hazen in December 1880. When a recalcitrant band of Utes refused to move from the Los Piños Agency in southwestern Colorado to the Uintah Reservation, Wagner's company was among those that formed a battalion under Captain Hamilton S. Hawkins detailed to force them onto the reservation. Confident in Wagner's abilities, Mackenzie placed him in command of the advance guard on the Gunnison River, where he prepared a ferry crossing in anticipation of the battalion's passage. During this operation Hawkins, too, found Wagner to be a capable officer, and entrusted him with the command of a supply depot on the Gunnison. As the last of the Utes moved to the Uintah Reservation, the battalion followed them via a circuitous route through Cheyenne, Wyoming, finally stopping at the confluence of the Green and Little Snake rivers in the northeastern corner of Utah. Here Wagner assisted in the construction of Fort Thornburgh, where he remained until late November 1881.[12]

Despite Wagner's reputable service in the West, during which Hawkins remarked that the lieutenant had made "no retrograde step," Wagner had tired of frontier duty. As early as January 1880 he was looking for a reassignment. He wrote to his friend and hometown advocate William Thomas, asking for some judicious lobbying on his behalf. Thomas agreed and wrote to U.S. Senator John A. Logan of Illinois, who recommended to the adjutant general that Wagner be assigned to detached service as an instructor of military science at the Illinois Industrial College in Champaign. Despite the fact that Logan was a well-known enemy of army professionalism, and an arch-antagonist of West Point, he seemed happy to perform this favor for Wagner. Logan was informed that the school already had an officer serving in that capacity, and his request was denied. When Logan heard, in March, that the instructor had resigned, he repeated his request, which was again denied. During the operations against the Utes Wagner had no time to seek a transfer, but when they were over he redoubled his efforts. In November 1881, Thomas again asked Logan that his friend be assigned somewhere as a college instructor. This time Logan was successful. A position was open at Louisiana State University, and Wagner got it. Logan's success no doubt impressed upon the young lieutenant the value of influential friends in high places, as his future campaigns for promotion would demonstrate.[13]

The appointment of officers to colleges and universities was no more unusual in Wagner's time than in the twentieth century. As a practical measure, these placements allowed officers who disliked or were unfit for field duty to stay in the army, while creating vacancies within the line. Thirty officers were allowed by law to serve at various colleges nationwide, and the number of instructors per state was determined by the population within the army's military departments. Wagner arrived in Baton Rouge on 19 December 1881, and no sooner had he done so than circumstances conspired to stymie his plans. Louisiana and Mississippi were normally allowed one officer each. Both positions were already filled, but since Florida, which was also allowed one officer and had a vacancy, had not requested an instructor, Adjutant General R. C. Drum decided to give to Louisiana Florida's allotment. While Wagner was en route to Baton Rouge, Florida unexpectedly applied to fill its vacancy, and Drum immediately revoked Wagner's assignment to Louisiana State University. Luckily for Wagner, Drum invited him to take an assignment at East Florida Seminary in Gainesville (today the University of Florida), which had applied for an army instructor. LSU's president, having found Wagner "satisfactory," implored Drum to change his mind, but to no avail, and Wagner arrived in Gainesville on 12 January 1882.[14]

Wagner's assignment at East Florida Seminary lasted three years. During this time he was promoted to first lieutenant and, on 5 September 1883, he married Annie B. Howard, daughter of the president of a Pittsburgh glass manufacturing company. He enjoyed teaching, and it lit a spark in him. Charged with teaching the military history of the

United States, Wagner began to think seriously about the nation's military policy. When, in 1884, the Military Service Institution of the United States announced a prize for the best article on the military necessities of the United States, Wagner put his talent as a writer to work. In so doing, he revealed a hitherto unknown capacity for scholarly research, and it established the temper of his career.

The article that emerged, "The Military Necessities of the United States, and the Best Provisions for Meeting Them," won the Institution's first gold medal and was published in the September 1884 issue of the *Journal of the Military Service Institution*. Among his fifty-five endnotes (the use of which was still rare even by professional historians of the day) were frequent references to Emory Upton's earlier *The Armies of Asia and Europe*, and to a fair extent Wagner repeated Upton's arguments for U.S. Army reform. That he did so has prompted Russell F. Weigley to characterize "Military Necessities" as "familiarly Uptonian." But while Wagner's article was Uptonian in spirit, it was not so much so in fact. Upton's call for reform was motivated by his anger that the United States, a burgeoning economic colossus, had a military establishment that was embarrassingly puny compared to that of England, France, or Germany. Upton appealed for an enlarged army despite his admission that America had few, if any, enemies that could threaten its security. His subsequent invective about civilian military leadership, in *The Military Policy of the United States*, was an indication that he prized militarism above democracy.[15]

Wagner's article was Uptonian to the degree that he expressed alarm over America's military unpreparedness. Like Upton, he dismissed the effectiveness of volunteers, and he embraced the desirability of postgraduate military education. But unlike his utopian predecessor, Wagner was motivated by what could practically be done to strengthen the nation's military establishment, without condemning its anti-military political heritage. Much of Wagner's argument was based on his perception of genuine military threats to American security, rather than advocating reform simply to keep up with more advanced European armies. Given American military unreadiness, and the tendency for modern wars to "arise quickly," Wagner feared that an armed confrontation with a foreign power would lead to a disaster. The condition of the navy and American seacoast fortifications particularly worried him; the obsolescence of both seemed predicated on the chimerical idea "that we were separated from all belligerent nations by an impassable sea of fire." It would be a simple thing, he suggested, for *any* naval power—

even Chile, which had a larger navy than that of the United States—to wreak havoc along the American coast, disrupt commercial shipping, and sink any ship the navy cared to send out. Although Wagner admitted that America was not in any immediate danger, he added that "in its present unprepared state, it is not clear that any effective resistance could be made, at first, to the attacks of any enemy." For those who argued that war with a foreign country was unlikely, Wagner suggested that enforcement of the Monroe Doctrine might easily lead to war with Mexico, England, or Spain over commercial interests south of the U.S. border, over a future isthmian canal, unrest in Cuba, or "a thousand unforeseen causes." Convinced that the navy "would soon be annihilated by [a] powerful antagonist," Wagner advocated a construction program to arm the fleet with modern, armored, steam-powered vessels. To protect harbors and inland waterways, he advanced ideas being proposed by army engineers that were later adopted by the Endicott Board.[16]

The army was not in such dire straits, and Wagner realized that not even the most powerful foreign army could manage an invasion of the American interior, much less land on its shores. If, however, the United States ever found itself embroiled in war against a foreign adversary, particularly Mexico, England, or Spain, Wagner advised that the army be able to launch immediately its own counterinvasion of Canada, Cuba, or Mexico. An army of one hundred thousand soldiers, he figured, formed mostly of volunteers from the civilian militia, would be sufficient for the task. Where Emory Upton refused to countenance the militia, Wagner understood that the American suspicion of standing armies made reliance on the militia an absolute necessity, and he thus disagreed with Upton's advocacy of conscription. The problem with the militia (in Wagner's day, the National Guard) was not, as Upton argued, that it was inherently incompetent. True, there were certain guardsmen who considered their service as little more than a costume ball; but the central obstacle was the guard's "wretched organization and the lack of a proper system of instruction." In a perfect world, the National Guard would be controlled by the War Department, but the Constitution forbade that. Wagner's solution was the formation of a civilian National Reserve that would complement, not replace, the National Guard. In all respects the reserve would be identical to the guard, except that its members would enlist for a specified period of time, could be called into overseas service, and would be answerable to the army, not the states. In order to stay within constitutional restraints,

Wagner advised that reserve units should be formed, regulated, and trained by the states, adding that the regular army should equip them on a par with its own soldiers and that it should determine the nature and amount of training applied. He even suggested that reserve officers be allowed to attend the Infantry and Cavalry School at Fort Leavenworth. By noting the restrictions imposed upon the army by the Constitution, Wagner demonstrated even at this early stage of his career a sensitivity for ideas that worked, rather than a romantic vision of how things ought to be. This pragmatic spirit would become the hallmark of Wagner's scholarly bent.[17]

In order that the army be capable of executing offensive military operations, Wagner promoted several simple reforms. Chief among them was better education, within and outside the army. Arguing that the "highest function" of the army was to "constitute a school for officers and a model for the State troops," Wagner was appalled by the presence of officers "who could hardly hold the rank of sergeant" in a European army. He suggested that officers be examined for promotion and that enlisted men be thoroughly trained in combat duties and techniques. With the observation that the nation's defense rested, in the end, on its citizens, Wagner advocated a "uniform course of military instruction" at those colleges, like East Florida Seminary, that offered courses in military science—a far less drastic proposition than Upton's appeal for universal military service. Wagner was sufficiently Uptonian, though, to conclude "Military Necessities" by remarking that "the indifference of the American people in regard to the condition of the national defenses is utterly incomprehensible." Vigilance was key, and in an era of increasingly destructive armaments and potentially aggressive enemies, the nation's citizens could no longer afford to be complacent.

Wagner was by no means alone in these sentiments. At the time, the army had many champions for reform, and through the 1880s and 1890s the army's principal forum, the *Journal of the Military Service Institution*, was filled with articles by reform-minded "young Turks" advocating a wide range of improvements. The need for better tactics, an end to promotion by seniority, and more humane and generous treatment of enlisted men were prominent among the suggested improvements, but most reforms tended to be advanced toward the army's post-Indian fighting mission. An increasing number of articles advocated a new, socially acceptable mission for the army, perhaps predicated on the desire to deflect criticism of the army's Indian-killing role in the West. The advent of violent labor unrest in 1877, and its steady increase thereafter, seemed to many officers to be a saving grace. The frequency with which a succession of presidents called on the army to put down labor strikes, and the inefficiency of the National Guard in dealing with them, offered a perfect opportunity for the army to perform a valuable civic duty, to uphold traditional national values, and to perpetuate its own existence. Wagner, initially, agreed with this idea, noting in "Military Necessities" that "all thinking men and good citizens" would clearly see the benefit of such a policy.[18]

Two years later, however, he recanted his position and remarked that it was "pernicious" to regard the army "merely as a national police force." Other reformers, seeking to discourage the conditions that led to labor unrest, believed that adopting universal military service would enable the army to serve as a "school" for immigrant assimilation, teaching the principles of good citizenship and correct social behavior. Wagner dismissed these ideas and rejected even the idea of new missions. He asserted instead that the army's fundamental role was to wage war. The solid core of "Military Necessities" was an exposition on the necessity for the army to prepare better for that role. Nothing else, in Wagner's mind, was more important than this, and his entire military career was devoted to that single principle.[19]

Soon after "Military Necessities" appeared in print, Wagner's detail at East Florida Seminary expired. The school's director, Edwin P. Cater, requested in March 1885 that Wagner's appointment be extended for another three-year term, noting that the lieutenant's performance had been "highly satisfactory" and attended with "zeal and energy." Failing in this, Cater went to Florida Congressman Wilkinson Cull with the same request; Cull thereupon went to Secretary of War William C. Endicott. Even Endicott could not secure the extension, although he did get a special order allowing Wagner to complete the academic year at the school. Wagner was officially relieved of duty on 1 July and was ordered to return to the Sixth Infantry, then stationed at Fort Douglas, Utah.[20]

Despondent at the prospect of remaining on the frontier for an unknown duration, a year later Wagner applied for a twelve-month leave of absence. He had been offered employment in his father-in-law's firm, the Phoenix Glass Company, and he wanted to try his hand at business before making a final decision about leaving the army permanently. His request never even made it to the adjutant general's office. Major General Philip H. Sheridan instantly disapproved it and Wagner was stuck. Still unwilling to accept the permanence of this outcome,

Wagner appealed to the regiment's new commanding officer, Colonel Alexander McCook, for relief. By a happy coincidence, in May 1886, the Sixth Infantry had been transferred to Fort Leavenworth, Kansas, and McCook assumed command of the Infantry and Cavalry School there, which had been established five years earlier. Only the regimental headquarters and two companies were stationed at the post, but Wagner wasted no time in requesting the obvious solution to his plight. In September he wrote to McCook about the possibility of obtaining a teaching position at the school. With competent instructors at a premium, McCook willingly obliged. Noting that Wagner was "especially well-fitted" to instruct students in the art of war, "a subject for which he has a special liking," McCook requested that Wagner be transferred to the school immediately. Sheridan disapproved this, too. Through some bureaucratic sleight of hand, McCook simply transferred Wagner to one of the companies already at Fort Leavenworth, then surreptitiously placed him on the school's faculty. Safe at last from the hardships of frontier service, Wagner was again in an element he had grown to enjoy and for which he had already demonstrated an affinity. It was the turning point of his career.[21]

Chapter 2

The Kindergarten

The institution to which Wagner now belonged, and at which he would make his mark in the army, had been formed by commanding general William T. Sherman in 1881. Although the Civil War hero did not see a war with a foreign nation on the horizon, he thought it wise to be prepared for one. Not wishing to repeat the Union's costly search for inspired leadership, Sherman wanted a cadre of officers ready for high command, trained in strategy and the combined combat methodology of infantry, cavalry, and artillery. To ensure that all officers were similarly grounded in current tactics and strategy, Sherman ordered that they be detailed to the school in rotation, "so that in time the whole Army will thus be enabled to keep up with the rapid progress and practice of war."[1]

The method by which he planned to achieve that end was inadequate, even contradictory, to his goal. Sherman cautiously advised that the school's course of instruction emphasize practical work in basic field duties and remedial education in reading, writing, and mathematics—things he believed "every young gentleman should be presumed to know." Trailing Sherman's list of priorities was "the 'science and practice of war,' so far as they can be learned from books." Despite his professed goal for the school, he encouraged none of the prerequisites of high command and limited its student body to first and second lieutenants. As he envisioned it, course work would be divided between two classes, one basic and the other advanced. The student body was to comprise one lieutenant from each infantry and cavalry regiment, chosen by their respective commanders (artillerists went to their own school at Fort Monroe). The first class, consisting of officers with previous education and experience, would concentrate on such subjects as surveying, reconnaissance, fortifications, international and military law, and the "Lessons of War as taught by the great masters." The second, more remedial class would be charged with "correct reading aloud," handwriting, basic grammar and arithmetic, geometry, trigonometry, and history. Students who successfully completed this introductory course graduated to the other course. To assist both classes in practical work, four companies of infantry, four troops of cavalry, and a battery of artillery would be permanently stationed at the school to enable each student "to show himself proficient in the company and battalion drills of the arm of the service to which he belongs." Typical of Sherman's phobia of things political was his wish that the school not become "the subject of legislation." Unlike West Point, he wanted it to remain independent of congressional supervision; otherwise, he feared, "it will be made political and taken out of our control."[2]

Wagner's arrival at the school came at the height of a crisis in its mission and amidst growing criticism of its curriculum. Its first years of operation had not been hopeful. The school began classes in January 1882 under the direction of Colonel Elwell S. Otis. Almost instantly he encountered problems that plagued the school for some time. Although student officers were taking courses, the manner and content of instruction had not been determined, which meant there was no genuine objective other than Sherman's original broad design. Even the content for examinations was not resolved. A committee appointed to draft a curriculum and official regulations attempted to settle these problems, but the adjutant general rejected its proposal as "too advanced and complex." Sherman himself called the suggested curriculum "onerous," and he issued a special order that temporarily prescribed instruction. Otis, concerned that even this was not as comprehensive as he preferred, admitted that it was suitable enough for what he called the "average intelligence" of the first group of students. As for the overall concept of the Infantry and Cavalry School, Otis found it nearly impossible for officers of the three arms to cooperate without considerable conflict. He blamed this difficulty on the "antagonistic opinions" they entertained about one another, and his attempts to ameliorate their divisions were "attended with constant labor." Problems with instructors were equally bad. None was especially qualified for his post, particularly since Otis could only select instructors from the Fort Leavenworth garrison. Most were evidently mediocre at best, for Otis ended up assigning several of the students to teach. In addition to these problems, the school had no buildings of its own, classes were overcrowded, and the buildings that Otis did have were destroyed at midterm in a fire. Instructors had few tools with which to teach, and Otis could not increase the school's sparse funding. He complained that the library "existed only in name" and that money was not available to purchase books. All the same, Otis believed that success would eventually attend the school, and he was pleased to note that despite disappointments, the first students applied themselves with "zeal" and "industry."[3]

A year later, however, little had improved. Otis yet complained of "inconveniences and obstacles" to the efficient operation of the school, ranging from inadequate quarters and class buildings to a continued shortage of library books. Official regulations and an academic curriculum had still not been approved, and the dearth of qualified instructors forced Otis to continue levying students from the first class for that purpose. He tried to put the best face on this last matter, suggesting that it was proof that the school's "course of study, unaccompanied by outside or unusual requirements, is not difficult to master." But while Otis believed that the school's modest academic requirements were an advantage, a gathering crowd of critics declared that they were not. In November 1883 the first class openly complained that "the apparent theories on which this school was founded are false in principle and are bold contradictions of each other," adding that the ill-defined curriculum was so basic as to prepare students for little more than employment as "mere drill masters." Among the school's "glaring defects" was the use of outdated textbooks, a failure to acquaint students with modern methods in tactics and logistics, and the use of junior officers to teach other junior officers. Wagner himself, then in Gainesville, joined the chorus, although he believed a deeper problem lay at the heart of the school's deficiencies. Its academic requirements and objectives, he wrote, were "a mortifying comment on the [school] . . . that it should be necessary to teach arithmetic and 'correct reading aloud.'" Wagner was equally angry at the caliber of students at Leavenworth, adding that "worse than the necessity for teaching such studies is the fact that there are in the army . . . officers who have been found deficient in the second-class course . . . and have thus shown that they lack either the ability or the industry necessary to master studies with which a school boy should be familiar." For the Infantry and Cavalry School to succeed, and for the army to have competent officers, both would have to obtain and cultivate "worthy men" with substantial "intellectual acquirements."[4]

Lieutenant Colonel Henry M. Lazelle, commandant of cadets at West Point, was even more disappointed. In a lengthy editorial for the *Army and Navy Journal*, he suggested that "if the object of this school is to provide young 2d lieutenants with an education merely in subjects belonging to general knowledge, then its present name . . . ought to be changed to that of 'The Army English High School,' or some similar name, which would convey an idea of its course of study." Noting that the Infantry and Cavalry School was created to "impart a high professional knowledge, so advantageous that West Point graduates should be sent there," Lazelle accused the school of harboring "a general sentiment . . . bordering on indifference" to its charter. Like Wagner, Lazelle believed that only the "most carefully selected . . . most meritorious, intelligent, and . . . best fitted" officers should be sent to the school. Regarding the school's aimless curriculum, he offered a simple solution: "Nothing should be studied [that is] not useful in actual war, and . . . both theoretical and practical instruction [should] conform, as far as possible, to the modern methods of war." The school staff did not take Lazelle's criticisms graciously, and anonymous defenders, in two separate replies in the *Army and Navy Journal*, accused him of "half-concealed sarcasm" and petulantly suggested that by complaining he would "lose many friends."[5]

Several years would pass before the Infantry and Cavalry School could confidently declare that its problems and shortcomings were behind it, and between 1882 and 1888 the school labored under the derisive but appropriate nickname of the "Kindergarten." The most intractable problem was a parade of consistently inferior student officers arriving at the school. In February 1884 Otis was forced to remind new students that they were obliged to study, attend classes, appear in them promptly, obey and respect their instructors, and behave in and out of class like officers. Since Otis had no control over which officers regimental commanders sent to the school, complaints about the merits of its students went unanswered, and Otis did not disagree with them. Among the students at the school, he noted, were "artful dodgers" whose sole aim at Leavenworth was to avoid instruction. He added that some commanders were sending him their troublemakers and shirkers. Once they were there, the worst he could do to them was fail them. Colonel Charles King, the well-known author of popular army fiction, observed that such a student "could pitch his books into the fire, and face his examiners with the serene consciousness that, do their worst, they could only send him back to his regiment." Yet even King should have known that the school as it was constituted at the time did not draw much respect. To expect regimental commanders to send their better officers to a school of questionable repute was unreasonable, and until Leavenworth proved itself, inferior students would continue to be sent there.[6]

Colonel Thomas H. Ruger replaced Colonel Otis in June 1885. He spent only a year as commandant, and little improved during his brief tenure. While the library at last saw real growth, its collection growing to thirteen hundred volumes, student performance actually declined. Of nineteen lieutenants in the second class that year, ten failed. Like Otis, Ruger tried to make the best of an unhappy situation, suggesting that the failures would have a "salutary" effect on future students who might be disinclined to study. By the time Ruger left the school, in May 1886, there was still no approved curriculum or general regulations for the operation of the Infantry and Cavalry School.[7]

The arrival of Alexander McCook, with Wagner in tow, marked a new beginning for the school. McCook immediately took charge and plotted a new course to salvage the poor reputation the school had acquired. The first thing he did was to request from students, faculty, and staff their recommendations for improving the course of study, although he made no immediate changes in the ad hoc curriculum then in use. During the summer McCook overhauled and greatly expanded the curriculum, initiating the new one in September 1887. New regulations were drafted and implemented in March the next year. Remedial classes were eliminated and the two-track system of instruction was abandoned. In its place McCook instituted a single two-year course that expanded in subject and scope the former first-year course and emphasized attention to the tactics of combined arms, which, McCook declared, would be "thoroughly taught." McCook insisted that only lieutenants with "application and aptitude" be sent to the school and required that any without a West Point or other college diploma take an entrance examination first. Finally, McCook was determined to give students hands-on, practical experience in their military duties. To that end, he used the companies attached to the school to instruct students in such mundane but necessary field duties as outpost, advanced guard, convoy escort, and rear guard. Lieutenants were expected to learn everything about company operations and were introduced to the particulars of field service in infantry, cavalry, and artillery. A strict disciplinarian, McCook was especially insistent that his students work hard, and the schedule of classes reflected his demand. Classes were conducted six days a week from 11:00 A.M. to 3:00 P.M. and on Saturdays until 5:00 P.M. Mornings were dedicated to practical exercises. Instructors were expected to apply themselves appropriately. To reward diligent study and to inject a spirit of competition, McCook requested that the six highest-scoring graduates of the two-year course be referred to the adjutant general for preferential assignments.[8]

McCook's reforms won acclaim. In 1888 Colonel Charles King declared that "the 'Kindergarten' is no more." Whereas the Leavenworth school was formerly a laughing stock, he wrote, it had now reached a state where its graduates commanded respect and were preferred for promotion. Wesley Merritt, commanding the Department of the Missouri, thought that future Leavenworth graduates would easily display a "professional proficiency as high as any occupied by young officers of any army." But certainly more important than these necessary improvements was the complete overhaul of the school curriculum. Classes were organized under ten separate departments: military art, infantry, cavalry, artillery, law, engineering, military hygiene, surveying and administration, and English studies. The latter three were dropped in 1890, as was the Department of Artillery in 1891, when the Leavenworth battery moved to nearby Fort Riley. With a comprehensive and integrated curriculum finally in place, McCook was confident that with proper support the Infantry and Cavalry School would rapidly assume the character of "a valuable war college."[9]

Indeed, a war college was precisely what McCook had set out to create, and it was within the Department of Military Art, to which Wagner was assigned, that his purpose began to take shape. Here Wagner's career blossomed and grew, and he produced his best work. (Wagner might well have been chagrined to find, as company commander of one of the school garrisons, his West Point nemesis John F. Stritch.) The Department of Military Art, chaired by Major Jacob Kline, offered classes and exercises in military policy and institutions, strategy, tactics, "operations of a mixed character," military geography, military administration, and the "didactic study of campaigns and battles" (essentially, military history). Military policy and institutions dealt with the function, form, and comparison of American and foreign armies. The course in strategy had a distinctly Jominian flavor, concentrating on such topics as strategic lines and points, lines of operations and maneuver, marches of concentration, and so on, while lessons in tactics were subdivided into sections concentrating on the organization of modern armies, grand tactics, minor tactics, and reconnaissance. "Operations of a mixed character" was simply a grandiose term for miscellaneous: the course covered such topics as "crossing streams and rivers, retreats and pursuits, bivouacs, and camp security." Military geography concentrated on the topography of the United States, Canada, Mexico, Cuba, and Central America. Classes on military administration generally explained the Byzantine staff system of the American army. The last part, "didactic study of campaigns and battles," blended military history with practical applications to present circumstances of lessons learned from past wars. The faculty also expected students to undertake an independent research project, the object of which was to illuminate "the path which alone leads to veritable military instruction—the study of and meditation upon the campaigns of the great masters." The essays produced were read publicly and critiqued by both instructors and students.[10]

A month after Wagner arrived at Fort Leavenworth, he published his second article, "The Military and Naval Policy of the United States," in the *Journal of the Military Service Institution*. Still in an Uptonian mode, Wagner followed up his prize-winning work of 1884 with a format and thesis nearly identical to Emory Upton's *Military Policy of the United States*. The title alone suggests that Wagner had read Upton's unpublished manuscript, which had been passed from hand to hand in manuscript form since 1881. Wagner agreed with Upton that the civil leaders of the United States were, for the most part, incompetent to provide for the nation's security. America's military policy, if it could be called that, was marked by "a parsimonious and inadequate provision . . . for the necessities of war; an injudicious reliance upon raw troops; and a mischievous intermeddling [*sic*] by civil officials with the conduct of military operations." These things occurred, he added, with "amazing pertinacity." There then followed, à la Upton, a historical record of the American civil-military relationship in wartime, from the Revolution through the Civil War.[11]

Wagner identified himself closely enough with Upton's *Military Policy* that he condemned, as Upton had done, Abraham Lincoln's "intolerable interference" in military affairs during the Civil War and upheld George McClellan as a good soldier done in by "epauletted politicians." Having said this, however, Wagner again proceeded to diverge from Upton's fundamental military philosophy. While not especially hopeful for the future ("the American people seem to be waiting for the rude shock of national disaster to dispel their illusions of security"), he repudiated Upton's pessimism about the civil-military relationship, especially where civilian control was concerned. Upton, according to one of his critics, "failed to acknowledge that military policy must reflect the general policy of a nation and . . . reflect [its] general spirit." As an admirer of Prussia's military system who believed much of it should be adopted by the United States, Upton did not recognize that Prussia, a modern Sparta with predatory designs, existed only through its army.

Americans, however, would never tolerate such overt militarism in peacetime, and in their periodic seizures of militant expansionism, they expected the army to go away when their passion was spent. Wagner did understand this, and while he shared much of Upton's military idealism, he also argued for a level and manner of readiness that did not threaten America's egalitarian, anti-military traditions. As he had shown in "Military Necessities," Wagner demonstrated a growing realism in his perspective, preferring to advance ideas that were likely to work. In this respect he was probably a more practical and careful thinker than Emory Upton.[12]

For Wagner, Americans' fear of standing armies and the tradition of civilian control, while perplexing and even onerous to military men, was something officers would do well to accept. Whereas Upton had upheld the army as a paragon of patriotic virtue, and protested loudly against the perversity of civilian control, Wagner realized that however much the army chafed under these conditions, neither was going to change. There was nothing the army could do about it, and complaining was fruitless: "Our military future will not be shaped by theories based upon military principles alone. The military policy of the United States will be strongly affected by the popular predilection for economical expenditures in time of peace; by a jealousy of large standing armies; by a reliance upon volunteers in time of war; and by a more or less active influence of popular opinion in the direction of armies in the field." Rather than bemoan this situation, Wagner suggested, the army would do well to accept it and go about the unromantic but no less important task of educating the public about its own immediate needs and the security needs of the nation. It is worth noting that at no time did Wagner, as Upton had done, argue for military control of America's military policy. Despite his Uptonian leanings, Wagner may be described as such only in his view of military policy as it affected the army, not in how it affected the nation, and clearly he shared several of Upton's opinions in regard to effects on the army. But Wagner also recognized the shortcomings of this myopic view and attempted to adjust it to the broader needs of the country.[13]

The general content of Wagner's "Military and Naval Policy" suggests the reasons why McCook was so eager to place the lieutenant on the Leavenworth faculty. Wagner demonstrated two traits McCook needed in his instructors, especially among those in the Department of Military Art: a spirit of pragmatism and a single-minded dedication to scholarship. The department was where history, theory, and practice met, and they met especially in the person of Arthur Wagner.

As only one of four instructors in the largest and most wide-ranging department at Leavenworth, Wagner had his hands full as McCook's new curriculum got under way. It did not help that one of the four was recalled by his regiment for field service. During the 1887–88 academic year, Wagner was immersed in his duties as assistant instructor, and he did not fall short of McCook's estimate of his abilities. His responsibilities in the Department of Military Art prompted him to begin thinking seriously about the relationship between military history and the art of war. It was, after all, one thing to use the historical record as a means for confirming a point of view, as he had done in "Military Necessities" and "Military and Naval Policy"; it was quite another to use history as an educational tool in a result-driven institution like the army. Wagner sought a usable history, one with which he could demonstrate how the lessons of past conflicts were applied or ignored in the present and how one or the other could mean victory or defeat. Although armies have always had an inclination toward historical utilitarianism, Wagner was, by far, more interested in the "lessons" of history than was any other officer of his day. In time he would insist that all officers study military history as part of their professional advancement. This concept put Wagner, according to Dennis Vetock, "a half step ahead of his time." The zeal with which he pursued that ideal reinforced McCook's already high opinion of Wagner. Despite previous criticism about the inadvisability of junior officers instructing other junior officers at Leavenworth, Wagner was an obvious exception, and his talent would serve the school well in the future.[14]

After his first year at Leavenworth, Wagner became increasingly concerned that its curriculum emphasized European rather than American military experience, even though the army's tactical guides—Upton's infantry, cavalry, and artillery tactics—were drawn from the experience of the American Civil War. This struck Wagner as perverse, and he was chauvinistic enough to believe that officers of the U.S. Army should take their lessons from their own history. What made this Eurocentrism even more distressing to Wagner was the existence in the army of a clique of Prussophiles who, he observed, were "wont to bestow all possible admiration upon the military operations in recent European wars, not because they were excellent, but because they were European." The potential result, Wagner feared, was that the army was in danger of forgetting its own heritage.[15]

Wanting to affirm the validity of American lessons of war, and to distinguish them from the European ones, Wagner applied in February 1888 for six months' leave to travel to Europe. This time Sheridan approved. Wagner's aim was to study the recent Austro-Prussian campaign of 1866 and the Franco-Prussian War of 1870–71 and analyze European military doctrines against those of the Civil War. Upon his arrival abroad, Wagner visited the battlefields of Königgrätz, Mars-la-Tour, and Gravelotte, and the Napoleonic sites of Prague, Austerlitz, Wagram, and Waterloo. He also took advantage of the opportunity to study at close hand Prussian army organization and visited the *Kriegsakademie* in Berlin. Out of this visit, as he intended, Wagner produced his first major work, *The Campaign of Königgrätz*, in 1889.[16]

The thesis of *Königgrätz*, and the point Wagner was trying to make for his American audience, was summed up in his judgment that "European military writers . . . still fail to recognize in the developments of our [civil] war the germ, if not the prototype, of military features which are regarded as new in Europe." Wagner mocked Helmuth von Moltke's derisive (if apocryphal) comment about the Civil War's "armed mobs," claiming that had Prussia, France, or Austria-Hungary taken the trouble to study America's recent conflict, all sides could have avoided costly errors and could even have changed the outcome of their wars. Wagner deliberately used the battle of Königgrätz to test the correctness and modernity of American tactics and incidentally used the Franco-Prussian War to show how Prussia was forced by the conditions of battle to adopt offensive tactics nearly identical to those used by the Union toward the end of the Civil War.[17]

True to his pragmatic spirit, Wagner was happy to credit Europeans for military advances where credit was due, but during the Austro-Prussian War, at least, he found the belligerents woefully behind American practice. Among the innovations Wagner identified from the Civil War were the use of entrenchments, battlefield dispersion and adoption of heavy skirmish lines, the transformation of cavalry from a battle-oriented to a security and reconnaissance role, and the use of artillery to support the infantry's advance. Rather than discuss the campaign on its own merits, Wagner analyzed it from the perspective of how differently the war might have turned out been had the Austrians or Prussians applied the techniques used by armies an ocean away.

Despite his respect for the Prussian military, Wagner found its reputation overrated. That Prussia won at Königgrätz at all, he wrote, was due more to Austrian blundering than to Prussian cunning. Austrian commander Ludwig von Benedek failed to inform even his corps commanders of his battle plans; his soldiers failed to entrench; and Austrian infantry tactics, still based on the bayonet charge, "possessed the double attribute of antiquity and imbecility." The Prussians, for their part, multiplied their own losses by attacking in column rather than by an American-style skirmish line, misdirected their artillery, and completely wasted the potential of their cavalry. Had the Austrians only dug in and faced their opponents the next day, the Prussians might well have lost. "There was no reason, aside from demoralization," Wagner observed, "for the retreat of the Austrians far from the scene of their defeat. Their communications were neither intercepted nor seriously endangered; their losses had not been excessive; and, but for their discouragement and loss of morale, there is no reason why their defeat at Königgrätz should have been decisive."[18]

Wagner believed that European military leaders unjustifiably magnified their feats of arms above those of the Civil War. Many years later he pointed out that the Austro- and Franco-Prussian wars were "fought on an area scarcely equal to half the State of Kansas." He continued, "If a Prussian army had penetrated entirely through the Austrian empire and Servia [*sic*] . . . [or] had pushed through France across the Pyrenees to Madrid, the distance traversed would in each case have been about equal to that marched by the Union armies from Louisville to Savannah." In either case, a European army would have had to be "dependent upon a single line of railroad for its supplies for nearly five hundred miles of this distance, and to be entirely without [a] base or communications for the remainder," a feat he doubted even Prussia could equal. Very clearly, and with no small amount of patriotic chest-thumping, Wagner was claiming that recent European campaigns were nothing compared to the American Civil War, and he was challenging the vaunted armies of Europe to attempt what had already been done in the United States. More important, however, was his message to American officers that the lessons of their own military past were in themselves legitimate. During the Civil War, he concluded, "Our armies and generals grew in excellence as the war continued; and before the close of the conflict, the art of war had reached a higher development in America than it attained in Europe in 1866, and in some respects, higher than it reached in 1870."[19]

To be fair to Europeans, the Civil War was not completely ignored by their armies, as Wagner claimed. The English devoted a fair amount of attention to the Civil War, the Germans somewhat less, and the

French none at all. Of the two principal textbooks used by Leavenworth's Department of Military Art, Sir Edward Hamley's *Operations
of War* and Robert Home's *Précis of Modern Tactics*, the former was the
more generous about lessons from the Civil War. Jay Luvaas observes
that Hamley "did not regard the lessons of that war as in any way
unique." Home covered the Civil War even more briefly than Hamley,
preferring to stress European conflicts. In Germany, writes Luvaas, interest in the Civil War "was confined to a handful of individuals," and
for the most part "basic military texts slighted the Civil War or else
failed to mention it altogether." The general consensus in England and
Germany was that the Civil War simply confirmed the established doctrines of their respective armies. France's failure to scrutinize the Civil
War, and the reason that the Germans and English underrated it, derived principally from the more recent wars of German unification.
Germany's stunning successes against Austria-Hungary and France
obscured the Civil War from view; besides, Europeans were more apt
to pay attention to their own wars than to anything American, and in
this light Wagner's prejudice against European doctrine appears somewhat conceited. It was the lack of attention, of course, that irked Wagner most, and he was fairly justified in claiming that nothing had happened in 1866 or 1870 that had not already been demonstrated between
1861 and 1865.[20]

The Campaign of Königgrätz was well received on both sides of the
Atlantic. A reviewer for the English *Army and Navy Gazette* found the
book to be highly informative and said of its author, "if the American
Army of to-day contains a large proportion of officers as zealous and
well-informed in their profession as Lieutenant Wagner . . . the United
States may depend with confidence upon her Army in any struggle that
may await the Republic." The London *Broad Arrow* noted that
"Lieut[enant] Wagner enunciates opinions diametrically opposed to
those of some of the best recognized authorities on the Seven Weeks'
War," adding that in many cases he had "the best of the argument in opposition" to them. A domestic review in the *Journal of the United States
Cavalry Association*, responding to Wagner's overall intent, hoped "that
this effort to place the art of the American soldier in its proper light may
receive the encouragement it deserves." The reviewer warmed to Wagner's analysis of the role of modern cavalry, saying that Wagner had
made "an accurate statement of the cavalry *idea* as it exists to-day." One
of Wagner's long-time friends, Captain Tasker H. Bliss, then serving as
commanding general John M. Schofield's aide-de-camp, wrote that he

"was very much pleased" with *Königgrätz* and urged Wagner to continue writing. "We want *American* books on the art of war," he said, hoping that "the preparation of such a book for Leavenworth may be undertaken by you. There may not be much money in it, but there will be a great deal of reputation." Bliss later talked Nelson A. Miles, who succeeded Schofield as commanding general, into purchasing two hundred copies of *Königgrätz* for general distribution within the army. But no author can please everyone. Writing for the *Journal of the Military Service Institution*, Lieutenant John P. Wisser, First Artillery, thought Wagner was prejudiced against the Prussians and found his criticism of the Austrians "uncharitable." While acknowledging the originality of *Königgrätz*, Wisser believed it was unfair to expect the Prussians or Austrians to have digested anything from the Civil War so soon after its conclusion. Still, Wisser generally liked the work; but this would not be the last time an officer of artillery found Wagner's ideas objectionable.[21]

The publication of *Königgrätz* also began a period of sustained scholarly writing by Wagner, all of it marked by his fundamental idea of the practical role of history. By 1889 Wagner was well on the way to establishing himself as the most thoughtful and energetic instructor at Leavenworth, even though he good-naturedly averred to the chair of his department, Major Kline, whom he said had "made a careful study of the art of war" himself. With two years' experience behind them, Kline and his assistants broadened appreciably the scope of practical field instruction in their department. Previously such applications were limited, despite the goals of the curriculum, to once-weekly exercises in minor tactics during the fall. Kline introduced the use of maps for instruction in problems that could not be solved with the school garrison. In the academic year 1889–90, practical applications included forming advance guards, establishing outposts, leading patrols, and conducting marches on an objective, all according to Upton's tactics. McCook was so pleased with the overall performance of the school's separate departments that he began including their progress reports in his own annual reports to the commanding general.[22]

With the Leavenworth school now well established and evidently going from strength to strength, Wagner published in July 1889 "An American War College," which outlined the school's achievements to date, why its continued existence was desirable, and how its mission might be improved. Wagner declared that the Infantry and Cavalry School was quickly nearing maturity, adding that "everything that *could* be done *has* been done . . . to increase its efficiency, and to raise it

. . . to a veritable war college." With the art and science of war becoming ever more complex, he noted, the school was uniquely qualified to impart the "careful training in the many branches of human knowledge which are now used in every feature of the profession of arms." To support these claims, Wagner made use of his recent visit to Prussia and compared the Leavenworth curriculum to the three-year course at the Berlin *Kriegsakademie*; in every respect except the length of schooling, Leavenworth measured up to the best school for war in the world. He was especially proud to note that "the course in the Art of War (probably the most extended one taught in America) is not limited to military history and a theoretical study of campaigns; but, in its branch of minor tactics, embraces the solution of military problems in the field."[23]

The school was not perfect, however, and Wagner suggested several ways in which it could be improved. Of signal importance was a qualified student body. Like successive commandants, Wagner was frustrated that there were still officers enrolled at the school "whose educational deficiencies were deplorable." Despite previous attempts to discourage or prevent unqualified lieutenants from attending, such measures were still ignored, although he acknowledged they could not "completely remedy the evil." Simply requiring a West Point diploma, he thought, was not enough. Instead, he suggested a roundabout solution: all officers should be required to pass an examination for promotion, and only officers who had passed it should be admitted to the Infantry and Cavalry School. The idea was not adopted, although some time later the army made promotion conditional upon examination. Among Wagner's other suggestions were that instructors should be selected from the army as a whole, not just the Fort Leavenworth garrison; that graduates of the course receive special recognition in the annual Army Register; that two officers instead of one from each regiment be selected for the course; and that the school be made open to qualified National Guard officers. A final suggestion would have horrified William T. Sherman. In Wagner's opinion, Leavenworth needed the same legitimacy and prestige as West Point and hence the support of the entire nation. In other words, the Infantry and Cavalry School needed to be sanctioned by the U.S. Congress. Sherman, it will be recalled, created the school with a general order to keep it from becoming politicized. Wagner believed that congressional sanction would end the parsimony with which the army funded the Leavenworth school and would endow it with patrons who would safeguard its existence and ensure its expansion. Wagner's suggestion was never adopted, and

Leavenworth remained purely an army matter. As it happened, Wagner need not have bothered making the recommendation. Before long the school would have all the prestige Wagner and his colleagues craved.[24]

Despite its continuing success and the evolving sophistication of its curriculum, the school was still not without critics. Increasingly, however, they moved away from a narrow denunciation of its curriculum to a broad attack on the school's (and Wagner's) overall goal—the cultivation of educated officers. In June 1890, for example, Lieutenant Colonel Edwin V. Sumner suggested that the Infantry and Cavalry School emphasized the infantry at the expense of the cavalry and should thus be called the "Infantry School only." But what really upset Sumner was that Leavenworth was propagating what he considered "artificial military intelligence," which he defined as "that which induces a novice, after reading Jomini, [and English writers] Hamley and Shaw, to become a military writer, suggesting theories of war, rehashing and continuing errors, real intelligence not being the guide." As far as Sumner was concerned, "real soldiers" did not need theory but only a clear head and an offensive spirit.[25] Sumner was not alone in his reactionary opinions. Among the most visible, prolific, and persistent naysayers was Major James Chester, Third Artillery, who practically embodied the conservative reaction against theoretical education in the army. A native of Scotland, Chester began his army career as a private in 1854. During the Civil War, his conspicuous bravery at Gettysburg and Kearneysville earned him a commission, and after the war he rose to the rank of major, to which he was promoted a year before he retired in 1898.

Chester vigorously opposed the idea that the principles of war could be taught and stubbornly refused to yield his position despite frequent and reasonable arguments to the contrary. He contemptuously referred to those who thought otherwise as *kriegsspielers* (war gamers) and called the tactical exercise, being used with success at Leavenworth, "an absurdity. . . . a soulless sham to everyone capable of discerning veracity." For Chester, the art of war was a vocation that could be neither taught nor learned, and the concept of leadership was a mystical and undecipherable phenomenon that some men had and others did not. A commander, he wrote, "may be learned, brilliant, familiar with all the formulas of war, a strict disciplinarian and a good tactician, but if he lacks the spirit of command his proper place is in the rear rank. A real captain . . . controls the spirits of his men *silently, mysteriously, magnetically*" (emphasis added). In Chester's view, only men endowed with these attributes—geniuses, in other words—could win battles. Theory was all right in its place, but it could never bring success in war: "While a man may be educated into a *kriegsspieler*, he cannot be educated into a commander of men any more than he can into a poet, or an artist, or a Christian." Only *kriegsspielers*, he wrote, believed in "book-made generals." He advised the army's theorists to "stick to parade maneuvers and sham battles; and the country, if it knew the facts, might devoutly pray that it may never have any other occasion for your services."[26]

To a degree, Chester was justified in his opinions, at least in the case of war games. The Prussian strategist Carl von Clausewitz, author of *On War*, noted that in combat, "reason is refracted in a manner quite different" than in exercises and that "peacetime maneuvers are a feeble substitute for the real thing." Clausewitz went on to say, however, that it was "immensely important that no soldier . . . should wait for war to expose him to those aspects of active service that amaze and confuse him when he first comes across them." In the end, Chester was on the losing end of the argument. In 1879, for example, John William De-Forest wrote in the *Atlantic Monthly* that "the solemn fact is that to know much of the science of war the cleverest man needs years of study and experience; and another solemn fact is that . . . we had better look for supreme guidance to experts, and to experts alone." In 1889, Captain William H. Carter wrote with some pride that "there is more reading and study of a professional character done in the army to-day than ever before, and its effect is visible in every garrison . . . of the army." Several years later he wrote that the value of a Leavenworth education was that it provided officers with "a happy combination" of theory and practice. In what might have been a courtesy to Chester, Carter added that "while no books will supply the place of instinctive genius for war, the best type of soldier will always be he who can on the field of battle, with its turmoil and strange scenes, turn theory into practice."[27]

Wagner's response to Chesteresque opponents of education was less generous. How else than by theoretical study, he asked, echoing Clausewitz, might an officer acquire knowledge of the art of war, unless he lived "to be as old as Methuselah, [engaged] in a hundred wars, and [passed] through every grade from private to field-marshal"? The pursuit of theoretical study evidently worked well enough for such Prussian masters as von Moltke and Gneisenau; why, then, should such preparation be evaded by American officers? In Wagner's mind, to ignore theory was to ignore history; he argued that "all theories as to what *may be* done must, if sound, be based upon what *has been* done." Chester and his ilk, men "who pose as practical soldiers and affect to despise all theory," were "generally ignorant and obstinate men who know as little of the practice as they do of the theory of war," and the sooner they disappeared, the better. Wagner almost desperately wished for the day when "the old 'Ireland-Army' man, whose military education was acquired in following the company swill-cart" gave way to "the ambitious, well-educated man who enlisted for promotion."[28]

Getting rid of the "Ireland-Army man" became a chief preoccupation for Wagner. He became ever more convinced that the American army had to root its war-making capabilities in the lessons of the past while simultaneously forging ahead in the modernization of its tactical methodology. Wagner may well have counted himself lucky that he was at Fort Leavenworth in 1891, when a newly appointed tactical board arrived, charged with the overhaul of the army's manual of tactics. Their work would soon make Wagner a household name among the army's officers.

Chapter 3

Enthusiastic Prusso-Maniacs

Wagner's struggle against those one might call anti-educators consumed his entire career. As noted, a key element of his academic passion was to make history and theory practical, and that meant making both disciplines applicable to the battlefield. For Wagner, and for many other officers keen on profiting from the experience of the Civil War, a central question was: How shall the army fight?

Although by no means unsophisticated, the tactics those officers had used between 1861 and 1865 were fairly straightforward. Moreover, considering the prevalence of volunteer officers who received little, if any, actual training in leading troops in combat, battle tactics often seemed not much more than marching a large body of troops toward the enemy, in the hope that simple numbers would suffice to overwhelm the other side. For the most part during the war, tactics meant drill—the art of maneuvering those troops as a single body. And therein lay a central problem of Civil War battle; the dense double-ranked formations in use at the time offered inviting targets to defenders, who were able to inflict grievous casualties on any would-be attacker. That such casualties accrued was not due to the heartlessness or incompetence of commanders; many believed there had to be a more efficient solution, and some (like Upton) attempted to find one. Rather, the Napoleonic-style tactics in the Civil War had been handed down like received wisdom, and while there were those who found them wasteful, few were willing to dispense with a tactical regimen that had served the army well in the past.

After the war there developed a fairly broad consensus among veteran officers that the tactics they had used were, after all, crude and unnecessarily costly. Most agreed that combat formations had been too dense, and reference was made to the increased use of heavy skirmish lines, in which dispersed soldiers moved out in front of the attack, rushed from cover to cover, and kept up a harassing fire on the enemy. Since defenders tend to shoot at attackers to their immediate front, it was reasoned that a forward line of skirmishers would draw enemy fire away from the main body of troops that followed in close order, thus making the attack less hazardous. But these experiments were only that, for the army at that time had no method for disseminating workable alternatives to traditional tactics. Indeed, the army did not even have an official tactical doctrine. Although the manuals-of-arms by William J. Hardee and Silas Casey were nominally accepted by the northern and southern armies as the approved guides, officers were not required to use them, and many did not. This doctrinal indifference persisted throughout the war, and when it ended the army still had no approved method for combat.[1]

That situation did not last long, for after the war questions were raised increasingly about the utility of close-order tactics in a climate of escalating firepower. Under the patronage of William T. Sherman, Emory Upton set himself to the design of a new system that stressed battle-worthiness over control, while disestablishing the use of parade ground formations in combat. The result, published in 1867, was *A New System of Infantry Tactics, Double and Single Rank*. Upton espoused a new doctrine that emphasized flexibility, simplicity, and maximum firepower. He described a method of attack that took advantage of terrain and available cover, increased the attacker's economy of force, and inflicted maximum damage on the defender. Upton also incorporated a degree of dispersion in his formations, although he did not completely abandon the ranked attack.[2]

The War Department adopted Upton's tactics immediately.[3] With the stamp of official doctrine came the requirement that all units conform to them. The change was not effected without protest, but few disagreed with the overall system that Upton introduced; most officers understood the need to extend the battle line, and the concept was generally accepted as simple common sense. But as technology pushed the lethality of modern weapons to higher levels, Upton's tactics began to fall behind, and increasing attention was devoted to the weapons-driven tactical advances in Europe. There, in the Austro-Prussian, Franco-Prussian and Russo-Turkish Wars, the use of breech-fired magazine rifles and the newfound accuracy and destructiveness of artillery called into question the continued effectiveness of Uptonian tactics. The dispersal of the battle line was still a recognized necessity, but was it dispersed enough? And if not, how dispersed could it become and yet retain its cohesiveness, firepower, and ability to deliver a shock to the enemy? Faced with new levels of battlefield mortality, and the enormous din of combat, how could company commanders impel their men to go forward or even make themselves heard to their dispersed soldiers?

As American officers watched the European debate on tactics un-
fold, they saw two completely different ideas emerge: one French, the
other German. The French, reacting to their humbling defeat by Prussia in 1870, concluded that too much emphasis had been given to
achieving fire superiority and too little to the cultivation of an offensive
spirit. The chief proponents of this view were Charles Ardant du Picq
and Ferdinand Foch, who argued that no defense could withstand the
psychological terror of an aggressive and impassioned attack. Firepower mattered not; victory came to the side with the will to conquer.
In order to exert the maximum psychological shock on the enemy, the
French rejected the trend toward dispersion, condensed their battle
line, and emphasized the bayonet attack in order to impress upon the
enemy the ardor and steadfastness of French soldiers. Said du Picq, "the
French have never met anyone who has resisted a bayonet charge."[4]

Germany took an entirely different path. Dispersed (or, as it was increasingly called, extended) order was emphasized. Portions of the battle line advanced alternately toward the enemy in rushes, seeking cover
and stopping to fire while other sections advanced. Company commanders were given a high degree of autonomy, and non-commissioned officers were charged with the control of smaller units. From
this, the squad system was eventually adopted, each squad being completely independent and widely separated from other squads. The soldiers within each squad were dispersed to assure maximum safety. Like
the French, the Germans also counted on the effect of an offensive
spirit, but while they cultivated this, they did not rely on it alone. Instead, they recognized that in any contest the side that produced the
most fire had a potent advantage, and they accordingly encouraged an
extremely high rate of fire to subdue the enemy.

As European armies instituted these changes, the American military
press was filled with articles on what a future war might look like and
how a new generation of weapons would affect combat. Writers on tactics, including Wagner, noted the increasing power of the defense,
which led to new questions about how to neutralize it. Related topics
on technical innovations that enhanced the defense, like smokeless
powder, magazine-fed rifles, and machine-guns, likewise received frequent attention. Because of the tactical difficulties in meeting such challenges, no consensus emerged among American officers. Unanswered
also, given the variety of foreign tactical doctrine, was determining
whether one mode was more appropriate than another. As tactical theory in the United States matured, however, the tendency was toward

the German model since it resembled much of American practice, with a healthy dose of French audacity.[5]

The chorus of voices heralding the increased lethality and complexity of battle was equaled only by those who argued that Upton's tactics were no longer capable of meeting the task required of them. The U.S. Army was falling farther and farther behind the armies of Europe, and the inevitable question was raised: What would happen if Americans ever met Europeans in battle? According to a pessimistic American officer in 1878, the obvious answer was "disaster and defeat." Upton himself did little to resolve the issue. Arguing that European advances were little different from his own tactics, he made no overt changes in a revision of *Infantry Tactics*. While recognizing the utility of Germany's extended order, he rejected it in favor of maintaining greater control in the attack, advising that "the safety of an army cannot be trusted to men in open order with whom it is difficult to communicate." Near the end of his life Upton changed his mind, but he killed himself before he could publish his new thinking. In his absence the modernization of American tactics stalled for ten years.[6]

Immediately after his suicide in March 1881, Upton's tactics came under a mounting barrage of criticism, and the cry went up for a completely new system. An anonymous officer, writing to the *Army and Navy Journal* scant weeks after Upton's death, believed that there were "radical difficulties with Gen. Upton's tactics." Later that year Lieutenant Colonel Henry M. Lazelle wrote to General William T. Sherman, confessing that "it is plain that our present tactical depth of rank must yield . . . to improved fire-arms, in order that we shall not present live targets, easily decimated, to an enemy. . . . Obviously, exposure to a severe, or even moderate fire, would at once destroy . . . any single rank formation, and probably would greatly cut up that of a double rank." Lazelle claimed that "the present system is very pretty for drills, but it has never been exclusively tested in the field." The *Army and Navy Journal*, which had vigorously defended Upton against his critics when his new system was introduced in 1867, printed Lazelle's letter and then commented that Upton's tactics had finally "outlived their uses."[7]

Lazelle advised Sherman that he should appoint a board of officers to oversee a revision of the army's tactics. Sherman, whose reply to Lazelle was also printed in the *Army and Navy Journal*, agreed that there were "defects" in the present system, but he objected to the idea that tactics by committee was the best way to correct them. Noting that there were already "a number of officers engaged upon the subject" of revision, Sherman thought that Lazelle's idea was impractical and suggested instead that "the work of preparing tactics is better accomplished by the spontaneous effort of one individual than by a board, or even by a single individual appointed to do it." Nor did the commanding general want a simple correction of the errors in Upton. If new tactics were to be adopted, he wanted them to supersede Upton completely; anything else, he concluded, was "not worth the time and labor."[8]

Sherman's proposal sent officers scurrying to claim the title as Upton's successor, and their ideas were received at the adjutant general's Office by the dozen. While none were particularly objectionable, few took into account the problems and obstacles of modern combat or offered adequate means to overcome them. By late 1883 the *Army and Navy Journal* expressed its impatience at the creeping pace at which tactical reform was proceeding, noting that by now "the subject should be in order." To make matters worse, the paper later complained that the proposed revisions were so burdened with complex drill maneuvers that "no living man could master them in their entirety." What was needed, the journal advised, was simplicity and common sense. Nevertheless, the tactical debate went on for several more years. Only a few submissions received serious consideration, and some were published in the service journals, yet even they eventually wound up in the bulging files in the Adjutant General's Office. In 1887 Sherman's successor, Philip H. Sheridan, took the step Sherman had refused by creating a board of officers to "prepare or recommend such revisions of the tactics as will place them more completely in harmony with the advanced methods of conducting war." The board was charged with studying not only the many suggestions in the Adjutant General's Office but also the tactical systems of other military powers. Out of this, it was hoped, would emerge a modern tactical guide that adhered to the most current doctrine and that suited American custom.[9]

Eight officers were appointed to the Board of Revision, which met for the first time in Washington DC in February 1888. They collected the proposals on file with the adjutant general and announced that they would also entertain new submissions; twenty-one were eventually received. In addition to these, the board purchased drill manuals of the English, French, German, Austrian, and Italian armies and twenty-three other European works on tactics; several of these were translated into English for the first time by board members. These works were consulted until April 1889, when the board moved to Fort Leavenworth in order to make use of the Infantry and Cavalry School's growing library and to test various tactical ideas with the post garrison.[10]

The board's arrival at Fort Leavenworth drew Wagner into the revision debate. He collaborated, in an unofficial capacity, in the board's deliberations, the content and scope of which are unknown. Wagner was not, of course, a newcomer to tactical theory or to the evolution of European methodology. His position at the school required him to stay abreast of tactical innovations, and *The Campaign of Königgrätz* had already established him as tactical critic of some repute. Since its appearance, Wagner had also written a groundbreaking article on Germany's tactical system based on his observations at the *Kriegsakademie* in Berlin. Published in the March 1889 issue of the *Journal of the United States Cavalry Association*, "The New German Drill Book and Some Deductions Therefrom" offered a current and detailed explanation of how the German army conducted battle. Wagner brought his findings, and his own suggestions, to the board's deliberations.

Comparing Germany's new tactics with Upton's, Wagner announced that "our drill system contains a useless amount of mere 'embroidery' [and] . . . lugubrious tactical nonsense." Here he echoed Lazelle's letter to General Sherman, saying that "we should imitate [the Germans] in recognizing the fact that drilling is simply *preparing to fight*, and that everything that does not have a direct bearing upon the duties of a soldier in actual war is a mere superfluity." In achieving this end, Wagner praised the German drill for its simplicity, efficiency, and above all, training. While American soldiers labored under what he called Upton's "extended and intricate manual," forcing them to "waste so much time in obtaining a nice execution" of drill movements, German soldiers were leaving the parade ground actually to learn how to conduct battle. This Wagner believed was the greatest advance Germany had made to the art of war, and he urged the U.S. Army to adopt the practice. Germany's battle tactics, he noted, were regulated according to the terrain on which its soldiers fought, emphasized the extended order, and did not cavil about maintaining precise intervals between soldiers or even an accurate alignment of the battle line. To all intents, Germany had done away with the battle line entirely, opting instead for a continuous advance by semi-independent bodies (squads) of skirmishers. This meant that individual soldiers had to be extremely well trained, with the outcome of battle heavily dependent upon their intelligence, creativity, and willingness to press forward the attack. Dissolution of command to such an extent gave enormous freedom to com-

pany commanders and platoon leaders, an innovation Wagner ap-
plauded profusely. Noting the German army's "wonderful decentraliz-
ation" of command, Wagner countered that there was a "growing tendency toward centralization" in the American army, an inclination he
deplored. He complained that "an American captain is, too often,
scarcely more than a lieutenant." Considering that in any future war the
American army would consist of men "suddenly called from the count-
ing-houses, the work-shop and the plow," he concluded that it was an
absolute necessity to emulate the simplicity found in Germany's new
tactics. The fact that the extended order was a Prussian innovation mattered little to Wagner, who had already criticized its army's conduct in
battle. What did matter was that it offered a reasonable solution to the
"infantry impasse."[11]

The board completed its assignment in May 1890 and brought forth
a completely new tactical manual. Wagner was quite pleased with the
result, noting that he had formed a "high opinion" of the board, probably because it heeded his advice. While retaining Upton's double rank
of fours for parade ground drill, the regulations broke with American
tradition and adopted the German method of extended order for combat. They also incorporated the squad and its requisite dependence on
individualism. By extending the chain of command down to the small-
est units, the board hoped to exert battlefield control over all units even
when dispersed. As Wagner had advised in "The New German Drill
Book," training was paramount, and a lengthy section on how training
should be conducted was included. A key object of the manual was "to
give [any] corporal the confidence and experience necessary to qualify
him as a squad leader." Troops were to be thoroughly instructed in the
principles of extended order through simulated combat situations. Exercises on varied ground were emphasized, soldiers being taught how
best to use any means of cover and concealment to protect them from
the enemy's fire and to aid them in their advance. Thorough guidelines
for advance under fire, as well as for defense, were included for the
company and battalion, in order to demonstrate the overall method by
which extended order was to be used in combat.[12]

Before the new regulations were recommended for adoption, the final draft was submitted to Generals Thomas H. Ruger (infantry),
Wesley Merritt (cavalry), and Colonel Henry W. Closson (artillery),
for their criticism and suggestions. While Merritt and Closson expressed general approval of the tactics that applied to their arms
(though Merritt was fully aware that any new system would not escape

censure in some quarters), Ruger had the most reservations. In a thirty-page letter to the adjutant general, he advised that the new regulations contained many "changes and omissions which seem of such importance as to require careful consideration." The bulk of these, however, were problems of language and definition, for Ruger wanted the instructions for the extended order to be absolutely clear and unambiguous. He admitted, though, that it was "not possible, even if desirable, to state precise rules applicable to all cases," and generally he found the new regulations to be "so superior in essentials to the Tactics now in use . . . that their adoption is advisable, but not definitely and unqualifiedly."[13]

The Board of Revision made such alterations as it thought justified, and in September the army's new commanding general, John M. Schofield, ordered that the new *Infantry Drill Regulations* be adopted immediately, inviting "free criticism . . . with a view to their ultimate perfection." Criticism there was, in abundance. Not surprisingly, the adoption of extended order on the German model, its reliance upon individuality, and the assignment of elements of command to non-commissioned and enlisted personnel generated the most protest. Critics objected to the idea that sufficient firepower could be developed from a dispersed assault to overwhelm an enemy and asked how such an attack could be controlled and maneuvered with troops so spread out. Some noted that the extended order was in retreat among some European armies, principally the French, and so questioned whether its use was truly advantageous. Doubters also scoffed at the idea that an average soldier had the wherewithal to control himself under fire, much less direct the movement of others. The very idea that mere soldiers were now expected to do what officers did was considered an insult to the officer corps. Asked one, "Can the direction of a line of battle be entrusted to a corporal?" He thought not.[14]

Major James Chester was among the most vocal in condemning the trend toward individuality. Chester was not one to trust soldiers (even though he had once been an enlisted man himself), writing that reliance upon their judgment was "the most dangerous element that could be introduced into modern war. It is inconsistent with discipline and detrimental to efficiency, and would convert any army into an armed mob." Discipline did not come from below, among soldiers in the ranks, but from a stern and courageous officer above. Therefore, he concluded, a single cowardly soldier could ruin any attack: "If men were [allowed to be] guided by their personal opinions, the most timid man . . . would be the first to think that his position was untenable. And if individual action were permitted he would be the first to retire." Such men were the first to seek shelter under cover, the implication being that cover was therefore evil. Chester went so far as to suggest that a soldier with self-preservation on his mind "must be called into the open, and held there . . . until his courage comes back to him. It is astonishing how soon nervousness will disappear under such treatment." And the idea that an individual soldier should actually aim at the enemy Chester found "altogether worthless," its usefulness "misunderstood and very much exaggerated." But then, Chester admitted, "I have always been something of a heretic," and he did not expect the loathsome *kriegsspielers* to understand the validity of his opinions.[15]

The 1891 *Regulations* weathered attacks like these, but there were other problems of a structural nature that gave even officers who supported the regulations reason for pause. A major problem was the board's assumption that attack formations would be based on a regimental system of three battalions of four companies each, like Germany's. The army's prevailing organization consisted of ten-company battalions, but board members naively assumed that Congress would accept a reorganization bill that established their preferred four-company battalion. Officers, Wagner among them, had long recommended just such a reorganization, citing the ease of controlling smaller battalions and the fact that European armies had taken that path. Congress, however, did not embrace the concept until after the Spanish-American War. The board's adoption of extended-order tactics was thus seriously compromised by the continued use of large battalions; a commander could easily have managed four companies in extended order, but coping with ten was recognized as a practical impossibility.[16]

Another less prohibitive, but no less troublesome, deficiency was the board's decision to delete altogether provisions for attacks in single rank on the old Uptonian model. Critics who did not believe that extended-order formations could generate sufficient firepower to take an enemy position focused on this issue, some adding that they could accept the extended order if provisions were made to re-form extended units into a single rank if necessary. This, they argued, would allow commanders to advance squads of skirmishers to draw the enemy's fire, while successive lines in single rank moved forward to deliver the final blow—an idea highly reminiscent of Upton's defunct tactics. Moreover, critics insisted, the inclusion of the single rank would allow officers to maintain direct control over their units. The only problem with this recommendation was that the chain of command would be confused in such either/or conditions, possibly leading to greater confusion in combat. Still, a revised edition of the *Regulations* in 1895 allowed the single rank, but it was permanently deleted after the war with Spain.[17]

The controversy over the *Regulations* did not soon abate. Officers across the country inundated the *Army and Navy Journal* and the Adjutant General's Office with criticism and requests for clarification on certain points. The tactical backwardness of many officers, and the desultory effect of frontier duty, was demonstrated by their repeated questions on trivial matters of parade ground drill. Officers asked how the sword knot should be worn, where a soldier's cartridge box should be positioned on parade, and why the *Regulations* made no mention of the proper manner for salutes. In 1895 a captain asked where his position should be if his company was marching in column on a city street too narrow for him to take his proper place, and in 1900 the commander of the Twentieth Infantry at Fort Sheridan, Illinois, asked if his troops should stand at attention during the playing of the "Star Spangled Banner." More troubling than these banalities was the continued resistance to the combat doctrine as espoused by the *Regulations*. Much of this can be attributed to the fact that the Board of Revision offered no justifications for its sweeping changes and failed to provide any tactical context that would explain the benefit or necessity of those changes. The staff of the Department of Military Art at the Infantry and Cavalry School ran up against this problem very quickly. Their classes in tactics, application, and military history were altered to incorporate the *Infantry Drill Regulations* even before these were officially adopted, and in order to explain the theoretical concepts of the revised tactics therein, they also had to explain how the new tactics were connected to the general evolution of combat doctrine.[18]

The department's principal texts—Sir Edward Hamley's *Operations of War* and Robert Home's *Précis of Modern Tactics*—were insufficient to this task. Not only were the books outdated, but the department's instructors were increasingly frustrated by their exclusion of American military history and lessons of war. Wagner had long been acquainted with this deficiency. In an 1890 letter to Tasker Bliss, he complained that the principles explained in European textbooks often could not be applied to American practice. Even more troubling, he wrote, was the existence of certain "enthusiastic Prusso-maniacs" in the army who "would have us draw all our tactical lessons from '66 or '70, instead of allowing us to take at least *some* from '64–'65." He then informed Bliss that "Major [Jacob] Kline and I are now engaged on a work on modern tactics which we hope to make of sufficient value to warrant its substitution for [Hamley] and Home." In October 1891 Colonel McCook officially assigned Wagner to the production of this work, after Kline dropped out of it.[19]

What had originally been conceived as a single volume on minor tactics eventually became two, and they were Wagner's most seminal works: *The Service of Security and Information* and *Organization and Tactics*. If their publishing history is a fair indication, they were also his most widely read; between them, the books went through twenty-one editions and six revisions between 1893 and 1907. Their appearance catapulted Wagner to instant renown within the army and established him as the legitimate successor to Emory Upton. Their purpose was four-fold: to replace Leavenworth's British works on warfare and tactics with American texts; to validate American military history and tactical innovation; to establish a uniform guide for the instruction of small-unit duties; and most important, to provide the historical and theoretical groundwork for the 1891 *Infantry Drill Regulations*.

While preparing the direction of his assignment, Wagner was promoted to captain in April 1892. At about the same time his health declined, and he requested an extended leave of absence so that he could "complete the work in question at some salubrious place in the Allegheny region." There, he was sure, he could recover his health and "obtain better results than would be possible here [at Leavenworth]—especially in a saving of time." His request approved, he decamped in May for Cumberland,. Maryland, taking with him a personal library in excess of 150 books.[20]

Wagner's first volume, *The Service of Security and Information*, was already well in hand when he arrived in Cumberland, and he promised to have it finished by August. Upon its completion, Wagner offered the manuscript to Generals Thomas Ruger and Wesley Merritt, as well as to other less senior officers, for their criticisms. He sent the corrected manuscript to his publisher and waited expectantly. Weeks went by with no word, and shortly before Christmas an exasperated Wagner wrote to Tasker Bliss, asking Bliss to intercede on his behalf to discover what was taking so long. His letter to Bliss and good news from his publisher crossed paths, and the book was finally published in April 1893. In his preface, Wagner revealed that even in a work of this importance, he had not lost his sense of humor. He had insisted to his publisher that the book be printed in an easy-to-read typeface. He explained to readers that military books of the day were typically printed in very small type to facilitate portability in one's pocket—in which, he noted, "they are never carried." He went on to observe that "anyone who has noticed the impaired eyesight of many of the graduates of our officers' schools must find much to condemn in a typographical style which seems designed mainly for the benefit of the oculist." Perversely, this was all printed in extremely small type. [21]

As *The Service of Security and Information* went to press, Wagner was busily writing the second volume, but things did not go as planned. His year's leave was up and he had not yet finished the project, so he requested an extension through 1 July. Even with this, however, he could not promise the book's completion before September, although he hastened to add that he was making "steady progress." Annoyed by another request for leave, the adjutant general reminded Wagner that he had promised both works "in not less than eight months and not more than a year." Still, the leave was granted and Wagner did not return to Fort Leavenworth until July. [22]

This second volume, titled *Organization and Tactics*, was used in manuscript form for a year by Leavenworth students to test its applicability to courses in the Department of Military Art. The book was printed for public consumption in December 1894. Both *Organization and Tactics* and *The Service of Security and Information* were immediately adopted by the school to replace its foreign texts. They remained in steady use at Leavenworth until 1908 and 1910, respectively, and were approved by the War Department for use by the National Guard. *Organization and Tactics* has endured even to the present day. English military historian Paddy Griffith notes that Wagner's "framework and examples from the Civil War have been excessively borrowed by modern students in a hurry," and instructors at the United States Military Academy still occasionally use it for its battle analyses. [23]

Wagner intended each book to fulfill a certain function, one practical and the other theoretical. In *The Service of Security and Information*, which met the first requirement, Wagner dispensed with theory and produced something on the order of a "how-to" manual. Essentially, it was a guide to the various noncombat duties of infantry and cavalry units in the field during wartime and was directed primarily at platoon and company commanders. Key portions of the book were later condensed into a pocket manual titled *A Catechism of Outpost Duty; Includ-*

ing Reconnaissance, Independent Cavalry, Advance Guards, Rear Guards, Outposts, Etc., replacing the venerable Dennis Hart Mahan's *Elementary Treatise on Advanced-Guard, Out-Post, and Detachment Service of Troops,* which had been in use since before the Civil War. Wagner's guidebook alone went through more than twenty reprintings.

While *The Service of Security and Information* was oriented toward such routine operational duties as patrolling and reconnaissance, its central theme was vigilance. All the duties outlined in the book revolved around the necessity for an army in the field to remain safe from surprise attack, to have up-to-the-minute information on the whereabouts, dispositions, and strength of the enemy, and to be constantly alert for opportunities and obstacles that might affect its mission. Ever the practical historian, Wagner offered the examples of Great Britain's blunders in the Crimean War, Brigadier General John E. Wool's abortive expedition in Chihuahua during the Mexican-American War, and Major General George B. McClellan's errant 1862 Peninsula Campaign as evidence for the fundamental importance of military information. Wherever possible, Wagner provided examples from both European and American military history to illustrate the concepts treated in each chapter. To fulfill the dual mission of ensuring security and gathering information, Wagner advised that "contact with [the enemy] should be quickly gained and never lost." Doing so required aggressive and constant reconnaissance, and it was in the application of this duty that Wagner concentrated his discussion of the functions of an army on campaign.[24]

Although Wagner provided examples of and instructions for the various activities he covered, a central feature of *The Service of Security and Information* was his reluctance to provide the reader with ironclad, absolute rules of action. He was fully aware that war was full of intangibles and that no canon could possibly meet every conceivable situation. Rather, Wagner reminded his audience that conditions of the moment must dictate the appropriate response. He advised, for example, that "no absolute rule for the strength of the advance guard can be given," that its proper distance from the main body "depends so entirely upon circumstances that it cannot be made subject to any rigid rule," and that "the strength of [an] outpost . . . depends upon so many considerations that no definite rule on the subject can be prescribed." The book was full of such intangibles. This was not a matter of evading difficult questions, for although Wagner declined to offer universal solutions, he provided general principles based on accepted practice that allowed an officer on the spot to proceed as conditions warranted. In doing so, Wagner actually affirmed, and sought to cultivate, the artistic aspects of war that were so important to James Chester. At the same time, however, Wagner upheld his conviction that a military education was the only viable alternative to personal experience. He fully expected his book to be used a training guide, from which certain principles could be established early in an officer's career. Men like Chester were not easily convinced, though, and Wagner would later have to challenge him directly on this point.[25]

Two of the three appendices that followed the main body of the work are worth noting for their novelty. The first, on the use of spies in gathering information about the enemy, was quite unusual in the military literature of the day but eminently reasonable considering the Wagner's subject. Regardless of their sometimes ignoble reputation, Wagner conceded that spies were "indispensably necessary," adding that the "commander will be victorious who has the best secret service." Wagner then went on to teach the would-be spymaster the delicate business of how to select spies, how to detect and use double spies, what sort of information spies should collect, and how to protect oneself against the spies of the enemy. Recognizing that spies were engaged in an occupation that required "habitual deceit and a want of principle," and practiced it for profit alone, Wagner strongly suggested that "a spy must always be well paid," with the admonition that "a badly paid spy will generally strike a bargain, sooner or later, with the enemy." As usual, he buttressed his recommendations with useful historical examples from the Civil War and Franco-Prussian War.[26]

Wagner probably intended no irony in the fact that with his counsel on the employment of spies, he included suggestions on how to manage the press. Declaring that newspapers were "the plague of modern armies," he advised that reporters be tightly controlled and that a press censor be appointed to approve reporters' stories; he prominently quoted Prussian general Bronsart von Schellendorf's declaration that "complete and unfettered freedom of the press is incompatible with a state of war." Wagner believed it a good idea to feed newspapers disinformation to mislead the enemy but warned that the practice should be employed judiciously. As he had done frequently in earlier chapters, Wagner cautioned the commander that there were no prescribed rules governing the management of the press; rather, circumstances of the moment had to guide one's actions, the objective always being to prevent "indiscreet publications."[27]

Even more unusual was Wagner's appendix on Indian scouting, considering the sparse contemporary literature on the subject. His interest in the matter was to demonstrate that even a primitive culture understood and had mastered the principles of security and information. The Apaches, he wrote, were "at their best when acting as *small infantry patrols*," adding that "absolutely nothing escape[s] their notice" and that they showed "surprising skill in the selection of positions and in the measures taken for defense." Turning to the Sioux, Wagner praised them as "perfect scout[s]" whose stealth and ingenuity had enabled them to observe General George Crook's two-hundred-mile march against them in 1876 without ever being seen.[28]

Wagner was so impressed by the Sioux that he went on to describe their combat tactics, judging them "simple and effective." Sioux attacks, he noted, typically "endeavor to surround, or, at least, to extend beyond the enemy, so as to bring upon him a convergent fire," their "chief object [being] to place themselves in such a position as to give them the most effective fire on the enemy, and, at the same time, to incur the least possible loss." Without actually saying so, Wagner demonstrated that Sioux battle formations were quite similar to the extended order promulgated by the 1891 *Infantry Drill Regulations*: "The fact that their own line is . . . thin and easily broken causes them no uneasiness; for their enemy's fire is . . . directed against a difficult target; and if the line is broken, they scamper away, quickly rally at a signal, and resume the same tactics as before."[29]

Returning to his main topic, Wagner offered an object lesson to the American army as practiced by its defeated enemy, while taking a swipe at the supposed superiority of European methods:

> It is not because of his courage, expertness with firearms, or celerity of movement that the Indian is a formidable foe—indeed, in the first two qualities he is greatly surpassed by our troops. He is formidable because his thorough knowledge of all the essential details of the science of security and information generally enables him to give battle when he chooses, and to avoid conflict when he sees fit. As a scout he is a model; and it may be said that the scouting methods prescribed by the best European authorities are valuable in proportion [only] to the degree of their approach to those of the North American Indians.[30]

Considering that the U.S. Army had not assembled in any single combat formation larger than a regiment since the 1876 Centennial

Campaign, and that a general war was a remote improbability, the overall subject matter of *The Service of Security and Information* at this point in the army's history was unique. At a time when some officers were advocating socially acceptable missions for the army, Wagner's was one of the few voices insisting that the army's proper and only mission was preparing for and waging war. While realizing that war was not likely, he persisted in arguing that the army could not be true to the nation if it were untrue to itself. An army untrained for war was a useless anachronism, whether or not enemies were on the horizon. Here, then, Wagner was not only reminding the army of its fundamental duty but also instructing it in how that duty was performed. For a host of junior officers who, like himself, had no actual wartime experience, Wagner furnished a practical alternative that transmitted the proven methods of generations of military history.

Like his first book, *The Service of Security and Information* was well received by officers. One of Wagner's West Point classmates, Colonel Hugh Lenox Scott, wrote in his memoirs that the publication of *The Service of Security and Information* meant that "a new era dawned for our army—a new epoch [was] ushered in—that was to progress until it found us, at the outbreak of the World War, with our officers the best instructed of any army in the world." Lieutenant George B. Davis, writing for the *Journal of the United States Cavalry Association*, gratefully acknowledged Wagner's comments about typeface and commended the author's "impartiality" on the subject matter. Best of all, he wrote, was that the book was "*readable*, and it should be a matter of pride to all officers to have an authorized American work of such excellence on this subject." A lengthy and surprisingly favorable review in the *Journal of the Military Service Institution* came from the hand of none other than James Chester, who nonetheless could not keep himself from scolding Wagner over small matters, such as the arcane duties of the commander of a vanguard, whether or not flags of truce should be received, and the evident hopelessness of setting "Tom, Dick and Harry to learn the business [of reconnaissance] from a text-book." On the subject of spies, Chester dutifully invoked his pet topic by maintaining that only a commander with the "requisite spiritual power" could tell a good spy from a bad one, noting that "the management of spies cannot be learned." In the end, Chester believed that "Captain Wagner's book ought to have an extensive circulation." But in a backhanded compliment, he added that Wagner's latest work would "find a broader field of usefulness in the national guards than it can hope to have in the regular army."[31]

The Service of Security and Information revealed a mind fully conversant with the technicalities of combat duty, able to present ideas in an understandable manner, and dedicated to the promotion of competence on the battlefield. The book's extended printing history is an indication that Wagner had reached a level of intellectual ability transcending that of most officers and that his peers found those accomplishments worthy of their attention. It was with the publication of *Organization and Tactics*, however, that Wagner's reputation as the army's most able historian and arbiter on matters of tactics was firmly secured.

Chapter 4

Organization and Tactics

As Wagner had previously complained to Bliss, the Infantry and Cavalry School and the army in general were hindered by their reliance on European texts, which duly emphasized the European military heritage. As an educator who applied appropriate tactical examples regardless of their source, Wagner found nothing fundamentally wrong with Hamley and Home. But to interested American officers, these English authors failed to consider seriously the experience of the American Civil War and the significant advances it had produced in the military art; nor were their books applicable to the army's *Infantry Drill Regulations*. Moreover, Wagner and others chafed under the supposed theoretical superiority of foreign-born military authors, and as Bliss had pointed out, great was the need for a comprehensive work on the art of war for American officers by one of their own kind. In early 1890, as Wagner looked ahead to the production of what he called a manual on "minor tactics," he told Bliss that it was one thing "to point out the shortcomings of other writers" but quite another "to make good their deficiencies by one's own work." Whatever his doubts, Wagner admirably succeeded in the task of correcting those deficiencies.[1]

The result was *Organization and Tactics*, and considering the near-universal acclaim that followed its publication, Wagner produced something for which the army had been waiting a long time. Where *The Service of Security and Information* provided a "how-to" approach to operations in the field, *Organization and Tactics* provided a detailed analysis of the army's new drill regulations, particularly the extended order. Furthermore, the book placed the army's new tactics in historical perspective, added novel ideas for the employment of cavalry and artillery, and enunciated for the first time a genuine doctrine of combined arms combat. Together, *The Service of Security and Information* and *Organization and Tactics* represented a codification of the rules, techniques, and theories of war for the American army, based on historical military experience. Because of these books Wagner quickly earned the reputation of being the army's final arbiter on matters of tactics, and before long both were required reading for any officer seeking advancement. So extensive was the readership of *Organization and Tactics*, and so valid and enduring were its lessons, that future fleet admiral Ernest J. King took from it "certain military concepts" and applied them to naval service.[2]

Wagner's principal aim as a military writer and educator was always to apply the lessons of the past to circumstances in the present. *Organization and Tactics* was no exception; indeed, it was as much a work of history as it was a tactical guide and textbook. Wagner was only one in a long line of military writers who insisted that example was the surest means of attaining an understanding of war. He wrote in his preface, "If an officer would prepare himself to be of service to his country, he must attentively consider the recorded experience of those who have learned war from the actual reality, and must accumulate by reading and reflection a fund of military knowledge based upon the experience of others." To that end, he "sought to give historical illustrations and examples as vouchers, so to speak, for the soundness of [my] premises or for the correctness of [my] assertions." Although Wagner was writing chiefly to defend and explain the 1891 *Infantry Drill Regulations*, he was careful to warn his readers that no system of war was absolute. "Every war has its surprises," he wrote, and even the most carefully conceived tactics might be demolished despite the best efforts of those who devised them. For that reason Wagner advised his readers not to place too much faith in "normal formations." Commanders who did so were inflexible and unimaginative and often found themselves overwhelmed when faced with a situation that required creative solutions. As he had done in *The Service of Security and Information*, Wagner refused to offer any more than broad generalizations on a commander's options in combat. Any system of tactics merely furnished "a standard . . . from which an officer in action can vary according to the conditions presented." The officer's ability to "vary," Wagner suggested, was dependent upon his knowledge of the history of war in general, so that he might have at his disposal a variety of possible tactical alternatives, which he might adopt or modify to meet the obstacle at hand.[3]

In large part, *Organization and Tactics* was a direct challenge to opponents of the extended order and critics of the new drill regulations. Wagner first provided a cogent "historical sketch of modern infantry," which demonstrated the interaction between weapons technology and attack formations. As weapons became more lethal over time, soldiers and officers naturally sought ways to avoid the effects of fire. According to Wagner, a turning point in modern infantry tactics was the innovation of skirmishing during the Napoleonic Wars, which brought flexibility and maneuver to the battlefield and enabled the attacker to bring increased firepower against the enemy. During the American Civil War, he continued, Union commanders increasingly employed skirmishing to reduce casualties. The great importance of skirmishing, however, was that it broke up the standard close-order line of battle into disorganized and dispersed formations; Prussia's extended order was merely an advanced refinement of the principle of dispersion. He concluded by observing that, over time, infantry formations of necessity became more dispersed, consequently requiring greater independence and discipline on the part of individual soldiers. The extended order described in the 1891 *Infantry Drill Regulations* was, therefore, simply the latest improvement of this trend and a timely answer to the deficiencies of Civil War–era combat tactics. To those who opposed the extended order, Wagner's overview made clear that they were bucking the tide of history. That alone, in Wagner's opinion, should be enough to demolish the criticism of tactical conservatives.[4]

But in case it was not, Wagner added an appendix in which he contemplated the contemporary European trend away from the extended order and a return to close-order tactics. *Organization and Tactics* appeared at the same time that the French army, under the influence of Charles Ardant du Picq and Ferdinand Foch, had turned onto the road that led inexorably to the infamous Plan 17. Integral to that plan was rejection of the extended order and a return to dense infantry formations on the assumption that this would raise the morale of the attackers. Wagner, too, affirmed the benefit of morale, but France's tactical regression seemed to him an absurdity. In describing what the French were advocating, he noted their belief that it was more important to maintain close control over soldiers during the attack than to emphasize "the greater security from loss afforded by a thinner line." Critics of the new American drill regulations took the French tactics to heart, arguing that dispersal required individual soldiers to act independently, and that it was foolhardy to assume they could do so. Although Wagner conceded that the backward-looking French system might well deliver greater firepower, he suggested that it would also "offer to the enemy a better target," and he hinted darkly that its actual use in combat would "necessitate further modifications which theory has not yet foreseen." Wagner did not live to see August 1914, or worse, the attacks of 1915–16, but he knew folly when he saw it and how costly it could be.[5]

The problems at hand were near-revolutionary "improvements in range and destructive effect of firearms." This rise in available firepower meant that "the defense has . . . gained enormously in comparison with the offensive," a confirmation of the Clausewitzian dictum that defense was the more powerful form of war. Against rapid-firing small arms and increasingly accurate artillery, the thick formations of old were now simply easy targets, making the offensive an ever more problematic affair. To succeed in the presence of a strong defense, Wagner declared that an attacker had to do several things at once: he must make the utmost use of his own fire while reducing the effect of the enemy's, present an unfavorable target, minimize the amount of time under fire, and then deliver a heavy blow at the end of the advance. The solution, of course, was the extended order.[6]

"Experience has shown," wrote Wagner, "that a firing line composed of skirmishers or of squads at suitable intervals best fulfills the first two conditions" noted. The only problem was that an entire battalion deployed in skirmish formation would be too extended to concentrate its fire on the enemy and would have insufficient mass to strike heavily at the end of its advance. To get around this conundrum, Wagner suggested a waved attack of three lines. A forward line of skirmishers advanced by squads, making use of natural cover for protection from the enemy, while laying down as heavy a fire as possible. A second, denser line of supports carefully followed, sending forward replacements for casualties ahead and contributing to fire upon the enemy as the attack closed on his position. Behind the second line followed a third, still denser, line of reserves. Wagner promoted the waved attack to limit casualties, to provide a steady supply of replacements, and importantly, to ensure that the attack went forward despite the intensity of enemy fire. Wagner knew well that cover could become an excuse to loiter; thus, he used the trailing lines to impel the soldiers in front onward toward the enemy. Wagner also counted on the waved attack's psychological effect upon the foe, noting that his morale would be "shaken by the spectacle of an unflinching advance which [his] fire does not stop."[7]

Wagner's concept of the waved attack, which employed the extended order as in the *Infantry Drill Regulations*, relied heavily upon the independent action of individual soldiers acting in small groups. As previously noted, individualism in combat was a near-revolutionary change in nineteenth-century tactics, and it met much resistance within the U.S. Army. Wagner, however, embraced individualism wholeheartedly, albeit not on its own merits. Individualism on the battlefield was necessary because the extended order required it. Since in Wagner's mind there was no reasonable alternative to the extended order, neither was there an alternative to individualism. He admitted that under extended order "each soldier is necessarily left more to his individual impulses than before," so he cautioned the reader that sedulous discipline was necessary to "prevent the men from getting completely out of hand." "The best evidences of true discipline," he wrote, "are found in the unmurmuring endurance of hardships by the soldiers, and in their willing, energetic, and intelligent efforts to perform their whole duty in the presence of the enemy." Cultivating that level of discipline was an officer's chief responsibility, and Wagner advised every commander, regardless of rank, to encourage the morale of his troops "as carefully as he provides for their food, clothing, and ammunition." Wagner acknowledged that there was "no law of universal application" in such matters, except that "a knowledge of human nature is half of the science of war."[8]

One of Wagner's principles of leadership was that a commander "should never give an order when there is reason to believe that its execution will be impossible." An effective assault depended on careful planning and realistic expectations of its prospects. Good commanders got results by avoiding unnecessary or wasteful attacks. For Wagner, the "least skillful" of all formations was the frontal attack, which, although occasionally expedient, required an enormous advantage in numbers, always accrued heavy casualties, and was "rarely decisive." Instead, he preferred the flank attack whenever possible. Such assaults weighed heavily on the defender's morale (especially if surprise was achieved) and enhanced the attacker's economy of force. When combined with a limited frontal attack that pinned the enemy in place and diverted his attention from the attack on his flank, Wagner suggested there was "no tactical combination that promises greater success." He added that "the increased range and power" of modern weapons made the flank attack more decisive than ever before, since such an assault actually diminished the power of the defense, which was generally oriented against a frontal attack. Caught in this disadvantage, the defender became vulnerable to the "increased range and power" of modern weapons, with advantage instead accruing to the offense.[9]

As an infantry officer, Wagner emphasized the importance of infantry by devoting many pages of *Organization and Tactics* to the theory and application of the extended order. However, he reminded readers that infantry by itself was a weak instrument. It had neither the range nor the firepower of artillery and could not reconnoiter, raid, or pursue like the cavalry. Left to its own devices on the battlefield, infantry was largely blind and, despite the extended order, unprotected. Yet infantry, in Wagner's view, was the decisive arm; it did most of the fighting, and it alone could seize, hold, or defend terrain. For Wagner, then, it was necessary to enhance infantry's qualities by uniting them with the qualities of artillery and cavalry; in other words, to apply the tactical properties of the three arms on the battlefield at the same time toward a single objective.[10]

The simultaneous use of the individual arms was certainly not unknown in the U.S. Army, but even during the Civil War, when such operations were common, there was no genuine unification of force.[11] Wagner, however, advocated the total integration of the three arms. Although he did not call it this, Wagner espoused a concept known to later soldiers as *combined arms*, in which each individual branch supports, and is in some way supported by, the action of the others. Wagner's own focus was somewhat narrower than this. Because he viewed the infantry as the critical arm, he maintained that under modern conditions, the cavalry and artillery existed mainly to support the infantry in its task (that is, that the others were auxiliary arms). In describing his theory of combined arms, Wagner first charted the histories of cavalry and artillery as he had done for the infantry, moved on to descriptions of their combat roles in the attack and defense, and then treated their use in combination with the infantry.

In the past, cavalry had been the agent of decision; its mobility, speed, and ability to inflict shock often made the difference between victory and defeat. The experience of the Civil War, however, indicated a decline in cavalry's efficacy in actual battle and an increase in noncombat but battle-related activities: reconnaissance, raids, pursuits, and operations against enemy communications. Because of the increasing defensive power of infantry, cavalry was forced to fight dismounted, assuming the formations and tactics of regular infantry. Cavalry that could not do so, Wagner charged, was "essentially a dependent arm . . . easily checked by insignificant bodies of hostile infantry." Indeed, Wagner practically wiped out the offensive mission of cavalry by suggesting that "good, intact, infantry, plentifully supplied with ammunition, and not taken by surprise, cannot be broken by a cavalry charge, however gallantly made." Cavalry action on the battlefield was effective only when the infantry was of poor quality, surprised, demoralized, already under attack by enemy infantry, or broken by the enemy's attack. Under Wagner's system of combined arms combat, the cavalry's new mission was to "reconnoiter the enemy, protect the flanks of the army . . . and reap the fruits of victory by an energetic pursuit."[12]

Wagner then turned to the artillery, which had traditionally been an anti-infantry weapon; its limited range and accuracy made it useful for little else. In most cases except at close range, cannon fire served mostly to inflict psychological terror on an attacker, to increase confusion, and quite literally to produce the smoky "fog of war" on the battlefield. As technology improved, however, introducing highly accurate long-range cannons and exploding shells, artillery fire against infantry became devastatingly deadly. As a result, Wagner saw the need, as did his European contemporaries, to protect one's own infantry in battle from the enemy's artillery. To resolve this issue Wagner adopted a new concept known as the artillery duel, in which one's artillery targeted that of the enemy before and during the infantry attack in order to "crush with a superior fire every hostile battery which opens upon the attacking infantry." Having done this, Wagner wrote, the artillery was to "turn its attention to the infantry of the defenders, which it must endeavor to overwhelm with such a storm of shrapnel as to shake its morale, impair the accuracy of is fire, and neutralize the advantage which it would otherwise have over the infantry of the attack."[13]

By introducing artillery support as an integral part of the infantry attack, Wagner pursued the late-nineteenth-century offensive ideal that firepower was the most important ingredient in battle and that fire superiority was the first requirement for a successful attack. The lethality of modern weapons made infantry highly vulnerable to a defender's combined infantry and artillery fire, despite the extended order. It was thus essential that attacking infantry have the continual support of artillery, making that arm the infantry's "indispensable companion." The importance of Wagner's description of the artillery's role in combined arms warfare was that artillery, like the cavalry, had become a support arm of the infantry (albeit an extraordinarily important one). Describing the general principles of the employment of artillery in battle, Wagner required that it be brought into action immediately and continuously, that it be massed for effect, and that its fire be accurate. He stressed that the artillery's "principal task" was to destroy the enemy's infantry and that fire upon the enemy's artillery, while essential, was merely to eliminate an obstacle that the attacking infantry could not overcome alone.[14]

Having defined the interrelated combat roles of the three arms, Wagner presented, at length, the manner in which they should be employed by a commander in a general attack. Referring to *The Service of Security and Information*, he reminded readers of the keen significance of timely and accurate intelligence on the enemy's intentions and dispositions. He then described precisely the characteristics of a successful assault: a clearly defined objective, a sound plan of attack, a pre-assault bombardment on the point(s) to be attacked, feints to confuse the enemy, the use of reserves at the right moment, and an aggressive pursuit by the cavalry once the enemy was broken. Although Wagner firmly advocated the offensive, he knew full well that not all attacks succeeded and that a withdrawal (he did not use the word *retreat*) might become necessary. On these occasions, he wrote, protecting the infantry was paramount. He advised that the cavalry "should not hesitate to sacrifice itself in desperate charges," and that the artillery should fire on the advancing enemy and hold its position "regardless of any loss of guns," in order to give the infantry time to regroup in a defensive position. Aside from these few brief suggestions, Wagner as usual refrained from offering more specific advice on the matter, since so much depended on individual circumstance. He then proceeded to describe the features of an effective defense, and the varied defensive duties of the three arms, with the same rigor and care with which he described the offense.[15]

Throughout *Organization and Tactics*, Wagner provided simplified résumés of the general principles governing the offensive and defensive use of the three arms alone and in concert. Although he was not one to make absolute rules for the conduct of battle, and recognized that there were always "exceptions to every general rule," condensing the essentials of infantry, cavalry, and artillery combat was not a bad idea. *Organization and Tactics* was a long book (more than five hundred pages), and the principles therein were many and detailed. Wagner's abbreviations gave the reader a solid foundation upon which to build a larger military vocabulary. Just as important, from his instructional point of view, was that upon completing the book, a diligent student officer would have read the most up-to-date American interpretation of the art of war, would have received a healthy dose of military theory, and would have taken a worthwhile history lesson in the process.

For the U.S. Army as a whole, though, *Organization and Tactics* represented an important watershed in its professional development. In addition to having a wholly new tactical regime that took it into the modern era of warfare, the army also had a comprehensive guidebook that would steer its tactics into the twentieth century. Although there were those, like James Chester, who believed that the army's burgeon-

ing educational system was creating "book-made generals," Wagner's
magnum opus began the slow process of ending the days when the army
had to rely on costly wartime trial and error to find talented commanders. But Chester was not willing to give way to this new era without a fight. In a lengthy criticism of *Organization and Tactics*, he scolded
Wagner that "experience cannot be purchased second hand," to which
Wagner responded, with justifiable scorn, that "it would be interesting,
but hardly profitable, to speculate upon the probable condition of the
art of war if every commander had to learn the art from his own experience." *Organization and Tactics* meant a more disciplined, systematic,
and historical approach to the American study of war, and to the American way of war as well. What mattered to Wagner more than anything
else was what worked and, equally important, how it worked. *Organization and Tactics* transferred to the army through the Infantry and Cavalry School this desire to produce results based on historical analysis
(regardless of how recent or from what source) and later became a doctrine of its own called "lesson-learning." As one of Wagner's colleagues
at the Infantry and Cavalry School wrote, through Wagner "the army
became students at once, and [his] books became as familiar as the drill
books." That said, however, it is important to note that Wagner's work
merely began the process by which the army took on an increasingly
sophisticated demeanor; it would be an exaggeration to suggest that
Organization and Tactics changed the army overnight.[16]

   Organization and Tactics aided the army's professional development
in another less evident but no less significant manner. Wagner, in his
way, was appealing for institutional legitimacy for the army—a mission statement of sorts—at a time when the army was seeking a viable
peacetime role. According to Wagner, by 1895 Indian fighting had all
but become a thing of the past, civil defense was a sham, coast defense a
task that did not require the army's undivided attention, and its recent
flirtation with strike breaking a barren pursuit. But with the decline of
these traditional missions, the army was an institution without a
clearly defined purpose and was flailing in the search of a new one. Numerous military authors filled the pages of the service journals with
heartfelt recommendations that the army should become the nation's
gendarmerie or become an institution (with the help of universal military service) for the inculcation of good citizenship and national service. Wagner deprecated all these "missions." Since the publication of
his first article in 1881, his persistent theme had been that the army's single function was defending the nation in war and that its paramount

mission in peacetime was preparing to wage the next war. The most notable aspect of *The Service of Security and Information* and *Organization and Tactics* was that both proceeded from the assumption of armies in the field—no minor outposts, no isolated regiments, but full-blown armies composed of corps, divisions, and brigades. This was a novel (perhaps even a quixotic) approach for an army of twenty-eight thousand soldiers who had not engaged in division-strength movements since 1865. Wagner was laying the operational groundwork for the conduct of large operations, while prompting his fellow officers to relearn concepts adopted during but abandoned after the Civil War. His goal in doing so was to ensure that the army understood and was ready to apply these concepts before a military emergency faced the country.

In seeking to advance the professional qualities of the army, Wagner plainly identified himself as a military progressive. By emphasizing continual education—whether in a dedicated institution or by simply keeping pace with current doctrine and innovations—and by prodding army officers to think seriously about their service and to act responsibly in it, Wagner shared identical tendencies with civilian professionals of the Progressive Era, who also sought their own institutional legitimacy. In his writing up until this point, Wagner had argued, in a roundabout way, that the military profession was a highly technical field dependent on specialized knowledge gained only by years of extensive education; that only military experts were capable of leading the nation in war, which was becoming increasingly complex; that officers had to understand the theory of war if they were to be successful in the practice of war; and that standards of officers' performance had to be maintained at a high level through periodic testing and efficiency reports. Wagner's progressivism in his search for a thoroughly professionalized officer corps is illustrated, in part, by his desire to combine a socially responsible service with a specific socially acceptable agenda—in this case, the defense of the United States in time of crisis. To encourage the growth of a professional ethic, Wagner, as Allan Millett writes, sought "the accumulation and systematic exploitation of specialized knowledge applied to specialized problems."[17]

With but one exception, *Organization and Tactics* was met with unrestrained acclaim. The editors of the *Journal of the U.S. Cavalry Association* were so impressed by Wagner's discussion of their arm that they printed, before the book's publication and without qualification, five chapters in two consecutive issues. A reviewer for the journal, noting that American officers once had to put up with the "prolix and tiresome style" of the Prussians, commended Wagner for writing his book in language so unambiguous that it could be "easily understood [even] by unprofessional readers." The exception noted was the redoubtable James Chester, who produced a negative review in the March 1895 issue of the *Journal of the Military Service Institution* (JMSI). Chester mounted his soapbox with a thinly veiled insinuation that Wagner believed "that the art of war can be acquired by books." Chester then proceeded to damn Wagner with faint praise, noting that while *Organization and Tactics* contained "excellent . . . teachings," it could "never make a tactician and may possibly spoil a few. . . . The art of war is a trade to be learned, and actual war is the best school to learn it in." For that reason, Chester thought the work was "too elaborate for a text-book," and "overloaded with details," no doubt suggesting that war was too complicated to be brought down to the level of the classroom or understood by any but geniuses.[18]

As an artillerist, Chester had specific reservations about the book, and he strenuously objected to Wagner's proposed abolition of an artillery reserve, which, for Chester, was "the thunderbolt which [the commander] holds in his hand, ready to be hurled at that part of the enemy's line which he has determined to attack." For Wagner, such concentration was all well and good, but he believed that withholding any guns from the action was an unconscionable waste of firepower and called the idea of the artillery reserve "ancient history." Chester, however, believed that "good infantry can get along with much less artillery than bad or indifferent infantry," somehow assuming that the quality of the attacking infantry should be the "controlling factor" in determining whether an artillery barrage was needed or not. Later, Chester attacked the extended order, noting that it had "recently fallen into disfavor in several European armies" and adding that its adoption by the U.S. Army was ill-advised because common soldiers could not be depended upon to follow even simple rules (which, he observed, were "so easy to lay down"). The only positive thing Chester had to say about *Organization and Tactics* was that it mentioned the importance of discipline. But even here his response had its sharp edge. Commenting that "the *few pages* devoted to this subject are the brightest in the book," Chester squarely aligned himself with the old school of iron discipline, not with enlightened instruction (emphasis added).[19]

Given Wagner's thin skin, he was by no means immune to Chester's criticism, which made its way into Wagner's correspondence with Tasker Bliss. Reminding Bliss of Chester's "idiosyncrasies," he suggested that his critic in the artillery had "not advanced beyond the smooth-bore era." Although Wagner tried to play the good sport by telling Bliss that he was "probably attaching too much importance to the review by noticing it at all," he was unable to let Chester's affront to his dignity go unchallenged. In the May 1895 issue of JMSI Wagner blasted Chester's criticisms in "'Organization and Tactics': A Review Reviewed." The outpouring was similar to Wagner's complaint about medical services rendered by Dr. Charles Richard three years earlier. Wagner contemptuously rebutted Chester's critique with refutatory evidence and suggested that Chester was delusional, ignorant, a careless reader, and guilty of grossly misrepresenting *Organization and Tactics* to JMSI's subscribers. So angry was Wagner at Chester's reproach that he devoted an entire article in the July 1895 issue of JMSI to rebutting Chester's arcane disagreement about the elimination of an artillery reserve (and for which Wagner was a awarded a hundred-dollar prize). Wagner, in his own mind, was always right, his detractors were uniformly wrong, and he considered it his duty to point out their errors. Although these antagonists did not cross swords again, they remained in each other's subsequent articles the anonymous embodiment of hidebound reaction, on the one hand, and impractical intellectualism on the other.[20]

In the long run, Chester's criticisms came to nothing, and *Organization and Tactics* was adopted immediately by the Infantry and Cavalry School upon Wagner's completion of the manuscript in September 1893. That month Wagner assumed the chair of the Department of Military Art at the school, beginning a new era every bit as significant as had been Colonel McCook's appointment as the school's commandant. Wagner immediately undertook a reorganization of his department, which McCook's successor, Edwin F. Townsend, found to be "remarkably successful." In his new position, Wagner's principal interest, not surprisingly, was an emphasis on tactical problems. Accordingly, he redesigned the department's applicatory methodology to include practical field exercises with troops, written exercises on selected tactical problems, and map problems, known at the time as *kriegsspiel*. The military principles upon which the exercises were based were rendered by recitations from *The Service of Security and Information* and *Organization and Tactics*.[21]

Wagner's practical field exercises applied the various fundamentals of small-unit duties as described in *The Service of Security and Information*, during which students commanded detachments of the Fort Leavenworth garrison. He included in these exercises "terrain rides," in which students solved "tactical problems on the actual terrain, various conditions being assumed, and the troops being . . . entirely imaginary." The latter was necessary since the army was not yet able or ready to conduct large-scale maneuvers and because the Leavenworth garrison was too small for Wagner's broader purposes. Written exercises were designed to acquaint the students with the important process of writing orders. The use of map problems Wagner realized was somewhat controversial. In his departmental report of 1894, he noted the "widely divergent views entertained by military critics as to the value of instruction by means of *Kriegsspiel*," a reference, no doubt, to James Chester. Wagner's intention was to acquaint his students with more abstract principles of tactics and strategy, and in so doing he prepared them for the sort of planning they might later perform on a military staff. Wagner believed it was a "significant fact" that those who excelled in *kriegsspiel* were also "the most intelligent, zealous, and commonsense" students at the school.[22]

Wagner was materially aided in these endeavors by his West Point friend and classmate, Captain Eben Swift. (Swift, incidentally, had been in attendance at Wagner's near-disastrous West Point graduation party.) A cavalry officer and champion pistol shot, Swift directed the practical exercises mentioned, designed the *kriegsspiel* scenarios, and in general organized the entire applicatory program at Fort Leavenworth. While Wagner judged his friend's work "invaluable," and praised him for "his able and zealous efforts," Swift was by no means Wagner's intellectual equal. But where Wagner excelled in theory and history, Swift was eminently talented in matters of military functionality; it was he who made Wagner's ideas work. Among Swift's most enduring contributions to the Infantry and Cavalry School—indeed, to the entire army—was designing a standardized system for the promulgation of orders, although Wagner had already indicated the necessity for "clear and definite instructions" in *The Service of Security and Information* and provided his own format for orders in *Organization and Tactics*. Swift's systematic procedure, however, was far more flexible and thorough than Wagner's and was easily integrated into the school's field exercises. Each order was written according to a five-paragraph form and described, in brief, unambiguous language, the dispositions of the enemy, the objective of the operation, the tasks of individual units assigned to the operation, preparations for logistical support, and information regarding the commander's exact location. As historian Timothy Nenninger has noted about Swift's innovation, "By standardizing tactical practices, the field order contributed to a better understanding among officers. It encouraged uniform doctrine and established standard tactical terminology, an obvious advantage in the stress and confusion of war." Equally important, Swift's use of a standardized, universal format for writing orders and Wagner's fastidious devotion to a sound tactical education based on the practical lessons of history combined to create a doctrine of "safe leadership" that advanced the general ideals of Wagner's military progressivism. Officers similarly trained, who spoke the same technical language and understood the same military principles, said Wagner, could be relied upon to "make command decisions based soundly on an appropriate principle of war."[23]

By 1896, Wagner and Swift had refined the applicatory system to such an extent that Wagner boasted in his report that year that "The benefit derived from such exercises can hardly be overestimated. . . . These exercises are well calculated to develop a young officer's self-reliance and confidence, more than any amount of ordinary garrison service." Moreover, following Wagner's personal reluctance to prescribe concrete maxims of war in any of his own works, students at Leavenworth were given "great latitude" in solving problems and conducting exercises. Wrote Wagner in 1895, "No hard and fast solution was assumed to which the students were compelled to conform, but any solution was accepted that was not in violation of correct military principles." His refusal to lay down "approved solutions" stressed the need for improvisation and quick and insightful thinking. Students were thus encouraged to use and cultivate their intuition, combining it with their knowledge of military history and theory. This was Wagner's way of developing a military intuition, that difficult-to-define *art* of war, which opponents of military education argued could not be learned in school.[24]

Yet even Wagner recognized that there were intangibles in war for which no set of general guidelines could be designed. It was for this reason that anti-intellectuals like Chester strenuously promoted the so-called inspired leadership principle of command. The rift between educators and *kriegsspielers* on the one hand and proponents of natural military genius on the other was caused by a struggle to maintain the *art* of war in the face of the increasing technological or scientific qualities of war and the problem of command: how it was defined, nurtured, and applied. As war became more complex and deadly, reactionaries could and did comfortably assert that its very complexity was an obstacle to mastering the art of waging it and that only native ability—what Chester called genius—could conquer it. This rule of leadership, sustained by the exploits of history's great captains, relied heavily on a commander's intuition and instinct, neither of which could be cultivated in school and which, proponents assumed, were perfected only in the churning cauldron of war. Wagner and Swift realized that simple "book learning" was hopelessly inadequate to the grave task of training officers to lead men in battle, which is why they pioneered the applicatory method—to learn, apply, criticize, relearn, reapply, and so on. By this insistence that junior officers be schooled in the appropriate theoretical, historical, and practical lessons of war, officers would be better equipped to undertake military operations than they would otherwise be. Talent was necessary in war, but undisciplined talent was unpredictable; it had to be refined and directed. Safety and good judgment were equally necessary, and Wagner insisted that learning from the examples of past success and failure was a better, less costly means of achieving an understanding of war. The goal of the Infantry and Cavalry School, then, was to equip officers with the fundamentals of command and the wherewithal to develop, through continual study and practice, an understanding of the operational art.

To extend Leavenworth's system of application, while seeking to inculcate students with historical examples of command decision in war, Wagner hoped to augment the courses he and Swift taught by allowing the best ten students of their department to visit selected Civil War battlefields, with a mind to making "a practical study of the terrain in connection with tactical movements." Wagner knew well the value of battlefield visits, having toured European sites extensively in 1887 and having used this experience to write *The Campaign of Königgrätz*. He sought approval of his plan in March 1895, noting that battlefield tours would be "a fitting cap-shief to the course of instruction in the classroom." He preferred that the entire class participate in these tours but realized the cost would likely be too great. His long-term intention was for the student visitors, having first read the available literature, to prepare monographs on individual battles based on historical accounts and their own inspection of the terrain. These would then be added to the Infantry and Cavalry School curriculum for use by future students as part of their regular course work. From a short-term, practical point of view, Wagner requested the visits as part of his ongoing application of map problems. By comparing historical accounts with maps of the area on the actual fields of battle, Wagner suggested, "object lessons in the

nature of positions for artillery and infantry, the topographical considerations affecting the security of flanks, the selection of points of attack,
etc." could be applied with an effectiveness not possible in other, more
academic settings. Wagner's proposal won the support of then commanding general John M. Schofield, who believed it would be "very
beneficial," but it was disapproved by Secretary of War Joseph R. Doe
for reasons of economy. Although battlefield visits were but a fond
hope for the moment, Wagner's idea did become a reality after his
death.[25]

Even as Wagner and Swift extended the sophistication of Leavenworth's primary function, the school still had its problems. In his 1895–
96 annual report, Wagner complained bitterly that certain regimental
commanders were still sending their least qualified and undisciplined
officers to the school. He was pleased to note that most commanders
understood the value of a Leavenworth education, but he hastened to
add that there were yet those who assumed that the school's mission
was to "remedy the educational deficiencies of a few men who are not
prepared to profit by an extended course of military study." Wagner
was not of a mind to allow the "mentally lame, halt, or blind . . . [to]
misrepresent his regiment and to make a vain attempt to remedy his
. . . deficiency in geography by the study of strategy." An evil equal to
this, he wrote, was the retention of students who had twice failed their
examinations for graduation but were sent back to Leavenworth yet
again by their regiments. Wagner asserted that "neglect of duty . . . or
hopeless incapacity" was the cause of such failures, and he wanted it
known that "the Infantry and Cavalry School is neither a pleasant resort for a lazy officer nor a convenient asylum for a stupid one." To allow a deficient student to remain at the school in the hope that he might
"learn *something*," he continued, would only convince the student of
"the idea that his military superiors view his deficiency as a matter of
small moment." It would also tie Leavenworth to the remediation of
problems that were not its responsibility, rather than allowing it specifically to train officers for command.[26]

That "something" that Leavenworth students were learning was becoming a matter of some debate in army circles. The question was increasingly raised whether the school was emphasizing pure theory at
the expense of its practical application; Wagner himself had some difficulty finding the correct balance between the two, and he was criticized
for not acting quickly to dispel such doubts. Captain William H. Carter
summarized the problem in a laudatory article on Leavenworth in the

July 1894 issue of JMSI: "Purely practical soldiers are apt to formulate false theories," he wrote, "while theorists are quite apt to make false application of good principles. A happy combination of theory and practice, as is contemplated at the Fort Leavenworth School, should . . . give the best results." Wagner himself, in his 1889 article "An American War College," noted that at Leavenworth "nothing is limited to mere theory." Increasingly, though, as Carter explained, some officers in the army were criticizing the school "because, it is claimed, there is too much theory and not enough practice." Carter did not believe this to be true, but he failed to dispel the idea, for he wrote of the need "to make the practical part of the instruction at the school far superior to any . . . obtained at any other station."[27]

Three years later, the misapprehension Carter had identified exploded on the Infantry and Cavalry School when the Military Service Institution awarded the gold medal in its annual essay competition to Captain James S. Pettit, of the First Infantry. Pettit's prize-winning article, "The Proper Military Instruction for Our Officers," was a lengthy, subjective and highly critical litany of recommendations to improve the quality of army education. Some of his criticism was directed at the Infantry and Cavalry School, which he found to be fundamentally flawed. While he believed it had "reached a high level of efficiency," and wished that every lieutenant of infantry and cavalry could attend, Pettit repeated the view that theory was overemphasized in its curriculum. He observed that courses in Wagner's Department of Military Art were emphasized to the near-total exclusion of every other department except engineering. Considering that it was called the *Infantry* and *Cavalry* School, Pettit wondered why Leavenworth did not "teach student officers, first, all the duties and functions of their own particular arms, and then such accessories as time and circumstances may permit?" If this was not the intent of the school, and if Wagner's department was instead the true acme therein, then Pettit suggested that "the name of the school should be changed to War College."[28]

Although Pettit's article had a number of serious flaws, not the least of which was making recommendations in one place and countermanding them later, his criticism of Leavenworth's educational objective was generally accurate. Wagner, following the ambition of former commandant Alexander McCook, was indeed attempting to create a war college and had said so openly several years before in "An American War College." In late 1897, Wagner's Department of Military Art became the Department of Strategy, signaling an abrupt shift in Leavenworth's curricular objectives. By the time this change took place Wagner had moved on, but it clearly bore his stamp. Instruction in the new department did away completely with applicatory field exercises; while these were still used at the school, they were moved to a completely new and separate Department of Tactics, which incorporated the old departments of infantry and cavalry. The Department of Strategy included courses in military policy and institutions, military geography, logistics, staff duties, the conduct of war, map maneuvers and war games, and military history and required a thesis. During the school year 1896–97, when Pettit wrote his article, the Department of Military Art conducted only nine field exercises over the last two months of the school year. Wagner began two new lecture series on "Strategical Operations" and the "Principles of Strategy," the first of which, interestingly enough, stressed Napoleonic, not American, campaigns.[29]

When Pettit's article appeared, Wagner had left the Infantry and Cavalry School for duty in Washington DC. By then he had been at Leavenworth so long, and had been so instrumental to its growth, that he and the school were practically indistinguishable. Wagner's anger was naturally aroused by Pettit's essay, and he typically took the captain's criticisms personally. In a long commentary in the March 1897 number of the JMSI, Wagner vented himself on Pettit, taking issue with him on matters both insignificant and profound. Much of Wagner's refutation was over Pettit's reproach that too much attention was given to things theoretical at Leavenworth and not enough to practical instruction and that the school was failing to instruct its students in the basic duties and functions of their own arms. In response to the latter, Wagner fumed that this was not the Infantry and Cavalry School's responsibility. Rather, he said, the school expected its students already to have acquired the basics in their own regiments. For Wagner, the primary objective of the Leavenworth school was "*to give instruction in those subjects which cannot be learned with equal facility or equal thoroughness at ordinary posts.*" As to the alleged preeminence of "an elaborate system of theoretical instruction," Wagner retorted that "rational practical instruction must be based on sound theory," adding that "theoretical instruction is first given in the different features of tactics, and a practical application of the theory is then made as far as possible *pari passu* with the lessons."[30]

The direction of Wagner's curriculum at Leavenworth, however, made this claim specious at best, for the net effect of the school's revised curriculum obscured its stated mission with Wagner's dream for it. Pettit had only made the mistake of exposing the growing disparity between Leavenworth's original aim and Wagner's obvious desire to turn it into an institution on the model of the German *Kriegsakademie*. Wagner could not disprove this, and he admitted as much by suggesting that changing the name of the Infantry and Cavalry School to War College "would [not] be at all objectionable." He concluded his rebuke with an indirect *ad hominem* attack on Pettit, observing that

> the school is doubtless held in slight esteem by the three following classes: 1. Ultra-conservative relics of the past, who dislike it because it represents something new; 2. Men who, owing to their own mental deficiencies or moral shortcomings, have been sent away from the school without a diploma, and who shield their wounded vanity behind an assumed contempt for the institution which found them unworthy; 3. Thoughtless officers who, without making use of their own intellect or powers of observation, accept without reflection the assertions of the two former classes.

Pettit did not fall into either of the first two classes, so one may assume that Wagner placed him in the third.[31]

The issue did not end there. Pettit responded to Wagner's attack with the telling suggestion that "the atmosphere at Leavenworth seems to be extremely sensitive and easily put in motion. It is impossible to determine which is most unpleasant to them, praise or fault-finding." Lieutenant Colonel Henry Lazelle, it will be recalled, encountered the same sensitivity when he criticized the school in 1883. Pettit's reply, like Wagner's, was blunt and uncharitable. Pettit accused Wagner of "'extracting' an article to suit his own purposes," of "personal abuse" and "blindness," and even opaquely questioned Wagner's sanity. He finally reminded Wagner that "people who live in glass houses should keep the panes frosted," and that "courtesy among military men is indispensable to discipline."[32]

Wagner was indignant and said so in a remarkable rejoinder to Pettit in the July 1897 issue of JMSI. Noting that "no institution . . . has been the victim of so much ignorant criticism as the United States Infantry and Cavalry School," he unwittingly confirmed Pettit's comment about Leavenworth sensitivity to criticism by saying that "the officers on duty at the Infantry and Cavalry School naturally object to unjust criticism, and . . . can be scarcely expected to relish praise when it is so qualified as to constitute the faint variety which implies damnation."

Wagner then accused Pettit of knowing "nothing about the school from his own experience or observation," remarking that no one he knew "would feel aggrieved at adverse criticism if it had at least the merit, like some works of fiction, of being 'founded upon fact.'" He took special note of Pettit's assertion that the army was not ready for a war college, stating that "such a college is needed by any nation that regards war as even a remote possibility." Of course, Wagner was one of the few officers in the army advocating such an institution. His personal reputation was intimately bound up in it, and he had never been one to leave insults unchallenged.[33]

The haste and fury with which Wagner replied to his detractors suggests a degree of insecurity about his own accomplishments to date. Considering that Wagner had been a marked underachiever at West Point, he had much to make up for, and he may well have found some relief for his past academic mediocrity by overcompensating later in life. It may also be true that Wagner was simply a "late bloomer" who needed a nudge in a certain direction before his qualities became evident, a phenomenon not uncommon among West Point graduates. Throughout his career, he never seemed to be completely satisfied with his own accomplishments, and he continually played the game of one-upmanship with anyone who challenged him. The taunting sarcasm he used to answer his critics is some evidence of his desire to demean them and, simultaneously, to magnify his own intellect. Admittedly, Wagner was a much different kind of officer than his peers. He taught, rather than practiced, the principles of command and the art of war, and this was an extremely uncommon vocation in the nineteenth-century army. Military academics were rare, and Wagner was one of the few whose reputation was built on his teaching and writing abilities alone. In time, his success in these areas would cause him considerable anguish. General George C. Marshall, a Leavenworth student in 1907 and 1908, recalled that "opposition to any studious preparation [among] older officers was very decided" and that they were "particularly critical" of Wagner's efforts toward that end. Wagner suspected that his talents were not wholly appreciated by higher-ups in the army, and he had reason to believe that there were those who actively sought to retard his advance in rank because he was not like other officers. Thus it is no surprise that Wagner would defend himself vigorously against all comers, if only to demonstrate the value of his unorthodox occupation. His feelings of being thwarted pursued him to the end of his career.[34]

Chapter 5

The View from Mount Pisgah

By the end of 1896, Wagner had climbed about as high as his rank would take him at the Infantry and Cavalry School. Although his work there had brought him acclaim within the army, Wagner had been at Leavenworth for ten years, and he was too ambitious an officer to stay put. When he heard, in the summer of that year, of a majority available in the Adjutant General's Office, he applied for it at once, even writing to Adjutant General George D. Ruggles personally for the favor. At this point Wagner began to lean seriously on his friends and superiors within the officer corps for their testimonials to the promotion board; in all, thirty-one such letters were sent, with a successful result. Wagner was promoted to major in November, and in March 1897 he left Fort Leavenworth for his new assignment as chief of the Military Information Division (MID) in Washington DC.[1]

The position was an appropriate one for Wagner. Formed in 1885, the MID was the army's first independent intelligence-gathering agency. With *The Service of Security and Information* to his credit and in wide circulation, and having expanded this work at Leavenworth with lectures in military geography and foreign military organizations, Wagner brought obvious qualifications to the MID, which was already applying concepts he taught at the Infantry and Cavalry School. In 1896, for example, one of Wagner's assistant lecturers—Lieutenant Joseph T. Dickman—delivered a lecture on "Military Policy and Institutions," which included a description of the German general staff. Germany's staff included a special "bureau of information," which compiled and disseminated "data concerning the organization of foreign armies (the press, literature, and other sources)." MID was already doing precisely this, and more, and had done since 1889. By the time Wagner took over, the division had posted military attachés at American embassies in nearly all the major capitals of Europe. These officers observed directly the progress of foreign armies and collected information not available in published form. Such information that was publicly obtainable was collected by MID on a reciprocal basis with foreign governments. The division periodically published reports on a variety of military subjects; in 1897 reports on the Swedish, Greek, and Turkish armies and the U.S. militia were printed. MID had also undertaken the long-neglected task of publishing current and accurate maps of foreign countries and certain regions of the United States, many of which were made available to the general public.[2]

Wagner was at MID for only a year, but he worked hard to increase the division's efficiency and importance. During his brief tenure new attachés drew assignments in Tokyo, Bern, and Istanbul and additional officers were assigned to existing legations elsewhere in Europe. Because the number of public and military requests for maps grew steadily, Wagner enlarged the staff and increased the production of MID's cartographic section, which printed, in early 1898, several detailed maps of Cuba and the cities of Havana and Santiago. He also increased the number of subscriptions to foreign military periodicals, made more discretionary funds available to the division's attachés in addition to an overall increase in MID's annual budget, and got larger and better office space for its Washington headquarters. Ten new publications were printed under Wagner's supervision, including a series of "Military Notes" on Cuba, Puerto Rico, the Philippines, and the Spanish forces in the Caribbean. Finally, to spread out the workload for his overtaxed personnel, Wagner authorized an increase of MID's clerical staff. He was rewarded for his efforts with promotion to lieutenant colonel in February 1898.[3]

Given the short duration of his assignment at MID, the bulk of Wagner's duties in Washington were administrative. By the end of 1897, however, the deteriorating political situation in Cuba had attracted his attention, and he penned a memorandum to Secretary of War Russell A. Alger requesting that "an officer be detailed to proceed to Cuba to examine . . . and report on the military situation" there. When Alger did not respond, Wagner wrote to him again in February, after the sinking of the battleship *Maine*. Anticipating the likelihood of American intervention in Cuba, Wagner was determined that the United States have at its disposal reliable information about the Cuban insurgency and Spanish forces on the island. Alger approved this second request, whereupon Wagner selected Lieutenant Andrew S. Rowan, who had previously performed confidential duty and whom Wagner found to possess "tact, discretion and good judgment," to make a secret reconnaissance to Cuba. He also arranged for another of his subordinates, Lieutenant Henry H. Whitney, "a young officer of unusual promise," to reconnoiter the island of Puerto Rico.[4]

What transpired from this decision brought national attention to

Rowan's so-called message to García. Rowan's mission was to land in Cuba and find resistance leader General Calixto García. The "message" was actually a request from Wagner for information of a military nature on the overall situation in the Oriente region of Cuba. Specifically, Wagner wanted intelligence on the positions occupied by the Spanish army; its numbers, condition, and morale; the quality of Spanish officers; a description of the geography; the condition of roads; and as Rowan himself put it, any other "information which would enable the American general staff to lay out a campaign" in Cuba. Rowan was also to ask García for his suggestions on mounting such a campaign. Since Rowan's mission was secret, Wagner insisted that he take nothing that would disclose his purpose should he be captured. Consequently, Wagner took Rowan to his home every night for two weeks and grilled him on the message to make sure he had every detail solidly memorized. Rowan sailed for Cuba on 8 April 1898 and returned on 14 May, bringing with him three of García's deputies and all the information Wagner requested. Although Wagner was responsible for the success of Rowan's mission, Rowan got much more mileage out of it than did Wagner. He was hailed as a national hero, lauded by the motivational writer of the day, Elbert S. Hubbard, and later promoted to colonel of volunteers.[5]

On 29 March, while Wagner was giving Rowan his instructions, Alger appointed Wagner to a two-man army-navy strategy board charged with preparing joint operational plans for the looming war with Spain. He was joined by navy Captain Albert S. Barker, and they were the only members of the board. Barker was already serving on the Naval War Board, which had determined that the first order of business should war break out was the destruction of the Spanish high seas fleet. Their duties on the army-navy board brought Wagner and Barker into regular contact with Alger, Secretary of the Navy John D. Long, and his assistant, Theodore Roosevelt.[6]

On 2 April Wagner and Barker meet with Roosevelt and the Naval War Board to define the duties of the army-navy board. Barker had a material advantage that Wagner did not, namely that the navy had already prepared its own war plans. Barker's role, then, was essentially to secure army cooperation for naval operations against Spain. The army's commanding general, Nelson A. Miles, was on record in opposition to an invasion of Cuba, preferring limited harassing attacks against the Spanish along the Cuban coast. Moreover, president William McKinley was noncommittal on the issue of an invasion and un certain about political and military objectives should war break out. In general, Secretary Alger anticipated defensive measures along the American coast, rather than offensive operations in Cuba, and spent the War Department's share of the $50 million congressional emergency defense appropriation accordingly. When public pressure forced McKinley to announce the probability of an invasion, the army was caught unprepared and Wagner in effect became responsible for conceiving the army's operational strategy. Despite help from Barker, Wagner had to operate in a near vacuum. Although this afforded him the luxury of drawing up a strategy as he saw fit—and based, among other things, on the information he had compiled at MID—there is no evidence to suggest that he was aided by Secretary Alger, General Miles, or any of the various army staff bureaus. Wagner thus by default became responsible for conceiving and enunciating general war plans and goals for the U.S. Army. He did have plenty of help from the better-prepared navy, though. Barker recalled that Secretary Long "was very complimentary in his remarks about the smooth way in which the Army and Navy Board worked, as Colonel Wagner and I had no friction whatever." In the coming weeks, Miles relied heavily on Wagner for strategic planning and implemented nearly all his recommendations without comment, although he was never particularly enthusiastic about it.[7]

Between 29 March and 25 April Barker and Wagner prepared a series of position papers that represented the course of action the joint services should take if and when war erupted. Since any military action would ostensibly be for the benefit of Cuba, Barker and Wagner interviewed a Cuban representative, known only as Señor Quesada, about Cuba's wishes should the United States intervene. Quesada did not want a large American invasion, believing it would create a feeling of inferiority and dependency among the Cuban people. He especially did not want Negro troops sent, for this "would make the Cubans feel that they were despised." To indicate American respect, Quesada suggested that Cuban guerrilla leaders accompany an American invasion force, and that rebel units be attached to army divisions. In the meantime, while waiting for the United States to act, Quesada requested artillery, horses and mules, forty thousand rifles, and five million rounds of ammunition. Should the U.S. Army indeed mount an invasion, he believed five thousand soldiers would be sufficient to put the Spanish occupation to flight. Quesada's extravagant requests prompted Barker to write in the notes of the meeting that the Cubans were evidently "jealous of us as a race and only want to use us."[8]

Neither Barker nor Wagner was favorably impressed by Quesada, but most of his requests nonetheless made their way into a report they prepared on 4 April. Several of their findings echoed an earlier memorandum that had advised the immediate destruction of the Spanish fleet and a total naval blockade of the island of Cuba. The report endorsed Quesada's demand for rifles and ammunition (albeit of the obsolete black powder Springfield .45 caliber variety) and accepted without question his opinion that an invasion force that included Negro troops would be "highly distasteful" and would "deaden the welcome" that might be extended to American soldiers. The report assumed that an invasion with the goal of capturing the capital city of Havana would be the most decisive, and that an expeditionary force of fifty thousand troops would be adequate to the task. Barker and Wagner considered Mariél, about thirty miles east of Havana, to be the best site for a landing. From there the army would march quickly on Havana itself. Once the city was deprived of its water supply, surrounded on land, and blockaded by sea, the two officers anticipated that its fall "would be certain, and probably speedy."[9]

Cognizant of one of the keys to tropical operations, the writers strongly advocated a delay in land operations until after the rainy season (at the time about six months away) for fear that an invasion might otherwise "be followed by an appalling sacrifice of life from disease, and might be the means of introducing . . . yellow fever into the United States." The board explicitly rejected Quesada's request that Cuban insurgents accompany the American army in the field. "Such a combination," thought Barker and Wagner, "would necessitate the adoption of Santiago de Cuba or Puerto Principe as a theater of *our* operations, and would carry us too far away from Havana, where our decisive efforts should at first be exerted." They were likewise convinced that Cuban guerrilla leaders would make "extravagant claims for command" and that they would be "reluctant to serve under the authority of our generals." By postponing the date of an invasion of Cuba, and by providing the insurgents with a lavish supply of arms, the board reinforced the opinion then entertained by the War Department that the army would have a limited role in a war against Spain—one directed against Cuba only and for the sole purpose of denying the Spanish their principal base of operations.[10]

For his part, Wagner believed an invasion would probably be necessary, but he knew that Miles was resistant to such an operation. He was also aware of the growing public clamor for an immediate invasion, which he believed would have disastrous results. He thus presented Miles with a detailed memorandum on 11 April that justified and explained the conclusions he and Captain Barker had reached a week before, especially regarding the issue of delay. Those who advocated an immediate invasion argued that a blockade of Cuba alone would hurt the island's civilian population, much of which had been herded into Spanish reconcentration camps and was therefore highly dependent upon outside sources of food. While the blockade wore on and the army waited for advantageous weather, the United States would be spending—or, it was feared, squandering—millions of dollars in a slow-motion war against Spain. The British, these advocates argued, had captured Havana during the rainy season in 1762; certainly Americans could do likewise. A delay, they continued, would make the United States look weak and indecisive abroad, would leave the American east coast vulnerable to a Spanish attack, and might lure some foreign competitor to intervene in Cuba, violating the Monroe Doctrine.[11]

Wagner conceded that all these things were possible but saw them as unlikely. An immediate invasion of Cuba was more dangerous than delay. Without a vaccine against yellow fever, the likelihood of significant casualties to this dread disease could not be exaggerated. Certainly the American public would not tolerate a decision that put American soldiers needlessly at risk. Although he was probably loath to admit it, Wagner pointed out that the army's present organization did not allow for an immediate invasion. Always the historian, he offered the Union's performance at First Bull Run as an object lesson in the fruits of unpreparedness, arguing that adequate preparation beforehand was sure protection against a debacle. As for the British seizure of Havana in 1762, Wagner countered with Napoleon Bonaparte's disastrous attempt to occupy nearby Haiti during the rainy season in 1802. While a similar fate might not befall American operations, under the circumstances Wagner was not willing to endorse such a decision. His memorandum was eminently to Miles's liking, for it reinforced Miles's preference that the navy strangle the Spanish into submission rather than that American troops be committed to a land war.[12]

Later that day (11 April), Wagner and Barker were summoned to the White House for a meeting with President McKinley and his cabinet. Barker informed the president that the navy was ready for war at any time. The army, of course, was another matter, and Wagner spoke honestly and at length about its deficiencies. For the most part, he reiterated for McKinley what he had already told General Miles, who was in attendance at the meeting. Although the president appreciated the army's shortcomings, he was noticeably disturbed by the recommendation for delay, given the growing public demand for an immediate invasion. Wagner acknowledged the obstacle, noting that chest-thumping war hawks were bragging that the United States "could put one hundred thousand soldiers . . . into Cuba in a few days." While this was technically possible, he quickly added that "they would not be soldiers but a mob." Wagner wanted a quick, uncomplicated victory, insisting that only professionals could do the job. At its present strength, however, the army would still need to be reinforced by the National Guard. This, too, would force delay. Wagner reminded the president that the army's lengthy sojourn on the frontier had prevented instruction "in the movements of large bodies, such as brigades and divisions." A period of appropriate training, particularly where the guard was concerned, was unavoidable. McKinley, Long, Alger, and other cabinet officials questioned Wagner carefully, and he stuck firmly to his conviction that the army could not be made ready for war any time soon. A delay might not be good politics, but it would certainly save lives. Barker recalled that Wagner's statements were "not pleasing to Secretary Alger," who had done little to prepare for a potential foreign expedition. Despite the possible political repercussions, McKinley accepted the Wagner-Barker proposal to concentrate against Havana after the rainy season, to Miles's chagrin. To his credit, McKinley refused to withhold black troops from the invasion. When the meeting was over, Wagner reportedly provided McKinley with a large situation map of Cuba, which the president used in his "war room" in the White House during the conflict.[13]

With the president's approval in hand, Wagner set to work drafting the army's order of battle and a schedule for mobilization. To assist him, he called on the services of two rising officers in the Adjutant General's Office, Majors Theodore Schwan and William H. Carter. Together, they compiled a long list of recommendations in a memorandum to General Miles that expanded upon the one Wagner had given Miles on 11 April. Although the commanding general was resisting an invasion of Cuba, it was evident to these officers, at least, that the U.S. Army would be engaged in a foreign war requiring the formation of a major expeditionary force in the very near future. This prospect was complicated when the so-called Hull bill, which would have increased the army to 104,000 troops, was defeated with the help of the National Guard Association. In its place the guard demanded, and got, a more limited increase of 60,000, with an additional 40,000 volunteers thrown in. With its regular establishment standing at only about 28,000 troops, Wagner faced the question of how to incorporate an additional 72,000 new recruits and volunteers without diluting the army's combat effectiveness. Having read Emory Upton's *Military Policy of the United States*, Wagner, Schwan, and Carter placed little faith in volunteers. In their memorandum, they reiterated that judgment by stating the "well known fact that raw troops cannot be depended upon to conduct offensive operations successfully." Wagner and his cohorts figured that the most efficient solution to this problem was to strip American coastal fortifications and interior garrisons of "every available man"—the regulars being "our best and most proficient troops"—and to replace them for the duration of the war with volunteers or national guardsmen, who could be "depended upon when acting upon a pure defensive, especially behind intrenchments." The memorandum proposed that garrisons be all but abandoned, leaving only "one officer . . . and two men from each company" at each and the posts guarded by hired civilian watchmen (preferably retired enlisted personnel).[14]

There was also the issue of army training, which the authors believed volunteers would complicate. While the delay agreed upon might enable the army to bring volunteers or guardsmen up to regular army standards, they were not certain that this could be accomplished in six months. Meanwhile, the army itself would be making ready for the invasion and for other military operations generally; training "raw troops" would be a time-consuming, frustrating, and potentially long-term pursuit. It would be better, then, to limit volunteers to uncomplicated duties, rather than to attempt to address their shortcomings hastily. Wagner, Schwan, and Carter did not completely eschew overseas participation by volunteers, but they allowed that only "the best regiments and batteries" should be authorized to accompany the invasion.[15]

That said, the writers envisioned an army organization based upon the long-established expansible army concept, which endorsed the inclusion of volunteers. Each regiment of the regular army would be accompanied by two trained regiments of volunteers; the former would provide organization and officers, while the latter provided mostly manpower. Given the fact that the coming war with Spain would be the first in which Americans experienced combat against modern weapons, the memorandum emphasized the importance of artillery and insisted that a minimum of twelve and a maximum of twenty batteries accompany each corps. Once formed into brigades of three regiments each, the brigades attached to independent divisions and these formed into corps, the expeditionary force would be concentrated at three ports for embarkation: Tampa, Mobile, and New Orleans. Nearly all the points of the memorandum were approved by the War Department (significantly, the suggestion about artillery was not) and enacted on 15 April. Twenty-two regiments were ordered to the three embarkation points, but over the next few weeks most of them wound up in Tampa, completely negating the desire of Wagner, Schwan, and Carter to minimize confusion and crowding during the buildup.[16]

Having gone this far in the service of his country, Wagner was determined not to be left behind when the shooting started. Following the American declaration of war on 25 April, he wrote to the adjutant general stating that it would be "humiliating" if he, an instructor in the art of war and a well-known author of books on the subject, was left behind at a desk job while his colleagues and former students went off to practice what he had preached. Despite an army surgeon's declaration that Wagner's frequent illness made him unfit for field duty, two weeks later he was in Tampa on special orders from Miles.[17]

Wagner's reward for his work during the planning stage of the invasion was the authority to create and command in the field a Bureau of Military Intelligence that would collect and distribute information on the enemy and his environs. Although not attached directly to the army in Cuba, Wagner was given permission to conduct whatever reconnaissance he deemed necessary to determine the dispositions and intentions of the enemy. The idea was not for his duties to supplant ordinary frontline combat reconnaissance. Rather, the bureau was to act as a central information clearinghouse that would ensure the overall safety of the army by disseminating critical intelligence to field commanders, and that would allow the expeditionary force to accomplish its goal in a competent and straightforward manner. Field commanders, in turn, were to forward to Wagner any intelligence that might be of value to the bureau. By overseeing the collection of field intelligence by the army, even in this semi-official capacity, Wagner—whose credentials in this matter were beyond dispute—would be able to guide those officers who had not had the benefit of a Leavenworth education. Even more important, from Wagner's personal perspective, was that he would have the opportunity to observe, and probably later report on, the tactical and organizational conduct of the army in its first conventional war in thirty-three years.[18]

Soon after Wagner arrived in Tampa, Spanish admiral Pascual Cervera slipped his fleet into the harbor of Santiago de Cuba. Cervera's presence there instantly changed everything, and Santiago, not Havana, became the focus of American designs. Furious that the Spanish fleet had sailed clear across the Atlantic and into Santiago harbor without detection, Rear Admiral William T. Sampson, commanding the navy's North Atlantic Squadron, now wanted the army's help to get Cervera. A minefield in the narrow channel at the harbor's mouth, observed from two sides by forts on the high bluffs that commanded the entrance, prevented Sampson from navigating into the bay's interior where Cervera was anchored. Sampson proposed that the army land troops nearby and march on and neutralize the forts, after which his ships could clear the minefield and steam into the harbor. With the army sluggishly and ineptly making ready for a campaign against Havana, and the navy clamoring for the army's help against Cervera before he got away, McKinley decided on 26 May to make the best of a bad situation. Despite the army's unreadiness and the threat of disease, he ordered the army to send what it had assembled at Tampa against Santiago immediately.

In Tampa, meanwhile, Wagner had wasted no time in getting his own start. By 21 May he had three lieutenants (with three additional officers en route), an interpreter, two guides, a stenographer, and a confidential clerk working for him. He was already compiling information on the Spanish positions in western Cuba per his original plans, having initiated secret communication with Cuban generals García and Máximo Gómez. Among his sources was Frederick Funston, a filibusterer who had recently returned from Cuba and had been ordered to Tampa to render whatever assistance he could provide. Funston was directed to Wagner, who, as Funston later recounted, "questioned me thoroughly on all points, and made copious notes, and after several days had succeeded in pumping me pretty dry." Once it became evident that Havana would not be the focus of the expedition, Wagner rebounded quickly, collecting additional information on the Santiago area to complement his previous MID material. He was also on the lookout for Spanish spies in Tampa and Key West, having heard that both were "honeycombed" with them; for this purpose, Wagner was given charge of two secret service agents.[19]

On 4 June the Adjutant General's Office sent a memorandum to Ma-

(*Above left*) Arthur Lockwood Wagner, Ottawa, Illinois, age fifteen (1868). Photo courtesy Shields family.

(*Above right*) Wagner prior to his graduation from West Point, 1875. Photo courtesy Shields family.

(*Left*) Wagner as second lieutenant, Sixth Infantry, Fort Buford. Photo courtesy Shields family.

83891

Staff of Brigadier General Henry W.
Lawton during the Santiago Campaign.
Wagner sits third from left, first row;
Lawton is seated at center. Photo
courtesy National Archives.

Colonel Arthur L. Wagner, Third
Division General Staff, probably 1904.
Photo courtesy National Archives.

Posthumous portrait of Wagner, painted for General Service and Staff School, Fort Leavenworth, Kansas. date unknown. Photo courtesy Frontier Army Museum.

jor General William R. Shafter, commander of the Fifth Corps in Tampa, describing in detail Wagner's assignment and noting that Wagner was under the direct command of General Miles. On the eleventh, Miles sent Wagner a personal memorandum that ordered Shafter to "afford him [Wagner] every facility for carrying out my instructions." Miles directed Wagner to present the memorandum to Shafter when the invasion began. Wagner had already introduced himself to Shafter and informed him verbally of his mission. Finding the general to be "cordial," and having been treated by him with "due courtesy and kindness," Wagner no doubt anticipated a fruitful collaboration with Shafter. When the Fifth Corps sailed to Daiquirí for the landing, Wagner sailed with it. He considered the site "judicious." A landing farther to the west at Cabañas or Aguadores, he believed, might have been better, but would have enabled the Spanish to concentrate quickly against the Americans before all units were brought ashore. Going in at Daiquirí at least gave Shafter time to assemble and concentrate his own force. As the landing got under way on the morning of 22 June, Wagner presented Shafter with Miles's order. Shafter simply announced that he was not interested in using the Bureau of Military Intelligence and that Wagner's services would be unnecessary. Shafter later excused himself by claiming that he thought Wagner had come along "simply [as] a spectator" and that he "had no idea he was down there for the purpose of taking notes for General Miles." Instead, Shafter gave the responsibility for reconnaissance to his chief engineer, Brigadier General William Ludlow, and ordered Wagner to turn over to Ludlow his notes on Santiago and its environs, including whatever information Wagner had collected on the landing site. Wagner dutifully complied. He was then informed that nonduty personnel (which Wagner suddenly was) would not be allowed to land until the beach was secured. Determined to be of help somehow, Wagner offered his services to Brigadier General Henry W. Lawton, commanding the Second Division, who welcomed Wagner's offer to direct the division's field reconnaissance.[20]

The Second Division was the first to land, and Lawton marched immediately on the coastal village of Siboney, the capture of which would provide Shafter with an additional debarkation and supply point. Wagner conducted a reconnaissance in that direction and discovered that Spaniards were nearby. Lawton gave Wagner command of the division's advance guard and ordered him to seize the town. Wagner was ready, but the regiment he was given was not, because of a "delay in preparing breakfast." Wagner asked for and got another regiment, but by then the Spanish—about six hundred strong—had withdrawn, to Wagner's extreme annoyance. The day was not a total loss, however. In their haste, the Spanish left their flag flying above a blockhouse; the flag ended up in Wagner's hands. He proudly announced thereafter, in his annual efficiency reports, that he had commanded the detail that captured the first enemy flag in the invasion of Cuba.[21]

With Siboney taken, the rest of the expeditionary force either landed there or came up from Daiquirí. Shafter's order of march was for Lawton's division to lead, Brigadier General Jacob F. Kent's First Division to follow, and ex-Confederate Major General Joseph P. Wheeler, commanding Fifth Corps' cavalry division, to bring up the rear. The Spanish had withdrawn to Las Guásimas, about three miles west of Siboney. Wheeler recklessly disobeyed orders by marching his dismounted troopers around Lawton's division during the night of 23–24 June, in order to be the first to draw blood in Cuba. Wagner somehow learned what Wheeler was up to and notified Lawton, who tried vainly to reach Shafter, still on board ship off Daiquirí. Wheeler, whose division included the Rough Riders, forced the Spanish to retire (which was their intent all along) but not without difficulty. As his attack progressed, he had to call on Lawton for assistance, and sixteen Americans were killed and twenty-five wounded. Wheeler's ill-considered skirmish was a major inconvenience for Shafter, since he had not intended to reach Las Guásimas on the twenty-fourth. Neither ammunition nor rations sufficient to resupply the troops had been unloaded, and only four wagons reached Las Guásimas that day. It took three days to bring up a comfortable supply of ammunition; only after this did the army begin to move forward again. Wheeler's attack, which drew the Fifth Corps away from the coast, also had the effect of committing Shafter to operations against Santiago itself rather than the batteries overlooking the mouth of its harbor.[22]

By the twenty-sixth Shafter had advanced no farther than Sevilla, about half a mile west of Las Guásimas, and there he stopped for several days, awaiting reinforcements. That day Wagner's personal situation grew worse. He had continued to reconnoiter in front of Lawton's division, enjoying himself immensely despite the setback for his intelligence bureau. As the Fifth Corps inched its way toward Santiago, Shafter designated another officer, Lieutenant Colonel George M. Derby, as his chief engineer. Shafter instructed Derby to direct the reconnaissance efforts of *all* units and to collect from them a daily report on their activities. This was essentially what Shafter had refused from

Wagner on the twenty-second. As a result of what Wagner called this "surprising and irritating" order, Derby retained for himself two aides whom Lawton had provided Wagner for his own reconnaissance work. Since he was senior by date of rank to Derby, and because he was acting in a purely voluntary capacity, Wagner refused to comply with Derby's consolidation effort. As the campaign progressed Derby completely botched his mission and even exposed American soldiers to Spanish fire drawn by an observation balloon sent aloft to uncover the Spanish positions on San Juan Hill. He was so inept that, having become lost during a routine patrol near the front, he indicated his whereabouts by "singing 'John Brown's Body' in a loud voice," which brought an instant response from a Spanish picket. General Lawton himself ended up having to find Derby and guide him back to the division's line. Wagner continued to do what reconnaissance work he could, but he lamented that Shafter's order had caused the "practical discontinuance" of his duties on Lawton's behalf.[23]

On 30 June the front had advanced to El Pozo, and General Shafter, who had finally come ashore, made a general reconnaissance with his division and brigade commanders. Shafter had determined to advance on Santiago from the front and flank. The plan was to attack and seize the San Juan Heights due east from Santiago and directly in front of the Fifth Corps, while Lawton's division and elements of Wheeler's cavalry swung around to the north via El Caney and then moved south to take Santiago. It was a classic military "bait and switch" maneuver, and despite the manner in which Shafter had treated him thus far, Wagner charitably viewed the general's plan of attack as being "as good as any that could have been devised." The assault, however, was not vigorously pushed, nor was it adequately supported by Shafter's artillery. Even worse, in Wagner's opinion, was the near-total absence of accurate frontline intelligence, which caused delays and tactical confusion.[24]

Realizing this, Wagner did his best to give Lawton as much information about his immediate front as possible. As Lawton was to march on Santiago after eliminating El Caney, Wagner reconnoitered two miles beyond the Second Division's lines to the Ducoureau House (Wagner knew it as the "Ducrot House"), a former French plantation home that bordered the north-south road from El Caney to Santiago. The house was assumed to be occupied by the Spanish; Wagner established that it was not, and Lawton sent a brigade forward to protect his planned line of advance on Santiago and to cut off a Spanish route of retreat. Alone, however, Wagner could only be of so much to help to Lawton, and reconnaissance of El Caney itself was superficial. When Lawton began his attack at dawn on 1 July, the result was an engagement that lasted all day, despite Wagner's own confidence that it would not last more than three hours.[25]

Lawton's attack on El Caney was ultimately successful, but with it Wagner's volunteer duties came to an end. Despite Shafter's last-minute hesitance to advance on Santiago, even to the point of contemplating a general withdrawal, the Spanish were already prepared to capitulate. Out in the harbor, Admiral Cervera made his ill-fated attempt to escape under Sampson's guns, and with that the campaign was over. Wagner, whose health was not good even before he left Tampa, suffered a relapse of malaria, which confined him to bed for several days. When General Miles arrived in Santiago on 11 July, he asked Wagner to accompany him for the invasion of Puerto Rico.[26]

Upon his return from duty in the Caribbean late in 1898, Wagner began preparing, at Miles's request, a report on his observations of the army's performance in Cuba. Work on the report was briefly delayed when Wagner's bout with malaria got the better of him, and he was transferred to a more temperate climate, serving as adjutant general of the Department of Dakota in St. Paul, Minnesota. He served in this capacity until November 1899 and wrote the report in that locale. What emerged was the first of its kind in the army's history and led directly to the establishment of the modern doctrine known as lesson-learning. Wagner could simply have drafted a generic after-action report, but he seized the opportunity to do more, since he was not one to sit around quietly when instead he could advocate positive change. Everything he had previously written was based on the lessons and practical use of military history for commanders, on the assumption already noted that following the lessons of the past was more advantageous than trial and error. However, the most recent action from which he had drawn tactical conclusions was the Russo-Turkish War of 1877. Considering his complaint that insufficient attention was given to American campaigns, the Santiago Campaign allowed new conclusions to be made in the application of modern tactical theory from an American perspective. Because American lives had been expended in its pursuit, those conclusions would have greater weight than any taken from someone else's experience. The objective of Wagner's report was not only to point out what went right in Cuba but also to note what went wrong and why, in order to perfect American combat techniques and safeguard future American lives in war. There was plenty to learn. From Wagner's perspective as a former Leavenworth instructor, nearly everything that could have gone wrong in Cuba did go wrong. Given the errors committed during the campaign, and the army's material disadvantages, it was fortunate that the army had not faced a more determined foe in Cuba, for even the demoralized and outnumbered Spaniards gave the Americans no end of trouble. But, realizing that failure is often a better tutor than success, Wagner saw clearly that the army could capitalize on its mistakes by learning how not to make them again.

It was evident that those mistakes began well before the Fifth Corps even began the landing, in the mismanaged concentration and embarkation of troops at Tampa. Like other observers of this very public debacle, Wagner harshly condemned the manner in which the expedition put to sea. "The lack of anything like a carefully-thought-out system was everywhere manifest," he wrote. The situation there was not only embarrassing but avoidable, since Wagner had emphasized in his memorandum to Miles the desirability of using three ports in order to eliminate confusion and ensure an efficient departure. His recommendation had gone unheeded, and Wagner rebuked the War Department for ignoring him. Because the army had no logistical doctrine for amphibious operations, it became necessary to improvise on the spot. Wagner complimented army engineers on their efforts, but the result overall was chaos, which Wagner described in some detail. He then suggested how the army might avoid another such debacle in the future: a single officer with absolute authority should be placed in charge of the port; ships should be loaded with freight first, soldiers and animals second; soldiers' equipment should be loaded with them on the same ship; one or two ships should be loaded with only high-priority supplies in case of emergency, and railroad cars arriving at the embarkation point should be clearly marked as to their contents. The list itself is suggestive of how much went wrong at Tampa.[27]

Wagner saved the bulk of his criticism, however, for more serious problems encountered in Cuba, the responsibility for which he laid at William Shafter's feet. Although Wagner commended the general for conceiving a sound plan of attack, he censured Shafter's exercise of command. Shafter had failed to execute that plan vigorously, which resulted in a confused, groping advance, unauthorized attacks and pursuits, miscommunication between units, and a dangerous absence of unity of command. Shafter gave only broad orders to his division commanders, while failing to apply the sort of control "that a commanding general is ordinarily expected to exert." When queried by Congress about errors made before and after the invasion, Shafter claimed that he neglected to commit his plan of attack to paper on the assumption that his commanders "were experienced officers who only needed to know the general plan, which was simple." But Wagner observed that Shafter never conveyed more than broadly what he wanted of his field officers. Shafter gave his aides little, if any, information about his intentions, which "compelled [them] . . . to give important orders on their own responsibility." Wagner compared the situation to "that of Braddock's command at the battle of Monongahela. With less resolute and efficient troops and less able and determined subordinate commanders," he wrote, "the [campaign] might have terminated as disastrously as the famous battle mentioned."[28]

Wagner's reproach was no doubt motivated by Shafter's brusque treatment at the landing site, but it was the issue of intelligence gathering that bothered him most. Much of his work at Fort Leavenworth, and the subject of *The Service of Security and Information*, dealt specifically with the issue of military security—on the march, in camp, on patrol, and especially in combat—the key to which was timely and accurate information on the enemy's whereabouts, movements, and intentions. With the exception of Lawton (to whom Wagner was indebted), Wagner noted that neither Shafter nor his division commanders made more than a perfunctory reconnaissance of the front. The little that was done, he remarked, "was not sufficient to locate the enemy's position or to gain a knowledge of the ground over which the troops must move in pushing forward to the attack." What irked him most was how easily that might have been accomplished. Sending out "a half-dozen patrols," he wrote, "would have resulted in gaining information that would have saved an infinitude of trouble" in the attacks against El Caney and San Juan Hill. From Shafter's position at El Pozo, Wagner sneered, "only such [a] general view of the country . . . was obtained as Moses may be supposed to have gotten of the Promised Land when he viewed it from Mount Pisgah." The cursory and incomplete reconnaissance of the objective rendered the terrain "a veritable *terra incognita* even to those in command," causing troops to be "pushed along blindly, not knowing where they were going." As a result, the attacks against El Caney and San Juan Hill took much longer than anticipated, encountered defenders where they were not expected, and drew an unnecessary number of American casualties. Confusion above bred misdirection below, which poisoned morale.[29]

Wagner must have been disappointed that his previous conclusions and admonishments about modern warfare had evidently not reached the army's upper echelons, where they might have had a more productive effect. To a degree, this was to be expected. The army's high command was still dominated by veterans of the Civil War, and many no doubt felt there was nothing new that the experience of that conflict had not already taught them. Wheeler, for example, simply galloped off with his troop in hell-for-leather style, confident that he would lick the enemy when he found them. As for Shafter, he should have known better. He had spent years fighting Indians on the frontier, where accurate information was imperative for successful operations. The fact that the lessons taught at Fort Leavenworth were not evident at the top rungs of the army's command ladder could easily be construed as an indictment against the Leavenworth school's curriculum and mission. It is, however, helpful to remember that Wagner's quest for an educated officer corps was still a novel idea. Although time was definitely on Wagner's side, it was too much to expect that an educational program oriented toward lieutenants and captains would have much effect on colonels and generals. The long-term benefit of a Leavenworth education would not become evident until attrition removed the army's "old school" of military leadership through death or retirement, and a younger, more progressive group of officers took its place. Wagner's attempt to transform the Infantry and Cavalry School into a genuine war academy indicates his desire to expand the school's student body to include field-grade officers. Given the army's prewar climate, however, such a proposition was unlikely to be accepted without a demonstrated need for it. Nonetheless, the army's lackluster performance in the Santiago Campaign played into Wagner's and other reformers' hands, for it provided a compelling reason to adopt their proposals. As the nation moved into the Progressive Era, which emphasized professional certification and rigorous academic training, army reformers would find new receptivity for their ideas. Yet it was external public support for army reform, rather than pressure from within, that ultimately brought the reform agenda to fruition.

Wagner may have sensed that the course of events had turned in his favor, for in his report he frequently referred to or quoted from his earlier publications, assigning a told-you-so attitude to his criticism. Few things can be more satisfying to a reformer than to have been right all along, and Wagner made the most of it. On a range of critical issues, from combat security, intelligence gathering, and the commander's role and responsibility in battle to the method for writing orders and the proper preparation and execution of a military campaign, the army had fallen woefully short in the application of these fundamental rules. Wagner's report, then, was both a reproach to critics of military education and a signal to the army at large that much work had yet to be done.

In that vein, Wagner concentrated on two technical advances that had significantly changed the conduct of battle: improved artillery and smokeless powder. Since the Civil War, artillery had become a weapon of unprecedented destructiveness, particularly when applied against attacking infantry. In order to spare the attackers from what might otherwise become a suicidal assault, Wagner had advised, in *Organization and Tactics*, that friendly artillery should first neutralize the enemy artillery, and then turn on enemy infantry. On the modern battlefield, artillery was the infantry's "indispensable companion." In Cuba, however, he found the performance of American artillery "very disappointing," noting that infantry was forced to make assaults "entirely unaided by the artillery preparation that infantry has a right to expect." Wagner pointed out that "in all armies under the sun," the ratio between infantry and artillery pieces was three to five guns per thousand men. In Cuba, however, there was only one gun per thousand men. At El Caney, where Wagner stated the need for twenty-four pieces, only four were available. He had even gone so far as to request specifically, in his prewar memorandum to Miles, that two to four batteries of artillery accompany each division, with six batteries in the corps reserve.[30]

Excuses had been made that the Cuban terrain made it impossible to employ a sufficient number of pieces, to which Wagner retorted that "no ground is so difficult that it will not afford positions for artillery *if there be a determination to find places for it*" (emphasis added). American guns were unaccountably kept well to the rear where they did no good at all, leading to biting comments among the infantry about the artillery's "timidity." So feeble were the results that Fifth Corps Gatling batteries were more effective. Wagner pointedly blamed the artillery for its own shortcomings, buttressing his previous claims that it was mired in the past. Quoting himself from *Organization and Tactics*, Wagner pointed out that artillery "should be actively employed as long as an enemy remains on the field" and must do so "from a position as close to the enemy [as possible] without incurring unnecessary and ruinous losses."[31]

Wagner admitted that the latter recommendation was a problem in Cuba, where even the few American guns employed were easy targets for Spanish counterbattery fire. He observed that American artillery was still using "anachronistic" black powder ammunition, which "at once rendered it a plain target for the enemy, and at the same time obscured its own aim." American guns at San Juan Hill, he noted, "received such a concentrated fire from the hostile . . . artillery that [they were] quickly compelled to withdraw." The Spanish, on the other hand, had the benefit of using smokeless powder, which only compounded American problems in neutralizing enemy pieces. Wagner's criticism of artillery in Cuba was justified, however, only on the basis of direct fire, and even he did not realize that the future for artillery lay in its indirect application. Smokeless powder made this necessary, even inevitable, if guns were to avoid fire from the enemy. To a degree, then, Wagner's comments betray a certain rigidity of thought, and an inability to see that the combination of range, smokeless powder, and telegraphic communication had the potential to make artillery even more powerful and effective than ever.[32]

The extent to which Wagner, like many of his contemporaries, was unable to sense the true potential of technological innovation was evident in what he had previously written about smokeless powder. Not seeing that artillery would be compelled to withdraw behind the front lines and fire indirectly, he assumed that advantageous use of smokeless powder would "probably rest [more] with the defensive rather than the offensive." Prior to the innovation of smokeless powder, counterbattery fire was simply a matter of targeting the enemy's plume of smoke. This advantage (and equal disadvantage) now was gone; artillerists could fire with relative impunity from the enemy, but targeting a similarly armed foe was more difficult. To compensate, Wagner's rather weak solution was to fix the general location of the enemy artillery and shower it with liberal quantities of shrapnel, in the hope that it could be disabled. He was equally shortsighted when it came to the effect of smokeless powder on the infantry. Whereas earlier battlefields had been obscured by a thick haze of smoke, which "concealed to a great degree" the horrors of combat, Wagner worried about how soldiers might react to the unobscured battlefield and fretted even more about how they would perform against an enemy they could not see, knowing that the enemy could easily see them. He tempered his nervous speculation by assuring himself that the new conditions should "not materially affect the troops. Men never despise danger, but their pride, combativeness and excitement neutralize the instinct of self preservation." During the Santiago Campaign, Wagner found that his fears about morale were groundless. Morale was actually improved, for "the absence of the bewilderment caused by smoke more than compensat[ed] for the clearer view of the casualties of battle."[33]

Whatever Wagner's own limitations, he understood clearly and had been writing for some time about the obstacles posed by a powerful defense aided by smokeless powder, improved artillery, and accurate, rapid-firing small arms. In an age when the cult of the offensive and belief in the power of morale was gaining increasing favor, Wagner was sufficiently aware to note that "the defense has, in late years, gained enormously in comparison with the offensive." Although he wrote that "there was not a single moment . . . when the issue [in Cuba] could be regarded as doubtful," he admitted that even he had "underestimated the stubbornness of the Spanish defense and the enormous advantages conferred upon troops in entrenched positions." Attacks were much more precarious affairs, and future commanders would do well to heed this lesson. Under such circumstances, Wagner emphasized the necessity of continuing with the extended order. Not lost on him was the irony that an entrenched enemy on San Juan Hill was taken by a frontal assault. He remarked that the attack was being used "by some ill-informed critics" to suggest that frontal attacks against strong positions were not hazardous after all and that the extended order might safely be discarded in favor of the dense, more manageable formations of old. This was little short of heresy to Wagner, who had taken great pains to demonstrate the folly of such attacks against modern weapons. In response to those critics, he replied that frontal attacks would almost always fail "unless the assailant has a great superiority in numbers or morale"; even then, there was no guarantee of success. He attributed the American victory at San Juan Hill to those factors and the influence of good fortune alone, and not to any "alteration of the theories" of war.[34]

In general, despite its handicaps in Cuba, Wagner thought the army performed well at the field level. He was pleased to report that American tactics were "well adapted to the circumstances of the action and the nature of the terrain." Soldiers did not demonstrate a "blind adherence to the drill book," and instead used personal initiative and imagination to solve problems. These qualities were particularly important to Wagner, for their use in battle were central themes of *Organization and Tactics* and the *Infantry Drill Regulations*. Giving individual soldiers greater responsibility and relying on them to think and act for themselves in battle were revolutionary ideas in the army. There were those who believed this would ruin the army and create an undisciplined, unreliable mob, but Santiago proved them wrong. Equally encouraging was the performance of Leavenworth-trained officers, who exhibited considerably more competence than their commander. In battle they skillfully followed the rules of command, control, and security taught at the Infantry and Cavalry School, which pleased Wagner no end.[35]

Wagner's former students supported his observations. After the war they frequently noted the difficulty of engaging an enemy they could not see and the problems brought on by well-hidden snipers. Once the enemy position was established, however, the principles of fire superiority and extended order served the army well. Captain Charles J. Crane of the Twenty-fourth Infantry, for instance, noted that his regiment had practiced battle formations and attacks at Fort Bayard, New Mexico, for which he credited the unit's success at San Juan Hill. Recalling the same engagement, Wagner's colleague in the Adjutant General's Office, Major William H. Carter, Sixth Cavalry, wrote that in the attack "the lines were very thin—mere skirmish lines." Major John Bigelow, Jr., with the Tenth Cavalry, concurred, saying that on San Juan Hill "there was hardly a semblance of a line—simply a broad swarm." Wagner himself was gladdened to see that the American tactics were "well adapted to the circumstances of the action and the nature of the terrain" and that soldiers did not demonstrate a "blind adherence to the drill book." Whatever the deficiencies of Shafter's brigade and regimental commanders, his Leavenworth-trained subordinates at the battalion and company levels exhibited considerably more competence.[36]

Given Wagner's growing stature in the army, and the comprehensive nature of his report, he undoubtedly hoped the army could yet benefit from his frustrated mission to Cuba. He wrote later that he believed his reconnaissance work for Lawton was "the most enterprising work of the kind in the campaign," and while he realized this might seem "egotistical and immodest," he declared that "it is the truth." How doubly frustrating it must have been, then, for Wagner to learn that "my report has never seen light; it is doubtless sleeping in the War Department, and if it ever gains publicity it will probably be too late to do me any good." He was more right than he could have known; the report was finally published as a "tribute" three years after his death. As it turned out,

however—despite the absence of official sanction—Wagner was ultimately able to transmit most of his report's observations to the army in
a more practical, hands-on fashion.[37]

Having completed and submitted his report, in October Wagner
was asked by Adjutant General Henry C. Corbin if he cared to be assigned to the Philippine Islands. Wagner jumped at the opportunity,
and in November he sailed with his family to Manila, where he remained for over two years. When he reported for duty in December,
American forces under former Infantry and Cavalry School commandant Elwell S. Otis were in the process of defeating the rebellious Filipino army of Emilio Aguinaldo on the island of Luzon. Wagner was
immediately designated adjutant general of the First Division, under
Major General John C. Bates, and served in that position during Bates's
campaign in the provinces of Cavite, Batangas, and Laguna. Described
by a participant as "a vigorously conducted triumphal procession for
the posting of garrisons," the operation could not have been a terribly
exerting one, even for an officer whose health was as frequently impaired as Wagner's. With the provinces successfully occupied, the
much more difficult task of pacifying them began. In April 1900 they
were incorporated into the Department of Southern Luzon, and Wagner was appointed as its adjutant general, a post he held through November 1901. He was, in the meantime, promoted to full colonel.[38]

Although he held fairly high rank in the Philippines, and served an
important administrative function, Wagner left few personal traces
during his two years in Luzon. He did, in 1900, pen a remarkable letter
to the department quartermaster, a mirthful, tongue-in-cheek request
for a new carriage (see appendix A), but aside from that Wagner practically dropped out of sight. Although an extremely efficient Division
of Military Intelligence was formed in the Philippines, there is no evidence that Wagner had a role in either its formation or its operation. As
adjutant general, he was responsible for all official correspondence to,
from, and within his department, and with active campaigning against
guerrillas and the onerous task of pacification, it kept him very busy.
He seldom had the opportunity to venture into the field, and while
overseas he produced nothing of a scholarly nature for publication back
home. Wagner was, however, a close observer of the army's counterinsurgency campaign in the Philippines. As adjutant general, he had the
opportunity to chart the progress of American operations on a daily
basis as field commanders funneled their reports through his office.
Brigadier General J. Franklin Bell noted that "there was no feature of

active warfare in the Philippine Islands which was not thoroughly grasped and understood by him."[39]

If that is true, then Wagner was surely confronted with the twentieth-century conundrum of fighting guerrillas with conventional tactics. Colonel Charles J. Crane, in his memoir of the Spanish-American and Philippine wars, noted how difficult it was to engage the Filipino rebels in open combat. They seldom gave "standard" battle; instead, when confronted by American forces, they generally fired off a ragged volley and ran away, after which they instantly became smiling "amigos." Clearly, extended order, fire superiority, and artillery support were of little use here, although anti-guerrilla warfare put a premium on security and information. By all accounts, the army succeeded admirably in learning these lessons, and it may be assumed, from Bell's statement, that Wagner was well acquainted with them. But if so, Wagner never published his observations. After his return to the United States, he had little time to compose thorough revisions of *The Service of Security and Information* or *Organization and Tactics*. Although the ninth and subsequent editions of the former included in the title "Revised in the Light of Recent American Campaigns," Wagner made the astonishing claim in his preface that "the recent campaigns of our armies in the West Indies and the Orient have evolved nothing new on the subject herein treated." In an "explanatory note" to the seventh and posthumous edition of the latter, General Bell noted that Wagner had "collected data and solicited the assistance of the [Army Staff] College [for] a proposed revision," but there is no record of what that data included. Wagner did not live to write it, and if he had planned to include lessons from those "Recent American Campaigns," they did not appear in this final edition.[40]

The only substantive recorded event during Wagner's Philippines sojourn was in connection with Bell's controversial policy of concentrating the Filipinos of southern Luzon in army-administered camps. Wagner came into direct contact with this policy in March 1902, just two weeks before he returned home. Wagner, then adjutant general of the Department of North Philippines, which had consolidated the formerly independent departments of northern and southern Luzon in November 1901, was ordered by its commander, Major General Loyd Wheaton, to inspect three camps in Santo Tomas and Tanauan. Wagner spent a day in each town, and his written report was characteristically exhaustive. Under the conditions of their forced resettlement, Wagner considered the inhabitants of the camps to be healthy, well-housed and

-fed, and "actually more happy and comfortable than they were in their own villages." Indeed, it seemed to him that "the *hombres*, or common people, are perfectly contented and have no desire to leave." This, he wrote, exercising the racist attitudes of the day, was because "they have scarcely more power of intelligent initiative than the same number of cattle." That being the case, Wagner was particularly pleased that concentration was hard on the aristocratic *principales*, who were well-known supporters of the insurgency. These people deserved "little sympathy in their unhappiness, for it is they who have sustained the war, and it is but just that the pinch of the concentration should be felt by them." The similar policy of Cuba's governor general, Valeriano Weyler, fresh in his memory, Wagner was well aware that "the term 'concentration' has doubtless become odious to the people of the United States." He hastened to add, however, that the material difference between Weyler's policy and Bell's was that "while many of the Cuban *reconcentrados* were starved, in [our] camps all are well fed." Wagner went so far as to assert that he had been "unable to find . . . any evidence in the slightest degree of the want, misery and squalor that are so evident in our best managed, and presumably humane, Indian Agencies."[41]

Three days after Wagner delivered his report he sailed for home. He had contracted tuberculosis while in the Philippines, and his health deteriorated steadily, to the extent that his former commander in the Department of Southern Luzon, Brigadier General James F. Wade, wrote that Wagner was "not in good physical condition." For that reason, Wagner was again given light duty in order to facilitate his recovery, this time as adjutant general of the Department of the Lakes in Chicago, a post he assumed in May. Wagner must have recuperated quickly, for on the twenty-eighth of that month he was subpoenaed to appear before the Senate Committee on the Philippines and asked to testify about Bell's concentration policy and the conduct of the war in the Philippines generally.[42]

Wagner appeared before the committee on 30 May. As a stalwart defender of the army, he could be depended upon to cast in the best possible light the Philippine concentration camps, which despite his March report seldom attained the sort of military perfection he described. For example, in explaining the rationale for the camps, Wagner testified that they had been established mostly to protect the inhabitants of southern Luzon from the local bandits, or *ladrones*, who lived off the townspeople through terrorism. Only incidentally were the camps a counterinsurgency measure, and Wagner said nothing about winning Filipino "hearts and minds." However, he remarked that the camps did make it possible for the army to destroy food supplies in the countryside, a tactic aimed directly at the insurgents. When questioned about the burning of native houses during the army's regular hunts for insurgents, Wagner was quick to point out the military necessity of property destruction whenever American troops came under fire, either to deprive the insurgents of shelter or to serve as a "retaliatory measure." The use of torture, which had been widely rumored and reported, was another matter, and Wagner went out of his way to state that those incidents with which he was familiar had either turned out to be stories told for the purpose of "jollying the old folks" back home or were the result of mental incapacity. For Wagner, there was "nothing in regard to the laws of war that justifies torture for the purpose of getting information," and that was enough for him; isolated cases of torture might occur, but in his opinion American soldiers obeyed the rules and behaved themselves appropriately. This was in keeping with the overall conduct of the war. Wagner did not pretend that the Filipinos did not suffer, but any grief they did experience he attributed again to "military necessity." He reminded the committee members that William T. Sherman's razing of Atlanta "was a cruel measure, but it was a measure of military necessity." In general, Wagner was satisfied that the Philippine War had been "conducted as humanely as any war that was ever waged." He took pains to inform the committee, however, that he was unable to comment about practices on islands other than Luzon. In Wagner's mind atrocities, torture, and "uncivilized" warfare did not occur, principally because no officer—and presumably no gentleman—would allow such things. "No officer could afford to be gratuitously cruel . . . even if he was so inclined, because it would damn him among his fellows. He could not afford to have it on his record that he had allowed people to be starved, or to be ill-treated, or to suffer." On this issue Wagner was either obtusely naive or willfully dissembling; it is difficult to believe he could have spent two years in Luzon and not run into reports of American atrocities against Filipinos.[43]

After his two-day interrogation in Washington, Wagner returned to Chicago. Having been arranged because of his continued ill health, his post as adjutant general of the Department of the Lakes was not a demanding one. As it turned out, the assignment was fortunate for Wagner, for it positioned him for a critical change in the army's fortunes. In the aftermath of the war with Spain, the congressional logjam that had blocked the passage of comprehensive army reform since 1877 began to break up. Much of this was due to the hearings of Senator Grenville M. Dodge's committee to investigate the army's conduct in that war. Out of it the army's disorganization and unreadiness for war finally became a matter of public debate and outrage, and the reforms that Wagner and others like him had advocated for so long at last became a genuine possibility. Coincident with this development was the appearance of Elihu Root, who replaced President McKinley's ineffective Secretary of War, Russell A. Alger, in 1899. Root improved the army's fortunes dramatically and prompted yet another turning point in Wagner's career.

Chapter 6

Master of the Art of War

During most of Wagner's career, the army neither emphasized nor practiced battle-readiness. Officers who had observed European armies occasionally brought up the concept, but not until after the Spanish-American War did the army deem it worthwhile to spend time actually training for war. When pleas were made for large tactical exercises, opponents of reform sneered at the potential of "sham battles," suggesting, as did the ever-acerbic James Chester, that they would only give young soldiers "false ideas of a terrible reality." Chester did not believe it possible really to prepare for war because "no safe programme of battle can be deduced from history." According to him, it was "absurd" to suppose that an exercise, mere playing at war, could do a soldier any good at all. "Of all the shams in existence, the sham battle is the most absurd. It lacks the only element which constitutes a battle, and is therefore a fraud and a teacher of falsehood." Battle alone could qualify an army to fight, or mold a recruit into a soldier; experience under fire was the only experience worth having.[1]

Wagner and other reform-minded officers, on the other hand, disagreed with Chester's views. Considering the disorganization, confusion, and unpreparedness encountered in the late war, the case for tactical simulations, paired with the logistical and organizational prerequisites for conducting them, was made all the more convincing. The U.S. Army was fortunate that it had faced a weakened and demoralized enemy in Cuba and that its failures in mobilization, transport, and supply were overshadowed by Spain's own inadequacies. Against a foe better trained, prepared, and supplied, the army might have fared much worse. Given the danger of the modern battlefield, peacetime training became the only reasonable preventative against a military disaster. For the American army, reliant mostly on vast numbers of untrained volunteers in time of war, allowing the test of battle to weed out the fit and unfit was fast becoming an intolerable anachronism. As an early proponent of sophisticated tactical training, Wagner wrote that "exercises in the field are as necessary for an understanding of the principles [of tactics] . . . as in the case of drill regulations." Critics might bleat about "mimicking war," but if mimicry gave Prussia its victories over Austria and France, then the U.S. Army would do well to take heed.[2]

Before the war with Spain, tactical exercises as a training method were only occasionally employed. Regular army and National Guard units would, irregularly, stage a demonstration for training purposes, but these were few and far between and rarely conducted in a systematic fashion. The one steady exception was the applicatory method at the Infantry and Cavalry School, where theoretical concepts were applied in small-unit exercises; but these were used to acquaint junior officers with certain techniques of field service, not to train an entire body of men. The troops used in these demonstrations were limited to the Fort Leavenworth and Fort Riley garrisons, and because the school seldom used soldiers from elsewhere, the long-term practical lessons learned were to the benefit of student officers alone. Regimental commanders here and there experimented with tactical exercises, notably Nelson Miles in Arizona in 1886 and Wesley Merritt in the Indian Territory (Oklahoma) in 1889, but hope that a methodical program of maneuvers would emerge from them was little more than a pipe dream. Major James B. Babcock, writing in the *Journal of the Military Service Institution* in 1891, tried to elicit support for such a program by promoting Merritt's successful and profitable exercises of 1889, but at the time regiments were still broken up by companies occupying scattered garrisons in the West, despite recent consolidation that eliminated many such posts. Hence it was highly unlikely that tactical exercises even on a regimental scale would be practiced any time soon, making the Infantry and Cavalry School the only location where they took place on a regular basis. Even there, tactical exercises were considered something of a novelty, a cutting-edge innovation not applicable elsewhere; given the opinions of anti-intellectual military reactionaries, the applicatory method alone was controversial despite its real-world orientation.[3]

The Spanish-American War and Elihu Root changed all that. Secretary Root is universally recognized as the single most influential figure in the army's transition to military modernity simply because he, unlike the army's progressives, was able to guide through Congress long-desired army reforms, the most important of which were the establishment of a general staff and an army war college. Equally important was that in Root, himself a progressive, the tenets of civilian and military progressivism merged, thus bestowing on the army the urgency and motivation of the civilian movement. Because of Root's influence, Wagner's own reform agenda, which was almost exclusively educational in nature, gained enormously in relevance. The so-called Root reforms heavily emphasized the need for an increasingly sophisticated military education, and it is noteworthy that the Army War College was the first of Root's major reforms to be enacted. But the Root reforms were not created from nothing, and Wagner's aggressive advocacy for advanced theoretical and practical military education helped prepare the way for the war college, and even the general staff, since future staff officers would of necessity be among the most academically proficient of the army's officers. Wagner's progressivism was evident here, too. The establishment of both a war college and a general staff would fulfill his goal for an effective and efficient officer corps, able to plan for and meet the security needs of the country and successfully chart the nation's course through war if it came. Wagner's place in this, as the army's preeminent educator, was to see that officers assigned to either the war college or the general staff were equal to their responsibilities. To a very large degree, the success of both institutions was dependent on the formal preparation that Wagner had worked so diligently to provide, and he was not disappointed. And because Wagner himself was eventually assigned to the Army War College and the War Department General Staff, he was partially responsible for their early direction and growth.

In 1899, however, there were more immediate issues to consider, and the major elements of the Root reforms were still some time away. Indeed, Root had not come to the War Department intent on reorganizing the army, but he was open to suggestions on how he might improve its image and effectiveness. The public, aroused by the scandal over "embalmed beef" and the army's blundered mobilization, certainly demanded it. Fortunately for Root and the army, Major William Harding Carter was stationed at the Adjutant General's Office in Washington at the time. One of the army's more assertive reformers, and previously one of Wagner's instructors at the Infantry and Cavalry School, Carter discussed with Root "what the trouble was in the Army." Carter informed him what progressive-minded officers had been advocating for the service since Emory Upton's day.[4]

Out of this timely and remarkable collaboration army reformers got practically everything they had been clamoring for since the 1870s: a substantially larger army, promotion (to an extent) by merit, a mandatory retirement age, an end to the line-staff impasse, a war college and general staff, a more effective civilian militia, and the opportunity to conduct large-scale maneuvers for the first time. In his first annual report, Root affirmed Wagner's long-established ideal by writing that "the real object of having an army is to provide for war." Among his proposals for ensuring that the army could do that, and subsequently avoid the mistakes evident in the Santiago campaign, was the "exercise and training of the officers and men of the army in the movements of large bodies of troops . . . under conditions approaching as nearly as possible those to be anticipated in . . . war." In making this statement, Root validated the Infantry and Cavalry School's applicatory method, and Wagner's own commitment to teaching the practical features of theoretical concepts. Root observed that "officers who have never seen a corps, division or brigade . . . cannot be expected to perform perfectly the duties required of them when war comes. The collection of large bodies of men presents . . . entirely new difficulties which only experience can qualify men to meet." It was desirable, therefore, to obtain this experience in peacetime by "approximating as nearly as possible . . . that which will be encountered when the war machinery is required to do its proper work." What this meant was the employment of maneuvers on the scale of those conducted by the armies of Europe, and Wagner would very soon play a central role in their development. He was also was expediently posted in the geographical department in which those maneuvers would take place.[5]

Arriving at a state of appropriate readiness and training would take time, and much practice and effort, but preparations began quickly. In late 1900, while Wagner was still in the Philippines, Root approved a War Department order that called for realistic training combined with field maneuvers "to simulate actual battle." Suitable locations were surveyed and plans made to purchase a permanent site for the purpose in 1901; Fort Riley, Kansas, was eventually chosen as the cheapest and most sensible location. Maneuvers did not take place that year, despite an increase in the army, because of continued commitments in the Philippines. By the summer of 1902, however, General Bell's successful campaign against the last Filipino insurgents in Batangas brought large numbers of American soldiers home, making possible a large maneuver that fall. Wagner by this time was at his new post in Chicago, and it was fortunate for the army that its acknowledged authority on matters of tactics and tactical exercises had returned to the United States. In August Wagner's former superior in the Philippines, Major General John C. Bates, then commanding the Department of Missouri (of which Fort Riley was a part), took command of the maneuver division, formed expressly to do what the name implied. Bates was ordered to ensure that the maneuvers, scheduled for September, simulated "as far as possible . . . war conditions." Secretary Root's desires notwithstanding, mock combat was not intended, but a demonstration of all procedures and actions leading up to violent confrontation was. To assist him in this task, Bates convened a board of officers to prepare the ground rules for the maneuvers, to design the tactical problems to be solved, and to determine the duties and responsibilities of the umpires guiding the exercise. To head the board Bates selected his former adjutant general, Arthur Wagner, knowing full well there was no one in the army more qualified to organize these first maneuvers.[6]

Wagner traveled with Bates to Omaha, Nebraska, where the full board met to deliberate on 1 September. Charged with determining exactly what sort of maneuvers the Fort Riley exercises would be, the board had among its options either something like European maneuvers, which solved a "general strategical problem" under simulated war conditions, or a more limited affair that emphasized separate daily exercises, encompassing a range of predetermined tactical problems. The board chose the practicability of the latter, despite the desirability of the former. This being the army's first foray into field maneuvers, and owing to the somewhat limited space available at Fort Riley, Wagner later admitted that the army could not yet attempt anything on the scale of European models. The expected participation of the National Guard complicated the issue because of that organization's attendant inadequacies. To get around this, the board prepared a week-long exercise for regular army troops alone, followed by another week in which regulars and guard troops cooperated in a joint maneuver. "The schedule of exercises," Wagner later wrote, "provided for regimental, brigade and division drills, lectures on military operations and field engineering, the practical construction of . . . various shelter trenches, a field bridge and a pontoon bridge, and a course of eleven practical field problems in tactics."[7]

The arrangement crafted by the board worked out well in practice, and Wagner was about as proud of the exercise as he was of his work at Leavenworth or in Cuba, noting the "many expressions of satisfaction heard from the most experienced and capable officers engaged therein." For Wagner the highest compliment was that "everybody had learned something." Indeed, the entire affair was simply a Leavenworth tactical exercise writ large, as the rules that regulated the exercise "were compiled mainly from those formerly in use at the Infantry and Cavalry School":

The officers of higher rank had an opportunity to exercise, in these maneuvers, the command of larger bodies of troops than could be assembled at their own posts, and to exercise such command, in *tactics* instead of *drill*, under circumstances approaching very closely to those of actual war. To the younger officers the mere fact of seeing and being a part of a large force of all arms was in itself a valuable experience . . . and all officers gained more or less from the interchange of military views inseparable from an association of different organizations with each other for a number of days in a course of active military work.

Of equal importance to Wagner was the validation of his conclusions from the Santiago campaign. Troops discovered reconnaissance in each day's exercise to be of enormous importance, and they reinforced Wagner's admonition about the "invisibility of intrenched infantry, using smokeless powder" to the extent that the combination "sent everybody back to camp a-thinking." For both regulars and guardsmen, the experience at Fort Riley provided a cheap alternative to fumbling attempts to learn the art of war under fire; and it was precisely this concept that Wagner had advocated for so many years.[8]

As chief umpire for the exercise, Wagner himself also had the opportunity to learn by doing. He left Fort Riley with many ideas on the conduct of future maneuvers and about the manner in which umpires should govern actions on the field. Wagner added much more to the already extensive list of umpires' duties that had been drawn up by the board at Omaha. In Wagner's field capacity as the final arbiter, the judge on whose decision everything depended, he was able to return to that which he enjoyed so much—teaching. Each night the officers were assembled and Wagner critiqued the conduct of and offered solutions or suggestions for the problems encountered during that day's exercise. "Interesting discussion" usually followed, and Wagner found these evening meetings "one of the most valuable features of the encampment." By order of General Bates, Wagner one evening delivered a lecture on the "Operations of War"; he later received the thanks of the National Guard officers in attendance for what they called a "most practical and brilliant lecture on military strategy." Bates himself was so impressed with the lecture that he wanted Wagner's future lessons recorded on an "electric stereopticon" at any future maneuvers.[9]

The success of the Fort Riley exercise inspired the immediate preparation for two more, one to take place at West Point, Kentucky (near Louisville), and the other at Fort Riley. Wagner again played a central part in their production. He insisted on, and got, a larger contingent of umpires. At Fort Riley he and his subordinates were stretched thin and occasionally hard-pressed to make prompt decisions, a phenomenon that led to several embarrassing "awkward pauses" interrupting the course of a day's exercise. Wagner also advocated the use of a much broader geographical area for the maneuvers, suggesting that it would be more realistic for the opposing "armies" to approach each other from a distance "in accordance with a general plan of campaign." This would give the cavalry an opportunity to employ screens and conduct long-range reconnaissance, and the infantry the chance to plan and execute an extended march with some sort of engagement at the end. Bates agreed, at least in principle, and made preparations for an increased number of participants by leasing forty thousand acres of land adjoining Fort Riley; he also leased an undisclosed amount of land near the Kentucky site. Despite the increased space and plans to the contrary, "friendly" and "enemy" (blue and brown) forces still camped on the same ground, and during exercises withdrew no more than a few miles apart, leaving Wagner still dissatisfied.[10]

The 1903 maneuvers improved on those of the previous year. Wagner again served as chief umpire and repeated the evening lyceums, giving regular and National Guard officers the benefit of his insight (a participant noted that discussions "were invariably keen and earnest and not infrequently vehement and exciting"). An observer of the well-planned 1903 maneuvers called the army's latest innovation a movable "military Chautauqua," and another heralded Wagner as its "directing genius." General Bates introduced his own innovations—a night march followed by a dawn attack on a defensive position at the Kentucky maneuver field and the attack and defense of a convoy at Fort Riley. Although everyone involved, both regulars and national guardsmen, thought the exercises another huge success, Wagner believed that he and his umpires got the proverbial short end of the stick. More umpires accompanied the exercises, but they still had more work than they could manage; and because they took, as Wagner put it, "the place of bullets," soldiers did not always appreciate their decisions; one officer noted that they were sometimes "despised . . . by some unfortunate participants." The experience proved that many more umpires would be needed in the future. Wagner added two suggestions regarding soldierly accouterments. In his report on the Santiago Campaign, he had directed attention to the value of an entrenching tool, to no avail. Perhaps because that report had been ignored, Wagner's report on the Kentucky and Fort Riley maneuvers repeated the necessity for such a life-saving tool. He fumed that the army's Board of Ordnance and Fortification, even after a year on the project, could not fabricate one that worked. Wagner also suggested that the time had come for officers to trade their swords and scabbards for something more utilitarian—a pistol. Complaining that the "'Saber vs. Revolver' [question] has been discussed *ad nauseam*," and that it had not "yet gotten beyond the realm of pure academic theory," Wagner wondered aloud if the question would ever "deserve *practical* consideration." His call for an entrenching tool, at least, got the attention it deserved not long after.[11]

If anything, Wagner's participation in these exercises only enhanced his reputation. In July 1903, for example, one month after the Kentucky maneuvers, Wagner sent through channels a request to be assigned as a military attaché in Russia or Japan (war was imminent between those two countries). Chief of Staff Adna R. Chaffee denied his request because he believed that "Colonel Wagner's services cannot . . . be spared" at this time in the army's development. For himself, however, Wagner believed his performance deserved a bigger reward. In late 1902 he began a campaign for promotion to brigadier general, and for two and a half years he relentlessly pursued anyone who might help him achieve the coveted rank. The number of endorsements he collected while chasing his major's oak-leaf clusters was dwarfed by those he accumulated for general. Since National Guard units regularly attended the army's maneuvers, Wagner took the opportunity to curry favor with guard commanders and the occasional politician who happened by (including Ohio governor Myron Wilmot, and Ohio congressman and National Guard patron Charles W. Dick), obtaining from each a commendatory letter attesting to Wagner's notable qualifications.[12]

In some cases these letters produced little more than hyperbole. Recalling Wagner's service in Cuba, for example, Major General J. C. Breckinridge wrote that "the unimaginable obstacles which seemed to obstruct field service, the ingenuity with which all obstacles were overcome, your persistent enthusiasm and determination to reach the very front, and your admirable bearing and skillful and gallant services . . . eminently deserve the highest recognition." Most, however, were honest and sincere, and Wagner probably had no better champion than J. Franklin Bell, who wrote that he considered Wagner "almost in a class by himself." Wagner even got the unprompted support of an anonymous writer to the *Army and Navy Journal*, who asked why the "Powers That Be" were holding up Wagner's promotion. "Ask the

Army who is the most abused man in it," the writer charged, "and ninety per cent will say Colonel Wagner. The [proposed] War College has been heard of for some time, but we all know that nothing will be done till Colonel Wagner is sent to Washington to take hold."[13]

Yet Wagner was not everywhere acclaimed. In the spring of 1904 General Bell heard a rumor that delays in Wagner's advancement hinged upon his not being a "practical" officer. Bell mentioned this to Wagner, who considered it the worst insult anyone had ever issued him. In a long, angry and anguished letter to Bell (see appendix B), Wagner spilled out his frustrations at being considered a mere "theorist." Even his enemies (and he acknowledged that he had some) could "not deny that my theories have been the basis of practical work on the part of the Army in time of war . . . and that a theory to be sound must be practical." It seemed to him that "the very work to which I have devoted myself for the good of the service . . . has been turned to my detriment, instead of my advantage. Surely it is not calculated to inspire young officers with a desire to cultivate their profession when they find a man's reputation as a military student used as a weapon against him." Wagner proudly recounted his long record of service in the field, from Fort Buford to the Philippines, admitting that he was "at a loss to know just when I ceased to be 'practical.'" Every officer in the army, he wrote, knew about his work at Fort Leavenworth, and junior- and field-grade officers up for promotion had to take an examination drawn from his books. If, however, none of this had any bearing on his own qualifications for promotion, he suggested that the army should "come out frankly and say that military study is prejudicial to an officer. Let us warn young officers to avoid study and caution them never to put [a] pen to paper. Then, being devoid of all evidence of a studious interest in their profession, they may possibly be recognized as 'practical' men, and escape being stigmatized as 'theorists.'"[14]

As usual, Wagner overreacted to the rumor, but Bell thought that Wagner's anger was justified. He sent a copy of the letter to Adna Chaffee, with the admonition that Wagner's "non-advancement cannot fail to create the impression that professional study and attainments are of little value in bringing about advancement in rank." It is unlikely that there was any sort of conspiracy to thwart Wagner's designs on general rank, but he did have a serious shortcoming. Although now a full colonel, Wagner had had no sustained command experience in the field since his days as a lieutenant in the West. His accomplishments, while bringing him much notice in and out of the army, were almost completely academic, and those that were not (chief of the Military Information Division, divisional and departmental adjutant general, chief umpire) had little direct connection to field command. Wagner could very well explain the *principles* of command, yet it was not evident that he knew how to *exercise* command himself. Although by 1904 staff positions had become much more important in the army due to the creation of the Army War College and War Department General Staff, it was still unusual to find general officers who had little or no command experience. Given his unorthodox occupation, Wagner undoubtedly knew he was bucking the traditional rules for promotion, particularly against officers who had more field experience than he. To counteract the conventional wisdom, he had gone well out of his way to ensure that he had good connections in securing his promotions. String pulling had been remarkably effective so far, and he may well have felt at this juncture that his sterling endorsements alone should smooth the way for a generalcy. In 1898 he had commented to a West Point classmate, Hugh Lenox Scott, that one's efficiency reports in promotion selections were "of slight weight" and that instead, "political influence was the main vehicle to advancement." In his own eyes, then, Wagner probably believed he had done everything right and that the coveted promotion should be his simply because he had called in his favors. But if he also believed that some unknown entity was blocking his advancement in spite of his assiduous efforts, Wagner did not say so. Significantly, he did not accuse anyone specifically of tripping him on his way to the top, and Bell could not identify the rumor's source.[15]

Despite the frustrations cited in his letter, Wagner's career continued to move forward. Soon after the Kentucky maneuvers in October 1903 he returned to Fort Leavenworth after an absence of seven years, now in the fairly exalted position of assistant commandant of the General Service and Staff School. He spent only three months at the post; in January he left for Washington and became senior director of the newly created Army War College, and scant weeks later he was assigned to a concurrent position as chief of the Third Division of the General Staff. Moreover, as he hoped, his diligent string pulling put him solidly on track for a brigadier's star.

Wagner's return to Leavenworth coincided with a major restructuring of the Infantry and Cavalry School, which had closed temporarily during war with Spain. When Elihu Root secured congressional approval for the Army War College in 1901, he mandated a new educational hierarchy in the army, beginning at West Point and culminating with the War College. In between, officers would receive elementary training in basic tactical and administrative duties at individual post schools and instruction appropriate to their branch at special service schools. The better graduates of these schools would move on to the General Service and Staff College, formerly the Infantry and Cavalry School, for instruction "in the administration and handling of higher commands of all arms." Selected distinguished graduates of the Staff College would advance to the Army War College.[16]

The Staff College opened on 1 September 1902, but it quickly disappointed anyone looking forward to a new era at Leavenworth. Two successive commandants, Colonels Jacob A. Augur and Charles W. Miner, had little to recommend them as school superintendents, and they were essentially seat-warmers. Few of the school's former instructors were recalled, and the program and curriculum were but thin shadows of their former selves. The school had only four departments: tactics (chaired by Wagner protégé Captain Joseph T. Dickman), engineering, law, and military hygiene. Despite claims to the contrary, in no way was any instruction in the "handling of higher commands of all arms" offered. Subjects in the department of tactics, for example, included regulations pertaining to outpost duties, infantry, cavalry, and small arms; lessons in riding; duties as officer of the day; and field artillery demonstrations. Assignments were unchallenging and most of the students were unqualified. Their performance reflected the school's deficiencies; the rate of failures and dropouts, as Leavenworth historian Timothy Nenninger notes, was "greater . . . than in any other class between 1881 and 1916." Reporting on tests in his department, Dickman wrote that "the handwriting of many of the papers is so poor as to be scarcely legible, and there is a noticeable deficiency in . . . grammar, while punctuation seems to be practically an unknown art." In his annual report Colonel Miner blamed these results on the old Infantry and Cavalry School grading system, which he thought was too hard, while offering a host of other excuses, among them students' lack of prior education and their inability to learn "technical knowledge" because they were too old. Major General Samuel B. M. Young, then president of the Army War College, wanted to deny diplomas to those students who did graduate because the course of instruction was so rudimentary.[17]

Wagner, watching these developments with some apprehension from St. Paul, wished he "could be in two or three places at the same time," one of them Fort Leavenworth. He got his wish. J. Franklin Bell, who returned from the Philippines in the summer of 1903, replaced the ill-suited Miner. Bell's arrival at Leavenworth was every bit as important to the school and to army education in general as had been Alexander McCook's in 1886. Bell quickly initiated a series of sweeping changes that returned focus to the school's operation. Convinced that it "had attained a high state of efficiency when [classes were] temporarily suspended in 1898," Bell insisted that the first priority "should be to get back, as soon as possible, to the conditions then existing, with a view to making further progress." To retrieve Leavenworth's lost direction, Bell sought Wagner's help, bringing him on board as the school's assistant commandant in November 1903, right after the second Fort Riley maneuver.[18]

With the 1903–4 school year upon him, Bell could institute only so much immediate reform. While en route to Leavenworth in July he visited Wagner to secure his assent to become assistant commandant and to get his views on what was needed to repair the Staff College. From this meeting Bell wrote a report in which he stated his intent to resume Leavenworth's practical orientation geared around the tactical exercise. He assumed that *"good, thorough, practical results* are required and enough of these tactical exercises should be given to afford officers [an] opportunity to acquire sufficient knowledge of terrain to enable them to make disposition of troops accurately and promptly." The greatest mistake, he believed, would be the introduction of "a 'stuffed' curriculum which embraced a vast amount of military knowledge" but which offered no opportunity actually to apply it. Until Wagner arrived and an entirely new curriculum was designed, Bell sought to reestablish, as far as possible, the school that Wagner had left in 1897. For the moment tactical instruction superseded the college's expressed goal of teaching staff and administrative duties.[19]

Wagner, meanwhile, prepared for Bell a memorandum of his own, offering his suggestions for a completely revamped curriculum. He envisioned a two-year course, divided between advanced practical education for infantry and cavalry officers the first year and an even more advanced, wider-ranging course designed generally to prepare officers for assignments at the War College. Wagner eliminated the rudimentary elements from the curriculum then in use on the assumption that officers should already have "easily acquired" such subjects at the post schools. First-year students at Leavenworth would learn to apply what they had already learned and would take an extended series of classes to acquaint them with the fundamental applications of field artillery, strategy and tactics, signaling, security and information, military law, and sanitation and hygiene. Classes in each subject would combine textbook recitations with hands-on demonstrations. Wagner expected the first course to emphasize the practical objectives of the old Infantry and Cavalry School by providing officers "with all the instruction that is needed for the proper performance" of the duties in those arms.[20]

The second course, he advised, "should be designed to give [officers] the further instruction needed to prepare them for the Army War College, or at least to give them a broad, advanced military education to fit them for higher command." Here Wagner continued to emphasize the applicatory method, particularly through map and live tactical problems, but at a more sophisticated level than in the first-year course. These classes, he wrote, would embrace the "higher features of tactics, with strategy, logistics, fortification, army organization, international law and . . . such elements of naval warfare as are involved in the consideration of the combined operations of the army and navy." The second-year course was ostensibly designed to produce staff officers, but Wagner did not include any classes of an administrative nature. It is probable that Wagner expected graduates to be able to perform appropriately on a staff, having taken two years of course work acquainting them with the functions of the army at various levels. The absence of staff work evidently did not worry Bell, who accepted Wagner's suggestions without criticism.[21]

Shortly after Wagner arrived at Leavenworth, he wrote to his old Infantry and Cavalry School colleague Eben Swift, commenting that "I scarcely recognize it as the place where we formerly served." Referring to his memorandum to Bell, and the task he and the new commandant had before them, he added that "it will be a matter of much labor to bring the course up to the standard it had attained when we were here." Unfortunately, Wagner had almost no time to do anything during his brief assignment.[22]

Bell wanted Wagner to stay on to supervise the implementation of their expected reforms for the 1904–5 school year, but Wagner was ordered to Washington three months after his arrival at Leavenworth. Bell could not replace Wagner's valuable oversight of the school, but he managed to get the next best thing by requesting that Eben Swift, then a major in the Adjutant General's Office, be assigned as the school's head of the Department of Tactics (later the Department of Military Art). Army Chief of Staff Adna Chaffee resisted Bell's request at first, and it took Bell until April 1904, after much pleading with Chaffee, fi-

nally to get Swift assigned to the school. Major William W. Wotherspoon, then head of the Department of Tactics, was promoted to lieutenant colonel and made assistant commandant. In October he, too,
was taken away by the Army War College, whereupon Swift became
assistant commandant. Even without Wagner, Bell reported that "grat-
ifying progress" was being made at the Staff College, remarking that
"within a year or two there is every reason to hope that [a] thorough
system will have been established."[23]

Fortunately for Bell, Wagner's departure for Washington did not end
his association with the schools at Leavenworth; indeed, the transfer in-
tensified it and assured that their reforms would proceed apace. As
noted, Wagner became senior director of the War College, second only
to its president and Wagner's long-time friend Tasker H. Bliss, then a
brigadier general. Wagner's concurrent position on the General Staff
was as chief of the Third Division, of which the War College was a part.
Lieutenant Colonel Wotherspoon joined the division as Wagner's immediate subordinate shortly thereafter. The War College, as originally
conceived by Colonel William H. Carter and endorsed by Elihu Root
in 1901, was to prepare and execute "an advanced course of professional
study for Army officers" and was governed by a War College Board.
But as Root had not yet been able to secure passage of a general staff, he
allowed (against Carter's wishes) that the board should function, as
much as possible, as an unofficial general staff. Chaired by General
Samuel B. M. Young, the War College Board had convened for the
first time in June 1902 and had spent the next year implementing the
new regulations for military education and preparing the organizational structure for an actual general staff, pending congressional approval. When this finally occurred, in February 1903 (the staff was not
activated until August), General Young became chief of staff, and Bliss
took over as president of the War College. Despite Root's intentions to
the contrary, Bliss did not see the duties of the War College as educational. Trained in Greek and Latin, Bliss interpreted the word *college* as a
"collegium—that is to say, a body of men associated together by a
community of interest and object for doing something rather than to
learn how to do it." In Bliss's opinion, the War College was not a rung
in the army's educational ladder; rather, he thought of it as "an institution of the General Staff to take up the solution of practical military
problems" for the army. In other words, the War College would be the
army's supreme planning agency for the direction of military policy. To
the extent that learning took place at all, it would be in the actual pro-

cess of solving those "practical military problems." A February 1904 War Department memorandum listed the function of the War College as conducting "studies of possible theaters of war, and preparation of plans of campaign including combined operations of the Army and Navy."[24]

Wagner's place in this scheme was twofold. As senior director of the War College, he was part of a three-man Strategy Board (Bliss, Wagner, and Wotherspoon) that reviewed and approved all work conducted by the War College. Much of this work involved the conduct of war games to test the applicability of plans made by students and permanent college staff. Wagner's extensive background in this area made him especially valuable to the fruitful operation of the War College. As chief of the Third Division of the General Staff, he indirectly supervised all the schools in the army except West Point. Wagner managed all aspects of army education not immediately related to administration, and he thus approved curriculum, methodology, regulations, student qualifications, and examinations. Among a host of other unrelated duties, Wagner was also responsible for the army's field maneuvers. Since the school at Fort Leavenworth fell under his purview, Wagner kept up a close relationship with Bell, assuring that he would retain a large degree of authority over its progress.[25]

As it happened, nearly all of Wagner's time in the Third Division was consumed by matters concerning Leavenworth. The paramount task he had before him when he took over in February 1904 was establishing a new educational regime at the General Service and Staff College. Wagner and Bell worked very closely in this process, and Bell brought in his department heads in order "to make them *particeps criminis* and rob them of any cause for complaint or excuse for non-compliance or enforcement when the time comes to put the scheme into operation." At the same time, Wagner had been charged with a complete top-to-bottom revision of the army educational system as first espoused by Elihu Root. Bell helpfully suggested that Wagner simplify compliance with this obligation "by using the General Orders relating to that subject [and] work[ing] up a schedule which will bring consistency . . . out of a mass of provisions which are now chaotic and inconsistent with each other."[26]

Always the diligent worker, by mid-March Wagner had completed a draft proposal for the revised system of military education and sent it to Bell for his approval of and recommendations for the sections relating to the Staff College. Bell distributed the proposal to his instructors, asking them to make sure that the courses envisioned were complete and that they allowed "sufficient time to cover thoroughly all of the instruction proposed." Wagner traveled to Leavenworth later that month to confer personally with Bell and his staff; he wrote to General Bliss that the "results will be very satisfactory."[27]

One of the thorniest problems Wagner encountered in reorganizing the General Service and Staff College was the disparity between its name and its mission under the army's present educational system. As Bell explained in his 1904 annual report, the school was not one for "general service," since it offered no courses applicable to the subject; indeed, the term had not even been defined. Instead, it acted as a school "for infantry and cavalry officers only, as other . . . special service schools." Nor was it a staff college, because it offered no courses of a staff-related nature despite Root's impending plans for a general staff. Since the college as originally conceived could not satisfy its charter, Wagner abandoned his original intention of implementing a two-year track at Leavenworth, deciding instead to create two completely independent schools under a single administration: one a resurrected Infantry and Cavalry School and the other a genuine staff college. Wagner's new proposal was based on, but went considerably further than, the suggestions he had made in his memorandum to Bell several months before. The first of the two institutions was a one-year service school at which the applicatory method would be applied to train officers in tactical theory and operations, organization, and strategy. Wagner's textbooks formed the core curriculum, and map problems and exercises were heavily emphasized. Distinguished graduates of the Infantry and Cavalry School would advance to the one-year course at the Staff College. Very simply, as Wagner explained, "The object of the Staff College is . . . to instruct especially selected officers . . . in the duties of general staff officers in time of war." Here too Wagner's books dominated the curriculum, but with a different emphasis. Students in the Staff College course prepared and directed problems in security and information for students of the Infantry and Cavalry School and critiqued their solutions; heard lectures on the employment of the three arms in combat and the comparative organizations of the American, Mexican, and German armies; and conducted exercises on mobilization and concentration. Other courses included logistics, grand tactics, military history and strategy, military geography, general staff duties, staff rides, and maneuvers. The latter consisted of a Civil War battlefield visit, which Wagner had wanted for some time, during which students would "study the terrain in connection with actual historical events but under modern conditions." Instruction in maneuvers would be almost completely practical, with students participating as umpires in the army's annual exercises. Finally, hoping to profit by the experience of the Spanish-American War, Wagner included a course in joint army-navy military operations. To ensure that each Staff College student clearly understood the concepts taught, Wagner required written or applied exercises in each subject. The new regulations eminently satisfied General Bell. In his 1905 annual report, the only major changes he anticipated were the deletions of all vestiges of elementary instruction and the course in security and information, on the assumption that it would be covered by the individual garrison schools.[28]

Wagner's proposal also included regulations for the Army War College, noting that "for the first time the nature and course of instruction at the War College are set forth in orders." Wagner hewed closely to Bliss's intentions for that institution, and his report unequivocally stated that "the object of the War College is not to impart academic instruction, but to make practical application of military knowledge already acquired." Although not a prerequisite, that knowledge, for the most part, would be acquired at the Staff College at Leavenworth. Students, if they could be called that, participated in ongoing work of the War College permanent staff, which included projects involving "the organization, mobilization and concentration of troops, general strategic plans and preliminary operations." They would also participate in "confidential strategical problems . . . [as] designated by the Chief of Staff," the preparation and "critical examination" of tactical problems to be solved by students of the garrison schools, and "the regulation and conduct of army maneuvers." The War College had no formal academic year and no examinations. Wagner's completed revision comprehensively set down regulations, described courses, approved methodology, and even prescribed administrative functions for every school operated by the army, from post schools for enlisted men to the War College. He left nothing out. Where Elihu Root's original 1901 order on army education totaled seven pages long, Wagner's proposal, when published, covered seventy-eight. The War Department accepted the entire revision and enacted it by General Order No. 115 in June 1904.[29]

Part of that order (and the original one it replaced) enjoined regimental commanders to send to Leavenworth only those officers "who have the most creditable record in the garrison schools" as well as conspicuous performance in other military duties. Compliance with the order

was another matter. Despite the lengthening history of army education, and the increasing esteem of Leavenworth, Wagner discovered
with unbridled exasperation that "there are still a few old moss-back
colonels who can not get the idea out of their heads that the Infantry
and Cavalry School is [only] for the benefit of officers who 'need instruction.'" Even after Wagner and Swift had turned the school into an
advanced center of army learning, and despite a secretary of war devoted to military study and a new general order that described an increasingly diverse and sophisticated educational system, this particular
reform was still being resisted in some quarters of the army. Even commanding general Nelson Miles—a soldier who by then ought to have
known better, considering that Wagner had served on his staff—in 1901
condemned the idea that "real soldiers" needed a formal military education. Wagner must have been extremely frustrated when, in February
1905, he received a letter from Captain Francis J. Koester at Fort Ethan
Allen in Vermont. Koester wanted to attend the Infantry and Cavalry
School, but his colonel, William M. Wallace, refused on the grounds
that "captains and graduates of West Point do not need this detail," suggesting instead "that no one but officers from the ranks of civil life
should be sent there." He concluded that regular army officers were
"not . . . especially in need of further education."[30]

   Wagner could scarcely believe it. He personally wrote to Koester and
instructed him to show Wallace the letter, in which he explained what
Leavenworth was for and called attention to the relevant paragraph in
General Order 115 about officer admissions. Koester did so, only to discover that Wallace's response "was as I feared." The colonel rejected
Wagner's explanation out of hand and insisted on his original decision.
Captains, he told Koester, were "competent and not in need of the instruction." At this, Wagner wrote to Bell at Leavenworth, informing
him of Wallace's "preposterous views," adding that if there were other
officers like Wallace, "I would like to hit them over the head with a club
as soon as possible." He asked Bell to request that the War Department
strengthen the language of the paragraph in question, noting that in
due time the matter would be "referred to this [the Third] Division,
[whereupon] we will draw up a memorandum that will cause a ray of
light to penetrate the skulls of some of these superannuated individuals
who . . . would give the detail at Leavenworth to the regimental idiot."
Bell took the matter very seriously and wrote to the War Department as
asked. Wagner, in committee with the Third Division, was invited to
report on the matter, and in early March he happily reported to Bell that

the revised order would "give some of the delinquent regimental commanders a rap over the knuckles that will instill the fear of the Lord in their hearts in regard to the order mentioned."[31]

Through the spring of 1904, after the proposed revision for army education was complete, Wagner spent most of his time writing the necessary orders and making arrangements for select National Guard officers to attend the Infantry and Cavalry School. Wagner had advocated guard participation at Leavenworth since 1884, when he published "The Military Necessities of the United States." At the time, he wrote, one of the weaknesses of the American militia was "the lack of a proper system of instruction." He suggested that such instruction "should be provided . . . by permitting a limited number of officers . . . to enter the School of Application at Leavenworth." In 1889, in "An American War College," he wrote that the nation's "military strength must be sought in the wide dissemination of military knowledge among the people." That being the case, "a number of officers of the National Guard might be instructed at Fort Leavenworth." The benefits of bringing the National Guard into the Leavenworth fold were, he believed, "beyond calculation. Military knowledge . . . would be disseminated among the militia; uniformity would be promoted among the various State organizations; and a leaven would be infused in the National Guard." With the passage of the Militia Act of 1903 (the so-called Dick Act, after Ohio congressman Charles W. Dick), the army finally gained control over guard training and organization, something Wagner and other army reformers had pursued for years. Wagner instantly lobbied to get National Guard officers posted to the Infantry and Cavalry School for instruction and successfully introduced language to that effect in the new general order on military education. After much negotiation with Bell and various guard units across the country, Wagner obtained approval for fifty-four guard officers to attend the Infantry and Cavalry School, starting on 15 September 1904.[32]

During the year that Wagner headed the Third Division, he chaired numerous committee meetings and approved dozens of reports and projects. He had able subordinates, among whom was Captain Joseph T. Dickman. Wagner knew Dickman well, for the captain had been a former student and later one of his instructors at Leavenworth. Dickman did good work for Wagner, being assigned to write the army's first *Field Service Regulations* (a manual prescribing the administrative, organizational, and tactical conduct of units in the field). Dickman later became one of General John J. Pershing's most effective division and corps commanders during the First World War. As during Wagner's previous assignments as adjutant general in St. Paul, the Philippines, and Chicago, administrative duties took up much of his time at the Third Division, but his responsibilities did allow him to get out of Washington from time to time. Among the division's responsibilities was the regulation and conduct of maneuvers, and Wagner—by then the unquestioned authority on how these things should be handled—traveled to direct them.

Only one joint army-militia maneuver took place in 1904, but it was the largest such exercise yet held. Wagner may have been the army's official "point man" where maneuvers were concerned, but if he had not learned this already, he certainly learned here that rank had its privileges. The army's exercises that year were held near Manassas in northern Virginia, the site of two catastrophic northern defeats in the Civil War, and were the brainchild of former Adjutant General Henry C. Corbin, then commanding the Division of the Atlantic. In December 1903 the War Department ordered Corbin and other like commanders to prepare "problems for military maneuvers within his division." One of the more progressive officers of the Civil War generation, Corbin interpreted the order broadly and made preparations for a massive exercise involving the 70,000 regular and National Guard troops under his command. The Fort Riley and Kentucky maneuvers, in contrast, never exceeded a total of 12,000 participants. In the end, only 26,000 soldiers arrived, but even this was twice as many as in any previous exercise. Corbin's prestige and residual power were evidently such that the army rolled over for him on this matter, accepting without question his desire to hold such an exercise.[33]

Corbin's big maneuver promised to be an expensive proposition, and Adna Chaffee appropriated one million dollars for the purpose. Corbin wanted the Manassas maneuvers to be more realistic than previous ones, intending to simulate two genuinely hostile forces although, as in all other maneuvers, no mock battles were planned. He proposed that the opposing forces maintain separate encampments so that each would constitute a "standing menace" to the other. Previous maneuvers had stopped at the moment when shots would be exchanged, and while the army, Wagner included, saw little need for combat simulation at this stage in the development of maneuvers, there was something to be said for giving the soldiers on opposite sides a genuine objective, rather than simply practicing the steps leading to battle. To make the necessary arrangements, Chaffee asked Bliss at the War

College to assemble a planning board; surprisingly, Wagner was not a member, but the board did all right without him. Corbin had the peculiar idea that umpires at Manassas would be unnecessary because there would be no actual problems for the troops to carry out; instead, the two opposing commanders were to conduct their commands in any way they saw fit as the circumstances warranted. From an *Organization and Tactics* standpoint, that was well and good, but the absence of supervision and tactical problems was too heretical an idea for the board, and its members rejected this part of Corbin's scheme.[34]

Wagner, accordingly, was brought in once more as chief umpire. He arranged for the fifteen highest graduates of the Infantry and Cavalry School, currently studying at the Staff College, to serve as umpires. Three weeks before the Manassas maneuvers took place Wagner and his senior umpires, Colonels Joseph Augur and Edgar Steever, went "quite carefully" over the terrain on which they would be held and "prepared the details of the problems with a long explanatory memorandum." Knowing that the maneuvers were Corbin's pet project, Wagner admitted that he did not know how his preparations would strike Corbin's staff, but he was prepared to give full support and aid. One thing did upset Wagner; since Corbin had originally wanted no umpires at all, his staff had made no calculations about how many might be needed. Wagner had already discovered that he could not have too many umpires, and although the War College board appointed to oversee the maneuvers insisted that they be used, far too few of them officiated at Manassas. Even worse, the board made no provision for Wagner and his umpires to assemble beforehand on the maneuver grounds for instruction and preparation, despite Wagner's continual urging in previous reports for such arrangements. Fortunately, under Dickman's direction, the Third Division had prepared a manual for the conduct of maneuvers based on prior experience, and this made up for some deficiencies. As he had done in his textbooks, Wagner advised his umpires not to follow the manual *too* closely, suggesting that common sense should override printed regulations. Most important, he told them, their duty required them to be neutral and impartial; an umpire was "not an advocate, but a judge," and on his decision rested the outcome of any particular engagement.[35]

The maneuvers began on 6 September and concluded on the tenth, with only two days of actual troop movements—hardly sufficient time to be constructive, considering the numbers of soldiers involved. Participants and umpires nonetheless found the maneuvers to be quite successful—Wagner wrote that they were probably "the most success-ful"—especially where the concentration of troops was involved. Wrote one participant, "Everything I saw relating to logistics was one hundred per cent better than it was in the Spanish concentration, and the equipment, condition, and training of the militia troops was several hundred per cent better than it was six years ago." Still, it became evident that the National Guard was woefully inadequate. Of the twenty-one thousand guardsmen involved, numerous units were untrained, some left necessary equipment at home, and others brought unusable or obsolete equipment with them. Straggling among guard units was rampant and endemic. An observer commented that "the militia need a certain amount of hardening," adding that "militia officers were not, as a rule, qualified." Wagner amplified these judgments with the suggestion that "only those militia organizations should be invited that have been duly declared 'qualified' for maneuvers." Because of the problems with the National Guard, the five thousand regulars "were so few as to practically lose their influence" and as a result got little more than field drill out of the exercise.[36]

The worst deficiency by far was the signal lack of umpires. Wagner found it "very exasperating . . . [and] extremely annoying" that he had only fifty of them to regulate the actions of the troops of both sides. One of the umpires later remarked that future maneuvers should be accompanied by at least one umpire per battalion rather than one per regiment, as was the case at Manassas. In addition, Wagner expressed his displeasure that neither he nor any of the other umpires had the opportunity to conduct after-action briefings with participating officers. Problems, as a result, went unsolved and suggestions went unmade. These issues aside, Wagner remained committed to the continued employment of maneuvers because they gave officers "valuable experience in the command of large bodies of troops" and because ordinary soldiers learned "to take care of themselves in camp and on the march and [the maneuvers gave] them a taste of real military conditions." Moreover, staff officers received much needed practical experience "in field administration, logistics and supply."[37]

A smaller maneuver over which Wagner presided two weeks before Manassas, held near Athens, Ohio, gave him more satisfaction. Only eight hundred regulars and six thousand guardsmen participated, a much more tractable number, the latter displaying much "earnestness." Referring to the problems encountered in Virginia in a report on the Ohio exercise, Wagner wrote that his experience with the smaller of the two was an "indication of the great use that can be made of such camps in preparing the militia for the more extended maneuvers in combination with the regular army." Organized by the state's National Guard, the Ohio exercise was not without problems of its own. A regular officer who observed the maneuvers complained that "there was . . . an intolerable amount of excited conversation in [the] ranks, and company officers were compelled to repeat their injunctions to preserve intervals, to take cover, to lie down, to quit talking, etc., many times before being obeyed." Another officer, however, commenting on the tactical problems "laid out by that master of the art of war, Colonel Arthur Wagner," was pleased to observe that "more can be learned by observation in one week . . . than can be imparted in a year of instruction in an armory." For Wagner, the inescapable conclusion drawn from the Ohio and all other maneuvers was that "practice makes perfect."[38]

Not everyone shared Wagner's enthusiasm about the utility of maneuvers. Though claimed a success, the Manassas exercise had cost roughly $700,000, and there were those, particularly in Congress, who wondered whether the army's latest innovation was worth the stunning expense. The proximity of Manassas to Washington, reminiscent of the Civil War battles fought there, drew large crowds, including numerous congressmen. They saw a great deal of activity and running about, but as battles were not simulated, they did not see any winners or losers. For the army, that was not the point, but congressmen needed more than just the assurance that such exercises were beneficial to military preparedness. For 1905 the General Staff, after study by the Third Division, planned three maneuvers, all of which would be smaller than the Manassas exercise but larger than those held at Fort Riley and West Point, Kentucky. Congress balked when the War Department asked for an appropriation of $1,250,000 for this purpose and refused to allocate any money for maneuvers in 1905. Stung by this seeming rebuke, Wagner published "Combined Maneuvers of the Regular Army and Organized Militia" in the January–February 1905 issue of the *Journal of the Military Service Institution,* in which he culled his official maneuver reports to plead for a continuance of annual exercises. "We must learn from our own experience," he wrote, with the injunction that "should [the United States] be involved in war it would be found that the experience gained by our officers in maneuvers had been of so much value as to repay the government with heavy interest for the expense incurred." Congress was not persuaded.[39]

Wagner certainly wanted maneuvers to continue because they gave him the opportunity to present scholarly papers. At the urging of General John C. Bates and other officers in attendance, Wagner published a paper on strategy, given at the 1903 Fort Riley and Kentucky maneuvers, later that year. As the last example of original scholarship on Wagner's part, the slim volume that resulted gives some insight into his maturing military thought. Considering the setting in which the lecture was delivered—at a tactical exercise—a lesson in strategy did not fit neatly. Wagner, however, wanted to broaden officers' horizons by demonstrating that tactical operations were but one part of a larger whole. He confessed, with "considerable embarrassment," that strategy was a difficult concept even for him to define, and he offered several definitions in vogue at the time. He preferred his own from *Organization and Tactics*, in which he explained strategy as "the art of moving an army in the theater of operations, with a view to placing it in such a position, relative to the enemy, as to increase the probability of victory, increase the consequences of victory, or lessen the consequences of defeat." This, he proposed, was a simple enough explanation. But while "in war everything is simple," he said, quoting Clausewitz, "the difficulty is to attain the requisite simplicity." Wagner then offered what he considered were "the two great underlying principles of Strategy": that soldiers on the march needed "food, clothing, medicine . . . [and] an unfailing supply of ammunition; and [that] . . . all other things equal, two or three men are able to whip one." Wagner believed that strategy was "based entirely on these propositions."[40]

For Wagner, it seems, logistics was strategy, or at least the engine that drove it, and the base of an army's supplies and communications was the most important factor in determining how strategy would be applied. Armies in the field, above all else, had to protect access to their base, especially as operations drew them away from it. The farther away an army ventured from its base, the more insecure and hesitant it became, lest the enemy find a way to intercept its lines of communications. Conversely, an army with its base nearby could act in the confident knowledge that it was never far away from its source of strength; but should the enemy draw too near, the army might find its options increasingly limited to defending its base. Civil War operations around Chattanooga, for example, Wagner found to have been completely dominated by logistics; the movements of both armies, North and South, were oriented not at each other, but at each other's lines of supply and communication. Sherman's march across Georgia was equally a matter of logistics, the movement itself merely the establishment of a new, more secure base on the Atlantic Ocean. This interpretation of strategy had clear Jominian connotations, and Wagner did discuss, briefly, the importance of strategic points and interior and exterior lines. However, the fact that they were Jominian did not make them wrong. In the cases noted, lines of communication were extraordinarily important, to the extent that the disruption of those lines might have caused entirely different outcomes. Nor was Wagner so Jominian that he did not recognize that *"the enemy's main army is always the true objective."* Various intermediary objectives might have to be seized before reaching the final object, but Wagner insisted that they be taken with that particular goal in mind. If operating against the enemy's lines of communications hastened the destruction of his army, that was all to the good; but they were important only to the extent by which they increased the prospects of victory. Such operations were thus not, in Wagner's view, valuable in themselves. General Ulysses S. Grant was Wagner's best (and the most obvious) example of this fundamental point: "[Grant's] predecessors sought to capture Richmond; but his object was to crush Lee, knowing that with the destruction of the Army of Northern Virginia, not only Richmond, but the entire Southern Confederacy, must fall."[41]

Wagner also offered his audience a few maxims on command. Sophisticated technology made it more and more difficult to achieve strategic surprise, so Wagner exhorted commanders to "make correct plans in the beginning." He echoed Grant's advice, "Always go ahead," and Prussian field marshal Helmuth von Moltke's dictum, "Having decided upon your plan, follow it energetically; and so long as it is working out satisfactorily, do not allow yourself to be distracted from it by any other plan, however alluring the latter may be." A commander had to be levelheaded and able to surmise the obstacles before him correctly without exaggeration. He must be willing to take calculated risks, for "a general who always plays for safety never achieves decisive results." He must also be willing to err; quoting Napoleon Bonaparte, Wagner wrote, "Show me a general who never made mistakes, and I will show you a general who never made war." Finally, Wagner advised the commander to accept the role of luck. It could not be controlled, but the wise commander made every reasonable attempt to plan for the unforeseen and took action accordingly. Having made these suggestions, Wagner closed by "stating what I believe to be the correct rule of Strategy":

Remember that your object is to meet and defeat the enemy, and endeavor to take the most direct means to accomplish this end. Look
carefully to the supply of your army; protect your flanks and guard
your communications; aim, if possible, at the flanks and communications of your adversary; remember that the enemy has as much
cause to worry about you as you have to feel anxiety about him. Having made your plan, stick to it unless compelled to change. Plan carefully and deliberately; then move quickly and strike hard.[42]

This sort of timeless advice was not a bad note on which to end a long
military career, and the premature end for Wagner's was approaching
quickly. The maneuvers proposed for 1905 were a dead letter, and Wagner's duties at the War College and with the Third Division became
routine in the extreme. Office work consumed the first weeks of 1905.
In February and March he was preoccupied over the matter between
Captain Koester and his recalcitrant colonel. As spring arrived he offered his advice on new regulations for officers' annual efficiency reports, began work on the end-of-term examinations at Leavenworth,
and studied a proposal to add a course in musketry at the Infantry and
Cavalry School. He continued lobbying hard for his advancement to
brigadier general, but it was becoming more and more doubtful that he
would get the promotion on merit alone. Wagner's second in command
at the Third Division, William W. Wotherspoon, wrote to Bell at Leavenworth that "someone is [still] getting in knocks about his [Wagner's]
being theoretical and not practical, and I really believe if he does get it, it
will be because they want a vacancy in a certain corps more than because he is the best man." Wotherspoon was correct; precisely such a
vacancy became available in late March, and Wagner's name was first
on the list of suitable officers for the promotion. Not long after, William H. Taft, Elihu Root's replacement as secretary of war, agreed that
Wagner would finally get his brigadier's star.[43]

About the same time, Wagner's health took an unexpected bad turn
due to an attack of appendicitis. Although he recovered without difficulty, his overall health deteriorated rapidly in April, when it was discovered that the tuberculosis he had contracted in the Philippines had
become advanced and was complicated by pneumonia. Wagner's doctor recommended a change in climate to Asheville, North Carolina,
where he confidently predicted that his patient's ailment could be "satisfactorily treated." When Wagner formally applied for a three-month
leave of absence on 11 May, his ordinarily firm signature was little more
than a scrawl. Accompanied by his wife and one of his five children,

Wagner arrived in Asheville shortly thereafter. Despite his doctor's best efforts, Wagner's health worsened, and on 17 June he died, one day after the thirtieth anniversary of his graduation from West Point. Wagner perished knowing that a promotion to brigadier general was his at last; what he could not know was that President Theodore Roosevelt was to have signed the order by the end of the same day. Wagner's body was buried, with full honors, in Arlington National Cemetery on 20 June 1905. The funeral was attended by the secretary of war and every senior officer of the General Staff Corps.[44]

Chapter 7

Among the Generals

Wagner's death left his wife and five children—the youngest of whom was only two years old—almost as needy as his mother and her children had been when Wagner's father died in 1866. With a survivor's pension of only thirty dollars a month and limited income from his books, Mrs. Wagner suffered financial discomfort. Wishing to ease this, General J. Franklin Bell and other Wagner friends saw to it that a bill was introduced in Congress that would retroactively reimburse Wagner three thousand dollars for his expenses while writing *The Service of Security and Information* and *Organization and Tactics.* Knowing also that Wagner had intended to revise *Organization and Tactics,* Bell arranged for a posthumous revision to be written, under his own guidance, by Captains Malin Craig and Herbert Brees and Lieutenant Leslie Chapman, all top graduates of the Staff College. In order to increase the royalty, the War Department, in turn, required every post library, every National Guard unit, all students at Leavenworth, and every officer up for promotion to purchase the new edition. These steps extended, at least for a while, Wagner's influence among his fellow officers.[1]

Bell and other army educators determined other ways to keep Wagner's immediate memory and influence alive, but had only limited success, and Wagner himself was partly to blame. When he returned to Leavenworth in late 1903, Wagner knew *Organization and Tactics* had become, as Bell later ruefully admitted, "somewhat obsolete, on account of recent advances . . . [in] warfare," and he hoped to use the staff and student body of the Staff College to effect a complete revision. His brief stay made this impossible, and as Bell recalled, once Wagner began work with the Third Division "he found himself so completely occupied that he could devote no attention to anything else." The revision that appeared was not a bad one under the circumstances, but it did little more than update Wagner's original work to then current doctrine as espoused by the 1904 *Infantry Drill Regulations* and by recent literature in the service journals. For example, the chapter "Infantry in Attack and Defense" eliminated Wagner's dated use of volley firing in favor of less-regulated individual fire and changed the distances between the lines of attack that Wagner had originally included to reflect recent modifications. The new book included Swift's well-established rule on orders and replaced Wagner's chapter on the employment of artillery with an artillery officer's lecture on the subject. Although Dickman's 1905 *Field Service Regulations* was included in the book's bibliography, there is no evidence that the manual influenced the revised *Organization and Tactics*, a serious omission. Moreover, the revision contained only the briefest references to the Russo-Turkish and Russo-Japanese wars and said nothing about the Spanish-American or Philippine wars. Had Wagner revised the book, he would likely have included a section on his own experience with the counterinsurgency in the Philippines and would definitely have made use of his report on the Santiago Campaign. With his death the army lost its most talented and reflective author on tactics and the art of war. As the revision that did appear had nothing of Wagner's contemplative spark, it was quickly replaced at Leavenworth by German works like Albert Buddecke's *Tactical Decisions and Orders*, Otto F. Griepenkerl's *Letters on Applied Tactics*, Fritz Bronsart von Schellendorff's *Duties of the General Staff*, and the in-house text *Studies in Minor Tactics*.[2]

While his principal text soon fell into disuse, *The Service of Security and Information* did not, remaining in print until around 1910. By the time that book fell from favor, Wagner's seminal works had trained regular and National Guard officers for nearly twenty years. More important is that the essential concepts Wagner introduced or affirmed in these works remained valid: reconnaissance and outpost duties, the extended order, intrenchments, firepower, close artillery support, soldierly initiative. When the United States entered the First World War, many of its army officers had received "basic training," as it were, in the principles of combat from Arthur Wagner.

Essential, too, was the long-term effect Wagner had on the Leavenworth schools. His passion for a usable, practical history that demonstrated theoretical military concepts, and his steadfast belief that knowledge acquired in the classroom must be applied in real-life situations, remained a central part of the Leavenworth and eventually the War College curricula. More than any single individual of his day, Wagner legitimized education in the army. Well into the First World War anti-intellectuals continued to challenge the pursuit of academic achievements, but Wagner's work was so credible and erudite that reactionaries were relegated to crank status. Even though Wagner was not a practitioner per se of the art of war, he overcame critics of military theory and education by successfully blending both endeavors with the operational art. Certainly Wagner was not the only educator or intellectual in the army, but he quickly became well known as the most influential among his contemporaries. Had he lived longer, Wagner undoubtedly would have played a central role in the army's continued professional development as it approached global war.

The tactical heritage Wagner left behind survived long after his death, and it is possible to connect the 1891 *Infantry Drill Regulations* and *Organization and Tactics* to General John J. Pershing's insistence upon "open warfare" in the First World War. The extended-order assault that Wagner described placed paramount emphasis on safety, maneuver, and firepower. Such attacks were employed in formations in depth, with utmost use of natural cover, and depended on the initiative of individual soldiers to press forward. When General Pershing arrived in France in 1917, he was convinced that the strength and morale of the French army had been sapped after years of trench warfare—which he believed was slow, unimaginative, and defeatist. As the American Expeditionary Force prepared for battle in the Meuse-Argonne, Pershing issued an order called *Combat Instructions*. It described, in some detail, Pershing's skepticism about trench warfare and included his preferred solution, known as "open warfare." As described in *Combat Instructions*, "Open warfare is marked by . . . irregularity of formations, . . . the greatest possible use of the infantry's own fire power to enable it to get forward, variable distances and intervals between units and individuals, use of every form of cover and accident of the ground during the advance, brief orders, and the greatest possible use of individual initiative by all troops engaged in the action." *Combat Instructions* urged that infantry not waste itself in futile frontal attacks against areas of strong resistance. The favored method, harking back to Wagner, was to pin the enemy frontally and destroy him on his flank. *Combat Instructions* also echoed Wagner's insistence that artillery help blast a way through for the infantry.[3]

Pershing has been widely criticized for attempting maneuver tactics on a static battlefield, although the Germans in their 1918 offensive, and the French in their counterattacks thereafter, used similar tactics with considerable success. The point to be made is not about the efficacy of "open warfare" but that Pershing was Arthur Wagner's logical tactical heir. It is doubtful that Wagner would have embraced the doctrine of trench warfare. Had he lived to retirement age, Wagner would have left the service in 1917, and it is hard to believe he would have stood by while Pershing battled the War Department over the AEF's proper tactical course. While he was an early advocate of entrenchments to strengthen the defense and to afford temporary shelter in an attack, he also believed that trenches had a tendency to make troops timid in the assault. Pershing believed much the same thing in 1917 and expanded this view to the overall condition of trench warfare on the Western Front. Pershing's subordinate, Robert L. Bullard, agreed, writing that trench warfare "took the offensive spirit out of the troops." Had he confronted the sickening reality of the Western Front, where artillery had usurped the infantry's dominance over the battlefield, Wagner might have moderated or revised his views, but that will never be known.[4]

Although Wagner is best remembered as a tactician, his work did have some effect on American strategy. As a product of his time, Wagner's view of strategy was purely military; although he had read Clausewitz, nothing in his writings suggests that he accepted the idea that military objectives were tied to political ends, because most of what he wrote focused on the operational level rather than on high-level strategy. The United States had not accumulated sufficient foreign foes to prompt speculation on national strategy, and most military writers of the day tended to concentrate instead on the more limited problems of attack and defense. In Wagner's case, the immediate question was how to make the offense work in an age when it was becoming more and more difficult a proposition. Thus Wagner's strategy was one of tactics, its aim to overwhelm (and perhaps to annihilate) the enemy army. This focus on the offensive part of war, paralleled in armies around the globe, had a significant influence on the U.S. Army as it developed through the twentieth century. More than any writer of his generation, Wagner established the ideal, born of Ulysses S. Grant's 1864–65 Virginia campaign, of the relentless and aggressively waged attack. The army's consistent offensive orientation through two world wars and beyond, while rooted in the experience of the Civil War, was defined and enunciated chiefly by Arthur L. Wagner. To a degree, Wagner may even be considered an American proto-Clausewitzian strategist; on page one of *Organization and Tactics* he paraphrased the Prussian by saying that "all strategical operations must terminate in a battle." For Wagner, the essence of strategy lay in the ability to make contact with the enemy advantageously and to succeed upon contact. That emphasis on battle was carried on, in part, by Wagner's son-in-law William K. Naylor, who in 1922 admonished an Army War College class to remember that "warfare means fighting and that war is never won by maneuver, not unless that maneuvering is carried out with the idea of culminating in battle."[5]

Although Wagner was by no means alone in his advocacy of the offensive, *Organization and Tactics* was the first American work of its kind to describe a systematic approach to the attack that combined all three arms and justified itself historically and theoretically. The only other contemporary book that came close was John Bigelow's *The Principles of Strategy*, published in 1893, two years before *Organization and Tactics*. Like Wagner, Bigelow also advocated an offense aimed at the enemy's army, but he was far more circumspect about it than Wagner. Bigelow's definition of strategy relied heavily on the Jominian concepts of maneuver and decisive points, whereas Wagner was almost completely battle oriented. Bigelow's brief discussion of tactical operations mentioned battle but did not describe it. Instead, he emphasized such things as the relative advantages conferred by the length of an army's front, the effect of interior versus exterior lines, and the tactical importance of the angles of road junctions. All these things had their place, but in Bigelow's hands advantageous battle seemed to be more a matter of geometry than of morale, firepower, and impulsion. While *The Principles of Strategy* was an important book for its day, it had nothing of the impact or endurance of Wagner's two seminal volumes, leaving Wagner clearly in command of the army's intellectual high ground.

As important as Wagner was to the army, his work was mostly that of an initiator. He died at a time of critical change in the army, too early to see his ideas and innovations mature. That was left to others, none of whom quite had the Wagner edge. But while Wagner was indeed indispensable to the army, he was not irreplaceable, and that in itself was one of Wagner's greatest achievements. His work at the Infantry and Cavalry School had gone a long way toward building up a corps of "safe" officers who were similarly grounded in military history, theory, tactics, the principles of strategy, and administrative duties. The army's educational system, meanwhile, had become increasingly institutionalized and was no longer reliant on single intellectual chieftains to prod the army along. The result was a self-perpetuating agency that could lose someone like Wagner without irreparable harm.

This is not to say that Wagner had become superfluous. The absence of the army's preeminent educator was acutely evident in the manner in which the Leavenworth schools and the Army War College continued to evolve. Bell and Swift left Leavenworth in 1906; Bell became army chief of staff, and Swift was assigned to the War College. The "dominant personality" at Leavenworth between 1906 and 1912, according to Timothy Nenninger, was Major John F. Morrison, who had been a student at the Infantry and Cavalry School a year before Wagner's arrival in 1886 and an instructor there a year after Wagner left in 1896. The interval is significant, for as head of the Department of Military Art, Morrison materially altered the tactical principles taught at the school.

Morrison was not a practitioner of the extended order or of tactical finesse. As an observer with the Japanese army in Manchuria in 1904, he noted that the Japanese had not adopted the extended order and used instead the principle of mass at the tactical level. The experience taught Morrison that "the right kind of infantry can carry anything if you have enough of it. It is cheaper to do it some other way than by frontal attack if possible *but frontal attacks can win*. . . . It isn't the [artillery] that does the killing, it is the little steel jacketed rifle bullet" (emphasis added). These were conclusions totally contrary to Wagner's, and it is no less significant that Morrison stopped using *Organization and Tactics* and adopted German texts that had backed away from extended-order formations. To be sure, Wagner had written that frontal attacks were not impossible, but he added the caveat that even with superior numbers and morale, they were still tactically backward. Although Morrison was lauded by his students as the "No. 1 tactician of the Army" and "a real authority on the modern methods of war," those methods practically exalted the frontal attack. Had Wagner not died when he did, it is almost certain that he would not have suffered such a drastic change in Leavenworth's tactical direction. Morrison at least retained the established use of the applicatory method at Leavenworth, expanded its course in tactics, and agreed with Wagner that standard tactical formations and solutions had no place on the modern battlefield. He was also instrumental in the development of the pivotal 1911 edition of the *Infantry Drill Regulations*, which emphasized command flexibility and fire superiority. To be fair to Morrison, he was following Wagner in the practical use of military history. In this case, however, regardless of the success of the Japanese in Manchuria, Morrison learned the wrong lesson, with disastrous results in 1918 despite Pershing's insistence on more Wagnerian techniques.[6]

The effect of Wagner's death on the War College was more subtle. In his new rank as brigadier general, Wagner was to have become president of the college in June 1905, but it is impossible to know what plans he may have had in that role. Certain things, however, are worth noting regarding its development in his absence. A 1907 order that redefined the War College's responsibilities deleted war planning and war gaming but retained its control over army education. In addition, the War College would "promote [the] advanced study of military subjects." Although the War College was still not an educational institution, Eben Swift, who had arrived there in 1906, used the clause to inaugurate there the applicatory method that he and Wagner had developed at Leavenworth. As chief of staff, J. Franklin Bell encouraged Swift in this endeavor. Swift's "Course of Military Art" was a series of map problems, combined with staff rides that explained certain tactical principles on real terrain. Although the map problems progressed in complexity from small-unit operations to others at division and corps level, Swift's course essentially duplicated that which was already being taught at Leavenworth. Swift also increasingly emphasized the teaching of military history at the War College, particularly from the American Civil War, adding the battlefield visits that Wagner had asked for at Leavenworth in 1895. Like Wagner, Swift emphasized the lesson-learning aspects of military history, with a mind to deducing some practical benefit from campaigns of the past.

The result of the applicatory method's introduction at the War College, as Harry P. Ball writes, was that "the collegium [of Tasker Bliss] had eroded." Although the War College still developed war plans, its emphasis had shifted to "the development of the individual student officer," meaning that the War College had become merely another of the army's schools. This might have been all right had the War College been preparing "a limited number of selected officers for the duties of higher command in war," as Swift intended his course to do, but increasingly, and with Wotherspoon's and Bell's approval, the War College simply repeated material found in the Leavenworth course. Ball writes that this had become necessary because the Staff College at Leavenworth was not producing graduates "competent in the military art." This divergence from the mission Bliss had articulated arose, in part, because Bliss himself had strayed from that which Elihu Root had planned for the War College. To a fair degree, Wotherspoon and Bell were simply returning the War College to its original purpose, but they failed to do so in a way that distinguished the War College from the Staff College or that prepared officers for high command.[7]

How Wagner would have approached the duties of the War College is impossible to say. But considering that he and Bliss were close friends and professional allies, that he had already written on the need for planning before the onset of war, and that he was fully committed to making the Staff College the necessary prerequisite to an assignment at the War College, it is probable that the War College under Wagner would not have taken the direction it did under Wotherspoon and Bell. Wagner may indeed have taken the War College in a more educational direction, but it is unlikely that he would have suffered a repetition of the Staff College course. Instead, he probably would have ordered an alteration or refinement of the Leavenworth curriculum and would have prepared an advanced course at the War College appropriate to its function.

Wagner's expected elevation to the presidency of the War College was a logical step for the army's most eloquent and determined advocate and practitioner of education, for it is in that field that he left his most enduring mark on the army. There were plenty of advocates for postgraduate military education before Wagner and many talented, motivated, and influential educators after him, but Wagner stands alone as *the* critical transitional figure in the development of a comprehensive and progressive educational system. He not only made the acquisition of a military education a matter of necessity, but his practical combination of military history, theory, and application laid the foundation for all army postgraduate education to come as well as for its general assumptions and objectives. His *Service of Security and Information* and *Organization and Tactics* were the army's first homegrown textbooks of their kind; their undogmatic style, insistence on good leadership, and prescriptions for safety and tactical prudence prepared the army for a new century of challenging combat. Wagner's insistence that history, both old and recent, be combed for its lessons in the present contributed directly to the twentieth-century doctrine of lesson-learning. Wagner's *Santiago Campaign* was the first applied instance of that doctrine, and the book's objective was echoed during the First World War in a series of *Notes on Recent Operations* compiled and published by the G-5 (training) section of Pershing's staff. Dennis J. Vetock writes that the *Notes* series "disseminated and prescribed information, doctrine, lessons, training methods and other combat matters, all mixed together, in effect as operational policy directives." Through the Second World War, Korea, and Vietnam, the army consistently employed frontline observers who reported on what worked and what did not, ensuring that Wagner's vision of a usable past remained constantly at the forefront of army tactical and strategic development.[8]

While Wagner, as noted, was not indispensable, no one rose to take his place as he had taken Emory Upton's place. His Leavenworth colleague Eben Swift was a good teacher and military historian, but he did not have Wagner's insight or ability to fuse history, theory, and practice into a recognizable whole. Swift, who was once described as an officer who was "not quick, but gets there," did not even particularly like military theory. J. Franklin Bell, for all his importance in the resuscitation of Leavenworth after the Spanish-American War, was more a facilitator than an educator, one who understood what needed to be done and knew who could do it. When he prepared to overhaul the Leavenworth course in 1903, the first person he called on for advice was Arthur Wagner. John F. Morrison, able and respected though he was, had his own peculiar deficiencies; and although Timothy Nenninger writes that "the Morrison years at Leavenworth . . . were fruitful, exciting, and important," his tendency toward the frontal attack is suspect. While he oversaw the production of a new American work on tactics, *Studies in Minor Tactics*, it was written by eight of his instructors and was not the creation of a single mind. The important and well-received *American Campaigns*, written by Wagner's friend Matthew Forney Steele in 1909, contained tactical analyses like Wagner's books but avoided discussion of doctrine or theory. Books published by other Leavenworth instructors—Henry E. Eames's *The Rifle in War* (1909); Oliver L. Spaulding's *Notes on Field Artillery* (1914); and Harold B. Fiske, Leroy Eltinge, and Augustus Bennett's *Notes on Infantry, Cavalry and Field Artillery* (1917), for example—were narrow, as their titles suggest. In 1925 Spaulding published *Warfare: A Study of Military Methods from the Earliest Times*, a work that resembled somewhat Wagner's *Organization and Tactics*, but it was co-authored with two other officers and ended with the campaigns of Frederick the Great. Wagner's only genuine intellectual peer was Tasker H. Bliss, whose work at the Army War College, while quickly reoriented, was of critical importance. Unlike Wagner, however, Bliss was not an educator, a theorist, or a tactician, nor was he among the army's more productive authors. No single officer was able to fill the void left by Wagner's death, and no subsequent individual books contained the historical and theoretical breadth that Wagner's did. Instead, an accumulation of officers and texts filled Wagner's shoes, and that in itself says something about his significance to the army.[9]

Wagner would have been extremely proud that "Leavenworth men" played so important a part during the First World War, a conflict he predicted must come. Perhaps no greater testament to Wagner's assiduous work in building up the Infantry and Cavalry School was given than

Major James A. Van Fleet's postwar reflection, "Thank God for Leavenworth." Wagner left an unmistakable impression not only on the army of his day but on the army that followed him, and his successors freely acknowledged their indebtedness to his single-minded occupation. Five years after Wagner's death, in 1909, his friend and colleague Major Eben Swift wrote a eulogy about Wagner's long career, suggesting that "we needed Wagner" to introduce to the army the "innovations . . . that were revolutionizing the art of war." Wagner's books, Swift wrote, had a "remarkable" effect on the army, and their author was a genuine "pioneer in the cause of military education." Major Elvid Hunt, author of the first history of Fort Leavenworth in 1926, credited Wagner for visualizing and then capitalizing upon the Infantry and Cavalry School's potential and for encouraging among its students an enthusiasm that was "quite beyond the ordinary." Oliver Spaulding, in *The United States Army in War and Peace* (1937), wrote that "largely through the influence of Colonel Arthur L. Wagner, the Army educational system was further developed and systematized." Colonel William K. Naylor's important 1921 work, *Principles of Strategy*, closely resembled his father-in-law's *Organization and Tactics*, with a heavy emphasis on historical examples and the works of American and European military authors—Wagner among them. Colonel William A. Ganoe was by far the most laudatory. In his famous 1924 work, *The Army of the United States*, Ganoe praised Wagner lavishly. He called Wagner the "Sylvanus Thayer of the General Service Schools" and "the foremost American strategist and military writer of his time." "What the service owes to him," Ganoe wrote, "can scarcely be estimated. Much of the success of our troops in the World War was due to his incipient efforts in awakening the officer back in the nineties to the realization of the unique and endless study and practice required by his magnificent profession."[10]

Far, far too late, in 1978, Wagner's dedicated service to military education and the advancement of a sound tactical doctrine was formally recognized by the army when he was inducted into the Command and General Staff College hall of fame. During the installation proceedings, the keynote speaker declared that Wagner's place in the army's history "truly ranks among the generals." Eben Swift probably said it best when he wrote that "if we ever have a great army it will be due, not to the work of one man but of many, and in the list the name of Wagner will have a good place."[11]

In his 1889 article "An American War College," Wagner wrote that "the army officer of the present day should differ as much from his predecessor of fifty years ago as a locomotive differs from a stage-coach, or a magazine rifle from a flint-lock musket." He concluded that article with the fond hope that it was not too "extravagant to believe that the time will come when the seed planted at Fort Leavenworth will have grown into a great tree."[12] Wagner's devotion to military education ensured that both dreams were realized, far beyond his imagining.

Appendix A

Wagner's Letter to the Depot Quartermaster

HEADQUARTERS DEPARTMENT OF SOUTHERN LUZON
Manila, P.I., July 6th, 1900

To the Depot Quartermaster, Manila, P.I.
Sir:—

I have the honor to invite your attention to the fact that though application was made some weeks ago for a suitable conveyance for the use of the Inspector General of this Department and myself, the only result thus far has been the "hope deferred" which "maketh the heart sick" and which, at the same time, makes the rest of one's individuality extremely tired.

The fact that the conveyance now in use by Major Beach and myself is an unattractive combination of a hearse and a chicken coop is one that I can endure in a becoming spirit of humility, though it might seem proper that there should be some visible evidence that in the matter of transportation the senior staff officer of an important department is given more consideration than is habitually extended to a company slop barrel; but it may be well doubted whether it accords with the best interests of the service to provide such a rickety and jolting conveyance for a staff officer that upon his arrival at his office he finds his inner man churned into an unlovely omelette composed of the wrecks of his viscera, his conscience and his professional attainments.

This request is neither inspired by pride nor prompted by the spirit of a sybarite. I do not aspire to an iron chariot such as baffled the Almighty in his campaign against the Canaanites in the Valley (Judges 1:19), nor even to a buck board of a pattern rendered famous in more recent military history. Nay more, I do not even aspire to a participation in the wheeled glory of my juniors in rank on duty at Division Headquarters nor to the vehicular grandeur of a newly created quartermaster; but I would like to have a conveyance which I could leave standing with a reasonable degree of confidence that it would not be removed, in my absence, by a police party, as an offense against the landscape, or a menace to sanitation.

The vehicle with which I am now provided offers an appearance of impending disintegration not unlike that presented by a man with his suspenders broken and ten Mexican dollars in his trouser pockets; and its imitation of the "One Hoss Shay" is doubtless delayed only by a Castilian spirit of procrastination acquired from its makers.

To be sure, there remains the alternative of walking through the burning rays of a tropical sun, which would be perfectly feasible if one could escape a *cabeza caliente* or consider his liver with the same indifference that the late Mr. Vanderbilt entertained for the public. But the alternative of my melting away in perspiration or fading away in an atmosphere of humilation [*sic*] is not attractive to me, though it may not be devoid of hopeful features for the junior officers of my corps.

Trusting that this delay in the matter of providing me with a suitable conveyance is due merely to a climatic spirit of "*manana*" and is not an evidence of original sin on the part of the Quartermaster's Department, I am,
Very respectfully,

Arthur Wagner,
Lieutenant Colonel
and Assistant Adjutant General, U.S.A.

Appendix B

Wagner's Letter to
General J. Franklin Bell

ARMY WAR COLLEGE
WASHINGTON

My Dear Bell: April 28, 1904

I have reflected a great deal upon the matter which you recently mentioned; namely, that you had heard an objection made to my promotion on the ground that while I am acknowledged to be well versed—even "deeply versed"—in the theory of my profession, I am not "practical." On what this statement is founded, unless it is based merely upon prejudice or ignorance of facts, I am at a loss to know.

Even my enemies—and though I am fond of believing that my friends in the service are legion, I have *some* enemies—acknowledge that the part I have taken in military education has been of great benefit to the Army; but granting this, they proceed to damn me as a "theorist." They can not deny that my theories have been the basis of practical work on the part of the Army in time of war, and that such work being good the theories must have been sound, and that a theory to be sound must be practical. They can not (or at least, do not) point definitely to a single thing in which my theories or my personal work have been impractical, but simply assert that I am a "theorist," presumably because I have devoted my time to an assiduous study of my profession and have expressed the results of my studies in print. Thus the very work to which I have devoted myself for the good of the service—work to which I have given all the intelligence with which the Almighty has seen fit to endow me and all the industry of which my physical powers are capable—has been turned to my detriment, instead of my advantage. Surely it is not calculated to inspire young officers with a desire to cultivate their profession when they find a man's reputation as a military student used as a weapon against him.

If anybody can demonstrate that I have shown in post or field a want of practical qualifications, I shall have nothing to say; but I should like them to specify instances in support of their claim that I am "not practical." When, years ago, General Hazen relieved my first lieutenant from duty in order that I (then a young second lieutenant) might take the company in charge of a large convoy through hostile Indian country, *he* did not deem me a mere theorist. When General Terry detailed me to take a large wagon-train to General Miles's command, through swollen streams and "bottomless" alkali flats, during the "spring break up," when it was necessary to push supplies through to the front, it did not occur to *him* that I was not practical. When later I was detailed to construct a military telegraph line, there does not seem to have been any lack of practical qualifications on my part. When General Mackenzie placed me in command of his advance guard to prepare a ferry crossing for his force at the Gunnison River, *he* had no idea that he was intrusting this work to a mere theorist, nor had he any such idea when he selected me for duty as depot quartermaster at Gunnison. I might, as you personally know, mention a score of similar instances during my service as a young lieutenant. I am at a loss to know just when I ceased to be "practical." It was not while I was on college duty, for my work as a practical organizer of the military department gained the commendation of the college authorities and caused them to apply for an extension of my detail. It was not when I was on duty at Fort Douglas and General McCook declared that the company of which I was in command was one of the best drilled and administered companies in the regiment. If *he* had deemed me impractical he would not have applied for my detail at the Infantry and Cavalry School at Fort Leavenworth, nor would I have been continued there for so many years at the request of Colonel Townsend or General Hawkins if my work had been that of a mere visionary. When the tactical board adopted all the suggestions that I offered in regard to the drill regulations (both infantry and cavalry) *it* surely did not deem me impractical. Nothing that I originated during my long tour of duty at the Infantry and Cavalry School has since been reversed. Nothing that I instituted when I was in charge of the Military Information Division has been changed.

When I was in Cuba there was nothing that I was allowed to do that I did not do. I left Tampa in the face of the declaration of the Surgeon that I was not well enough to go into the campaign. I was with the "point" on the march and on the firing line in battle, when had I been at home I should have been on the sick report. Yet my services were commended and I believe they were of value. With the sole exception of General Chaffee's splendid reconnaissance of El Caney, I believe my reconnaissance work on the 30th of June to have been the most enterprising work of the kind in the campaign. This may seem egotistical and immodest, but it is the truth; and I would like nothing better than to have my work in that campaign carefully examined. My report has never seen light; it is doubtless sleeping in the War Department, and if it ever gains publicity it will probably be too late to do me any good. When I was in Porto Rico I was commended for my work, and when I was Adjutant General (practically Chief of Staff) of a force of 15,000 men in the field, in Luzon, General Bates surely did not deem my work impractical. When I served as Chief Umpire at the first three great maneuvers we have ever had on this continent, if there was anything impractical in my duties in either the preparation or the conduct of the maneuvers it seems to have escaped the observation of General Bates and other officers with whom I came in contact. When General Chaffee recently declined to send me to Japan, because (as he said) I am needed here for work on matters of great importance to the Army and the Nation, *he* surely did not deem me a mere theorist, for of what earthly use would an impractical man be on such work?

Assuming in the face of facts and my actual record that I am only a "theorist" (which I do not grant), is not the servant worthy of his hire? If my theories are of value to the country ought I to be damned for possessing them, and not rewarded for the good they have done and are supposed to do? Is it not inconsistent on the part of my superiors to continue making use of my work if such work deserves to be characterized as impractical? If this is to be the case, let us come out frankly and say that military study is prejudicial to an officer. Let us warn young officers to avoid study and caution them never to put pen to paper. Then, being devoid of all evidence of a studious interest in their profession, they may possibly be recognized as "practical" men, and escape being stigmatized as "theorists."

There is not, so far as I have been able to ascertain, a single thing in my entire military career that has been made a matter of adverse record at the War Department. If any blemish exist[s] on my record it has never been called to my attention and I have never been given an opportunity for explanation or denial. The only comment to my detriment that has ever reached my ears was a verbal remark by General Corbin, criticising my conduct in leaving my desk at the War Department (though with his consent) for the purpose of going to war! Surely it is a heinous offense for a soldier to seek service in the field instead of remaining to play the part of "the man behind the desk." But if I have sinned I have the satisfaction of being in illustrious company, for the President himself did practically the same thing; and if I happen, in any respect, to resemble him rather than General Corbin it is not such a misfortune that I am inclined to waste any time in lamentations over it.

I acknowledge frankly that I desire promotion, and I have reason to desire it. In the first place a man would be unworthy to hold a position in military service if he did not honestly aspire to a higher one, but in my case there is even a more vital reason. The consolidation of the Adjutant General's Department and the Pension and Record Division has blocked the advancement that I had good reason to expect. The present Military Secretary is but six months older than I am; and instead of seeing my way clear to the head of the corps for five years, as formerly seemed certain, I now find myself shut out until almost the very date of my retirement. To be sure, life is full of uncertainties, but it is not safe to base hopes of promotion on the prospect of the death of one's superiors before reaching the age of sixty-four.

But while I acknowledge that I desire promotion and intend to strive for it so far as may be proper, *you* know (whether anyone else does or not) that I would not ask for anything for which I did not honestly believe myself to be fitted. Possibly the natural egotism inseparable from human nature might cause me to place too high an estimate on my own record, but I think the judgment of my superiors as expressed in official papers may be relied upon as a deliberate and dispassionate estimate of my qualifications. I ask nothing but a careful comparison of my work and its value to the Army with the services of other officers of my grade. I have not a word to say to the detriment of any other applicant for promotion, and I readily concede all that their friends may justly claim for them; but I do not wish to have my own services misrepresented, and I feel—and, as you know, I am not alone in the belief—that certain people, unable to deny my actual record, have attributed to me a lack of "practical" qualifications, though such imputation is belied by my career and is apparently based solely on the assumption that an officer who has devoted his life to the study of his profession must be lacking in the power to apply practically his own deductions, though they are practically applied by others. I wish to combat most earnestly this unjust representation of my personal qualities, and I know that I can rely on you to assist me in doing so; for you have known me for thirty years and are personally familiar with the manner in which I have performed my duties of various kinds under many different conditions.

But though I find myself shut out from the head of my corps and find the brigadier generalcies of the line rapidly filling up with my juniors, I am not yet ready to quote Woolsey and say, "Had I but served my God," and all that dismal sort of thing. I know that I have the endorsement of our best and ablest soldiers; and if (as I believe will be the case) we shall have war within the next decade, and I get half a chance, I will endeavor to demonstrate that a man can be a practical soldier even if he has not allowed his intellect to go to seed.

With cordial regards and best wishes, I am,
Sincerely yours,
Arthur L. Wagner

General J. Franklin Bell, U.S.A.,
Fort Leavenworth, Kansas

Abbreviations

ACP	Appointment, Commission, and Personnel Branch, War Department
AGO	Adjutant General's Office, U.S. Army
ANJ	*Army and Navy Journal*
ARSW	*Annual Reports of the Secretary of War*
JMSI	*Journal of the Military Service Institution*
JUSCA	*Journal of the United States Cavalry Association*
JUSIA	*Journal of the United States Infantry Association*
MID	Military Information Division
NARA	National Archives and Records Administration
RG	Record Group
USAMHI	United States Army Military History Institute
USM	*United Service Magazine*
USMA	United States Military Academy

Notes

INTRODUCTION

1. For the charge that Wagner was "impractical," see Arthur L. Wagner to J. Franklin Bell, 28 April 1904, file 2908, ACP 1882, RG 94, NARA.

2. Considering Wagner's stimulating legacy to the army, perhaps the most surprising thing about his career is that it has, by and large, been overlooked by the community of American military historians. Wagner has not been totally ignored, but examinations of his career are limited to a few brief and fairly broad synopses. The best among these is Timothy K. Nenninger's *The Leavenworth Schools and the Old Army: Education, Professionalism, and the Officer Corps of the United States Army, 1881–1918*. Nenninger, the first present-day writer to "discover" Wagner, gives him about eight pages, covering the highlights of his career and how and why he was so important to the establishment of the Infantry and Cavalry School. Nenninger writes that Wagner's work there "laid the basis for Leavenworth methods, course content, doctrine, and overall objectives until World War I." In "Arthur L. Wagner: Doctrine and Lessons from the Past," a 1978 article for *Military Review*, Major Michael D. Krause claims that Wagner "helped shape our [American combat] doctrine in the latter part of the 19th and early 20th century." Furthermore, says Krause, Wagner "emphasized the combined arms even before there was universal recognition of the need for [an] integrated application of the combatant arms in battle." Most recently, Carol A. Reardon, in her *Soldiers and Scholars: The U.S. Army and the Uses of Military History, 1865–1920*, recognizes that Wagner was "one of the army's first and most influential proponents of the new ['safe leadership'] command philosophy," and writes about Wagner's role as an author of military history. Other works, while no less complimentary to Wagner, are far briefer in their examination of his effect upon the army.

3. Chester, "Military Misconceptions and Absurdities," 510; Chester, "Impending Changes." See also Chester, "Geniuses."

4. Wagner, "'Organization and Tactics': A Review Reviewed," 560.

5. Swift, "An American Pioneer in the Cause of Military Education," 71.

6. For the army's burgeoning school of "safe" military leadership, see Reardon, *Soldiers and Scholars*, 21–23.

7. Millett, *Military Professionalism and Officership in America*, 13.

8. Abrahamson, *America Arms for a New Century*, 34–36.

1. A MIND WHICH MATURED SLOWLY

1. "Personal Memoranda of Major General Eben Swift," 38–40, Eben Swift Papers, USMA Archives.

2. Swift, "American Pioneer," 67; William Thomas to Senator William E. Mason, 17 April 1898; R. W. McClaughry to Senator William E. Mason, 2 May 1898, 2908 ACP 1882, NARA; General Court Martial, Order No. 56, 6 December 1870, in Department of War, *Index of General Court Martial Orders*, 2–5.

3. Association of the Graduates of the United States Military Academy, *Thirty-Eighth Annual Reunion*, 27; *Official Register of the Officers and Cadets of the U.S. Military Academy, West Point, N.Y., 1871–1875; Register of Delinquencies, Classes of the United States Military Academy* 16: 260, 298; *Register of Delinquencies* 17: 64, 167, 214; *Post Orders, United States Military Academy, January 2 1872 to June 30 1875* 8: 183, 296, 422; Mrs. Betty G. Y. Shields to the author, 10 December 1992, author's collection.

4. Swift, "Personal Memoranda," 42–43, Eben Swift Papers, USMA Archives. Copies of the only surviving issue of the the "Weekly Spyglass," 28 July 1874, may be found in Swift's papers and in "Absalom Baird's West Point Memories," USMA Archives; Swift, "American Pioneer," 67.

5. Swift, "American Pioneer," 72; "Efficiency Report of 1st Lieutenant A. L. Wagner," 31 December 1891, file 2908 ACP 1882, NARA.

6. Wagner to AGO, 28 January 1892, file 2908 ACP 1882, NARA.

7. Wagner to AGO, 4 February 1892 and 11 February 1892, file 2908 ACP 1882, NARA.

8. Wagner to J. Franklin Bell, 28 April 1904; Arthur L. Wagner, "Military Record of Captain Arthur L. Wagner, Sixth Infantry, with Extracts from Letters on File at the War Department with His Application as Major in the Adjutant General's Department," file 2908 ACP 1882, NARA.

9. ANJ, 25 January 1879, 44; William B. Hazen to James Garfield, 5 May 1872, quoted in Hutton, ed., *Soldiers West*, 203.

10. Special Orders, Fort Buford, Dakota Territory, 1876–78, RG 393, NARA; Col. S. W. Groesbeck to Wagner, 13 February 1903; Wagner to J. Franklin Bell, 28 April 1904, file 2908 ACP 1882, NARA; Post Returns, Fort Buford, Dakota Territory, August–October 1876, RG 393, NARA; Wagner, *Military Record*, file 2908 ACP 1882, NARA; Special Orders No. 170, August 1878, Fort Buford, Dakota Territory, RG 393, NARA. According to his descendants, on the Glendive Wagner met William F. Cody, who told him of plans to start a wild west show. Some years later, during Wagner's assignment at Fort Leavenworth, Cody sent a coach and Indian outriders to Wagner's quarters to take him and his family to one of the shows (Shields to author, 10 December 1992).

11. Rodenbough and Haskin, *The Army of the United States*, 496–97; Wagner to Bell, 28 April 1904; Wagner, *Military Record*; Hamilton S. Hawkins to Wagner, 2 July 1895, file 2908 ACP 1882, NARA.

12. Hawkins to General George D. Ruggles, 12 November 1896; John A. Logan to AGO, 13 January 1880; Logan to AGO, 11 March 1880; Logan to AGO, 4 November 1881, file 2908 ACP 1882, NARA. For a profile of Senator Logan, and his antagonism toward West Pointers, see Weigley, *Towards an American Army*, 127–36.

13. R. C. Drum to William Preston Johnston, President, Louisiana State University, 20 December 1881; Drum to Wagner, 19 December 1881; Edwin P. Cater, Prin-

cipal, East Florida Seminary, to Robert Sinclair, Secretary of War, 19 November 1881; Johnston to Drum, 19 December 1881, file 2908 ACP 1882, NARA.

14. Swift, "American Pioneer," 69; "Report of the Board of Award," JMSI 5 (September 1884): 232; Weigley, *Towards an American Army*, 145.

15. Upton, *Armies of Asia and Europe*, 369; Wagner, "Military Necessities," 237–49, passim.

16. Wagner, "Military Necessities," 241, 249–60, passim; Upton, *Military Policy*, 66–67, 85, 256–57.

17. Wagner, "Military Necessities," 261–65, 267; Upton, *Armies of Asia and Europe*, 327–29.

18. Wagner, "Military Necessities," 265–67.

19. Wagner, "The Military and Naval Policy of the United States," 396. For the use of the army in labor unrest, see Cooper, *The Army and Civil Disorder;* Cooper, "The Army as Strikebreaker"; Hacker, "The United States Army as a National Police Force." For the general tenor of army reform, see Abrahamson, *America Arms for a New Century*; Jerry M. Cooper, "The Army's Search for a Mission, 1865–1890," and William R. Roberts, "Reform and Revitalization, 1890–1903," both in Hagan and Roberts, eds., *Against All Enemies*, 173–95, 196–218; Foner, *The United States Soldier between Two Wars*; and Peter Karsten, "Armed Progressives," in Karsten, ed., *The Military in America*. Edward M. Coffman's *The Old Army: A Portrait of the American Army in Peacetime, 1784–1898* is the best overall work on this period.

20. Cater to AGO, 17 March 1885; Cater to Wilkinson Cull, 16 March 1885; Cull to William C. Endicott, 4 April 1885, file 2908 ACP 1882, NARA; War Department, Special Orders No. 119, 25 May 1885; Wagner to AGO, 5 June 1885, file 2908 ACP 1882, NARA.

21. Wagner to AGO, 8 July 1886; wrapper endorsement, "leave of absence disapproved," 20 July 1886; Alexander McD. McCook to AGO, 3 October 1886; AGO to McCook, 12 October 1882, all in file 8 ACP 1882, NARA.

2. THE KINDERGARTEN

1. General Order No. 42, 7 May 1881, in Department of War, *General Orders and Circulars of the Adjutant General's Office* 1881; William T. Sherman to Philip H. Sheridan, 22 November 1881, in Hunt, *History of Fort Leavenworth*, 161; Sherman, *Address of General W. T. Sherman*, 1–13.

2. General Order No. 8, 26 January 1882, and General Order No. 42, 1881, in Department of War, *General Orders*; Sherman to Sheridan, 22 November 1881, quoted in Hunt, *History of Fort Leavenworth*, 161.

3. War Department General Order No. 8; Department of War, *Annual Report of the Secretary of War* (ARSW) 1882, 1:173–77; Sherman to Otis, 26 January 1882, in Nenninger, *Leavenworth Schools*, 24.

4. ARSW 1883, 1:198–203; ANJ, 17 November 1883, 303–4; Wagner, "Military Necessities," 262. See also Wagner, "An American War College," 288.

5. ANJ, 15 December 1883, 387; 1 March 1884, 633; 5 April 1884, 740.

6. ANJ, 15 March 1884, 667; King, "The Leavenworth School," 790–91. See also Spiller, "The Beginnings of the Kindergarten."

7. ARSW 1885, 1:211–14.

8. ARSW 1886, 1:210–13; ARSW 1887, 1:205–9; Sherman to Sheridan, 22 November 1881, quoted in Hunt, *History of Fort Leavenworth*, 161; U.S. Army, Historical Division, *Register of the Officers and Student-Officers and Regulations and Programme of Instruction of the U.S. Infantry and Cavalry School, Fort Leavenworth, Kansas* 1888, 1–11; Hagemann, ed., *Fighting Rebels and Redskins*, 72–73. See also Nenninger, *Leavenworth Schools*, 28–29; ARSW 1886, 1:212.

9. King, "Leavenworth School," 792; ARSW 1887, 1:205–07; *Regulations and Programme* 1888, 3–4; ARSW 1888, 1:197.

10. *Regulations and Programme* 1888, 14–20; ARSW 1887, 1:206.

11. Wagner, "Military and Naval Policy," 371.

12. Wagner, "Military and Naval Policy," 390, 395, 399; Upton, *Military Policy*, 291–92, 295–97, 307–8; Weigley, *Towards an American Army*, 109.

13. Upton, *Military Policy*, 61–63, 238–40, 336, 417; Wagner, "Military and Naval Policy," 397–99; Ambrose, *Upton and the Army*, 132; Weigley, *Towards an American Army*, 110, 116.

14. Vetock, *Lessons Learned*, 27.

15. ARSW 1888, 1:197; McCook to AGO, 4 October 1896, 2908 ACP 1882, RG 94, NARA; Wagner, *Königgrätz*, 4. The principal texts used by the Department of Military Art were Sir Edward Hamley's *The Operations of War, Explained and Illustrated* and Robert Home's *A Précis of Modern Tactics*. See *Regulations and Programme* 1888, 4, and Wagner, "An American War College," 289. McCook noted, however, that "illustrations from our own . . . wars were given by the instructors whenever the conditions were applicable." See ARSW 1889, 1:202.

16. Wagner to AGO, 14 February 1888, 2908 ACP 1882, RG 94, NARA; Wagner, *Military Record*, 2908 ACP 1882, RG 94, NARA.

17. Wagner, *Königgrätz*, 3–4.

18. Wagner, *Königgrätz*,, 73, 84–86, 97.

19. Wagner, *Strategy*, 28–29; Wagner, *Königgrätz*, 99.

20. Luvaas, *Military Legacy of the Civil War*, 102–3, 115–17, 137, 149–50, 193.

21. Reviews of *The Campaign of Königgrätz*, in the London *Broad Arrow*, 22 March 1890, and in the *Army and Navy Gazette*, 12 April 1890; "Reviews and Exchanges," JUSCA 2 (December 1889): 430; Tasker H. Bliss to Wagner, 8 February 1890; Wagner to Bliss, 14 March 1890, Bliss Papers, USAMHI; John P. Wisser, "Reviews and Exchanges," JMSI 10 (May 1889): 277–79. See also a review in the *Nation*, 30 January 1890, 99.

22. Wagner to Bliss, 11 February 1890, Bliss Papers, USAMHI; ARSW 1888, 1:194–95; ARSW 1889, 1:202; ARSW 1890, 1:203–4.

23. Wagner, "An American War College," passim.

24. Wagner, "An American War College," passim.

25. Sumner, "American Practice and Foreign Theory," 142, 146.

26. Chester, "Military Misconceptions and Absurdities," 504–5, 510; Chester,

"The Invisible Factor," 357; Chester, "Impending Changes," 84–85. See also Chester, "Geniuses." For Chester's military career, see his dossier in file 75, ACP 1880, RG 94, NARA.

27. Clausewitz, *On War*, 113, 122; DeForest, "Our Military Past and Future," 575; William H. Carter, "One View of the Army Question," 576; Carter, "The Infantry and Cavalry School at Fort Leavenworth," 753.

28. Wagner, in critics' discussion of Sumner's"American Practice and Foreign Theory," JUSCA 3 (June 1890): 150, 154–55; Wagner to Bliss, 14 March 1890, Bliss Papers, USAMHI; Wagner, review of Reginald Clare Hart, *Reflections on the Art of War*, JMSI 18 (January 1896): 224.

3. ENTHUSIASTIC PRUSSO-MANIACS

1. Griffith, *Battle Tactics*, 73–90, 189–92.

2. Upton, *Infantry Tactics*, 22–98. See also Ambrose, *Upton and the Army*, 63–65.

3. General Order No. 73, 1 August 1867, in Department of War, *General Orders*.

4. Du Picq, *Battle Studies*, 127, 146.

5. Among the more prominent and thoughtful such essays on the modern art of war were H. Elsdale, "The Coming Revolution in Tactics and Strategy," USM 7, new series (October 1892): 355–67; Francis V. Greene, "The Important Improvements in the Art of War during the Past Twenty Years and Their Probable Effect on Future Military Operations," JMSI 4 (January 1883): 1–41; W. W. Knollys, "The Effect of Smokeless Powder on the Wars of the Future," USM 6, new series (November 1891): 451–58; Henry M. Lazelle, "Important Improvements in the Art of War during the Past Twenty Years and Their Probable Effect on Future Military Operations," JMSI 3 May 1882: 307–73; John P. Wisser, "The Battle-Tactics of To-Day," USM 3, new series (June 1890): 565–75 and (July 1890): 37–46.

6. ANJ, 16 November 1878, 234; Upton, *Armies of Asia and Europe*, 270; Upton, *Infantry Tactics*, rev. ed. (1873), viii.

7. ANJ, 16 November 1878, 234–35; ANJ, 30 April 1881, 817; Henry M. Lazelle to General Sherman, ANJ, 26 November 1881, 359–60; "Shall We Have New Tactics?" ANJ, 26 November 1881, 363.

8. Sherman to Lazelle, ANJ, 26 November 1881, 360.

9. ANJ, 21 January 1888, 501; ANJ, 15 September 1883, 123; ANJ, 12 April 1884, 758; ARSW 1887, 1:78.

10. Lieutenant George Andrews to General J. C. Kelton, Assistant Adjutant General, 17 February 1888, file 526 AGO 1888, RG 94, NARA.

11. Wagner, "The New German Drill Book," 43–60.

12. Department of War, *Infantry Drill Regulations* 1891, 44, 186–97, 207–26.

13. Wagner to Captain E. S. Godfrey, 15 December 1892; Lieutenant Colonel John C. Bates to AGO, 6 May 1890; Brigadier General Thomas H. Ruger to AGO, 1 July 1890, file 526 AGO 1888, RG 94, NARA.

14. Major General John M. Schofield to Secretary of War, 21 September 1891, file 526 AGO 1888, RG 94, NARA; Richards, "Is the Tendency of Modern Drill Regulations Salutary?" 903.

15. Chester, "Modern Bobadilism," 35; Chester, "Dispersed Order and Individual Initiative," 362; Chester, "Military Conceptions and Absurdities," 518; Chester, "Military Discipline," 272.

16. See Miller, "Recruiting and Training of the Company," 68; Wagner, "Is the Three-Battalion Organization Necessary for Us?" See also Crites, "Development of Infantry Tactical Doctrine," 104–5.

17. For criticism of the extended order versus single rank formations, see ANJ, 27 October 1892, 156, and 4 March 1893, 468; and Department of War, *Infantry Drill Regulations* 1895.

18. Captain Fred C. Wilson to AGO, 6 June 1891, AGO file 9345; Inspector General, California National Guard to AGO, 6 May 1892, PRD 1892, AGO file 32326; Commanding Officer, Washington Barracks to AGO, 29 March 1892, PRD 1892, AGO file 28734; Captain H. W. Hubbell to AGO, 10 May 1895, AGO 1895 file 19788; Colonel William S. McCaskey to AGO, 16 May 1900, AGO 1900 file 435117, RG 94, NARA.

19. Wagner to Bliss, 11 February 1890, Bliss Papers, USAMHI.

20. Wagner to AGO, 8 April 1892; Wagner to AGO, 5 May 1892, file 2908 ACP 1882, RG 94, NARA. Wagner originally planned a third volume, tentatively titled *Logistics and Supply*, which was never completed. See Wagner to AGO, 20 April 1893, file 2908 ACP 1882, RG 94, NARA.

21. Wagner to Bliss, 21 December 1892; Wagner to Bliss, 26 December 1892, Bliss Papers, USAMHI; Wagner, *Security and Information*, 6.

22. Wagner to AGO, 20 April 1893; AGO to Wagner, 24 April 1893, file 2908 ACP 1882, RG 94, NARA.

23. Griffith, *Battle Tactics*, 228.

24. Wagner, *Security and Information*, 3–5.

25. Wagner, *Security and Information*, 8, 13, 46.

26. Wagner, *Security and Information*, 200–10.

27. Wagner, *Security and Information*, 233–35.

28. Wagner, *Security and Information*, 221–24.

29. Wagner, *Security and Information*, 225–26.

30. Wagner, *Security and Information*, 227.

31. Scott, *Some Memories of a Soldier*, 145; "Book Notices and Exchanges," JUSCA 6 (June 1893): 213–15; "Reviews and Exchanges," JMSI 14 (July 1893): 884–88.

4. ORGANIZATION AND TACTICS

1. Wagner to Bliss, 11 February 1890, Bliss Papers, USAMHI.

2. King, *Fleet Admiral King*, 64.

3. Wagner, *Organization and Tactics*, vi–viii.

4. Wagner, *Organization and Tactics*, 69–104. Wagner wrote that tactics are "dependent upon the nature of the weapons used; with each change in arms the method of handling troops in battle changes, and a knowledge of tactics must be sought in the lessons of the most recent wars, and in the study of existing conditions."

5. Wagner, *Organization and Tactics*, 468–71.

6. Wagner, *Organization and Tactics*, 105.

7. Wagner, *Organization and Tactics*, 104–9; 116–17; 161.

8. Wagner, *Organization and Tactics*, 109, 40, 45.

9. Wagner, *Organization and Tactics*, 39, 141–44, 391–93.

10. Wagner, *Organization and Tactics*, 45–46, 55–57, 59.

11. See Ambrose, *Upton and the Army*, 76–82.

12. Wagner, *Organization and Tactics*, 215, 232–40.

13. Wagner, *Organization and Tactics*, 307.

14. Wagner, *Organization and Tactics*, 307, 387–88.

15. Regarding the three arms in the attack, see Wagner, *Organization and Tactics*, 388–414; for the defense, 414–25. Wagner discussed withdrawals at greater length on pages 161–63 and 361–65.

16. Swift, "American Pioneer," 71.

17. Millett, *Military Professionalism and Officership in America*, 2.

18. See Wagner, "Chapters from *Organization and Tactics*," "Historical Sketch of the Organization and Tactics of Modern Cavalry," and "Cavalry in Attack and Defense," all in JUSCA; [Eben Swift], review of *Organization and Tactics*, JUSCA 7 (December 1894): 365–66; James Chester, review of *Organization and Tactics* in "Reviews and Exchanges," JMSI 16 (March 1895): 403, 407.

19. Chester, review of *Organization and Tactics*, 404–6; Wagner, review of Hart, *Reflections on the Art of War*, JMSI 18 (January 1896): 228.

20. Chester's review, in "Reviews and Exchanges," JMSI 16 (March 1895): 403–407; Wagner, "'Organization and Tactics': A Review Reviewed," 559–64; Wagner, "An Antiquated Artillery Organization."

21. ARSW 1894, 1:169; Arthur L. Wagner, "Report of the Instructor, Department of Military Art," in U.S. Army, Infantry and Cavalry School, *Annual Report of the Commandant* 1894, 18–24. McCook had been replaced in 1890 by Colonel Edwin F. Townsend, who in turn was replaced by Colonel Hamilton S. Hawkins in 1894.

22. Wagner, "Report of the Instructor," in *Annual Report* 1894, 19–20, 23–24; Wagner, "Report of the Instructor," in *Annual Report* 1895, 18.

23. "Report of Captain A. L. Wagner," 11 July 1894, file 6144 ACP 1886, RG 94, NARA; Wagner, "Report of the Instructor" 1894, 21; Swift, *Orders*, 21–22. See also Nenninger, *Leavenworth Schools*, 45–46, and Carol Reardon, *Soldiers and Scholars*, 23, 41, 103. For Wagner's comments on and suggestions for orders, see *Security and Information*, 100, and *Organization and Tactics*, 402–3. Swift developed the concept of "safe leadership" in his *Remarks, Introductory to the Course in Military Art*.

24. "Report of Captain Arthur L. Wagner," appendix B in *Annual Report* 1896, 18; Wagner, "Report of the Instructor," in *Annual Report* 1895, 18.

25. Wagner, "Report of the Instructor," in *Annual Report* 1894, 25; Wagner to the Secretary of the Infantry and Cavalry School, 20 March 1895, file 17317 AGO 1895, RG 94, NARA. See also Reardon, *Soldiers and Scholars*, 53–54.

26. Wagner, "Report of the Instructor," in *Annual Report* 1895, 19–20; "Report of Captain Arthur L. Wagner," in *Annual Report* 1896, 26–27.

27. Carter, "The Infantry and Cavalry School at Fort Leavenworth," 290.

28. Pettit, "Proper Military Instruction," 29–31.

29. U.S. Army, Infantry and Cavalry School, *Register of the Officers and Student-Officers and Regulations and Programme of Instruction* 1897, 18–21; Wagner, "Report," appendix B in *Annual Report* 1897, 2–5. American campaigns *were* covered in the lecture series; six American battles were discussed, as opposed to fifteen Napoleonic campaigns and a lecture on the Franco-Prussian War engagements of Metz and Sedan. See Wagner et al., *Strategical Operations.*

30. Pettit, "Proper Military Instruction," 30–31; Wagner, "Proper Military Instruction," 424–25.

31. Wagner, "Proper Military Instruction," 428.

32. Pettit, "Proper Military Instruction," 631–34.

33. Wagner, "Proper Military Instruction," 205, 207.

34. Bland et al., eds., *George C. Marshall Interviews,* 152.

5. THE VIEW FROM MOUNT PISGAH

1. Arthur L. Wagner to George D. Ruggles, 9 October 1896, file 2908 ACP 1882, NARA. In January 1895, Wagner tried unsuccessfully to wangle an appointment to the Inspector General's Department; see Wagner to James H. Eckels, 5 January 1895, file 2908 ACP 1882, NARA. See also ARSW 1897, 1:215–16.

2. Wagner's lecture series on military geography included discussion of Canada, Chile, Mexico, and Central America and was later published as *Military Geography.* Dickman's lecture was published as *Military Policy and Institutions.* The status and duties of the Military Information Division (MID) in 1897 may be found in a staff memorandum to the adjutant general dated 28 September 1897, MID file 639–6, RG 165, NARA. A contemporary account of the MID's history is W. A. Simpson to the Secretary of War, 21 February 1902, MID file 639–13, RG 165, NARA. The most comprehensive present-day history of the MID is Bruce W. Bidwell's *History of the Military Intelligence Division, Department of the Army General Staff: 1775–1941,* although his treatment of the division's formative years (1885–98) is perfunctory. More suitable are Elizabeth Bethel's "The Military Information Division: Origin of the Intelligence Division," and Marc B. Powe's *The Emergence of the War Department Intelligence Agency: 1885–1918.*

3. Captain Carl Reichman to Arthur L. Wagner, 8 February 1897, MID file 639–7, RG 165, NARA; Reichman to Wagner, "Notes on the Military Information Division," 14 September 1897, MID file 639–5, RG 165, NARA; Staff Memorandum, Carl Reichman to Adjutant General, 28 September 1897, MID file 639–6, RG 165, NARA; ARSW 1898, "Report of the Adjutant General," 1:282–83. See also Powe, *War Department Intelligence Agency,* 28–29.

4. Arthur L. Wagner to Secretary of War, 28 December 1897 and 26 February 1898, Army War College file 6831–1, RG 165, NARA. For Wagner's judgment of Rowan and Whitney, and other officers on the MID staff, see Wagner to Adjutant General, 30 December 1897, file 2908 ACP 1882, RG 94, NARA. See also Powe, *War Department Intelligence Agency,* 29–30, and Alger, *The Spanish-American War,* 42. Whitney's Puerto Rican reconnaissance is described in Miles, "The War with

Spain—III," 125, and in Chadwick, *Relations of the United States and Spain*, 2:358–59.

5. For Rowan's mission, see his *How I Carried the Message to Garcia* and "My Ride across Cuba" and Hubbard, *A Message to Garcia*. Rowan's accounts of this episode were written in the "thrilling adventure" style of the day, and while he credited Wagner for selecting him for the mission, Rowan limited his chief to a brief appearance. Rowan's nightly preparation by Wagner is in Betty G. Y. Shields to author, 10 December 1992, in the author's collection. See also Peake, "Andrew Summers Rowan and the Message *from* Garcia."

6. Adjutant General to Lieutenant Colonel A. L. Wagner, 29 March 1898, file 2908 ACP 1882, RG 94, NARA. For the deliberations of Wagner and Barker on the joint board, see Barker, *Everyday Life in the Navy*, 277–80.

7. Barker, *Everyday Life in the Navy*, 277–78.

8. Barker, *Everyday Life in the Navy*, 277–78.

9. Army and Navy Board, "Report for the Honorable Secretary of War," 4 April 1898, file 198209 AGO 1899, RG 94, NARA.

10. Army and Navy Board, "Report for the Honorable Secretary of War." For War Department assumptions, see Trask, *War with Spain*, 146–48.

11. Arthur L. Wagner, memorandum to Nelson A. Miles, 11 April 1898, in Nelson A. Miles Papers, USAMHI.

12. Wagner memorandum to Miles. For Miles's use of Wagner's memorandum, see Trask, *War with Spain*, 153, and Wooster, *Nelson A. Miles*, 212. Wagner received a commendatory letter from Miles stating that things might have been even worse in Cuba had Wagner been totally ignored. See Miles to Wagner, 3 January 1899, Spanish-American War Miscellaneous Collection, USAMHI.

13. Barker, *Everyday Life in the Navy*, 279–80; Powe, *War Department Intelligence Agency*, 33.

14. Arthur L. Wagner, Theodore Schwan, and W. H. Carter, "Memorandum for the Commanding General," 14 April 1898, file 147558 AGO 1898, RG 94, NARA.

15. Wagner, Schwan, and Carter, "Memorandum."

16. Wagner, Schwan, and Carter, "Memorandum"; Trask, *War with Spain*, 151.

17. Arthur L. Wagner to Adjutant General, 7 May 1898, file 2908 ACP 1882, RG 94, NARA.

18. Miles's initial approval of Wagner's idea was verbal, which led to questions about Wagner's authority while he was in Tampa. Not until 4 June did Wagner receive a written order, which spelled out precisely what his duties in Cuba would be. A copy of the order may be found in Wagner's *Santiago Campaign*, 15–16.

19. Funston, *Memories of Two Wars*, 156; Wagner to Adjutant General, 21 May 1898, file 2908 ACP 1882, RG 94, NARA.

20. Adjutant General to William R. Shafter, 4 June 1898; Miles to Wagner, June 11, 1898, both in Wagner, *Santiago Campaign*, 13–16; Wagner to Adjutant General, 21 May 1898; Wagner to J. C. Gilmore, Assistant Adjutant General, 21 July 1898, both in file 2908 ACP 1882, RG 94, NARA; Shafter to Henry C. Corbin, 16 August 1898, Corbin Papers, USAMHI; Wagner, *Santiago Campaign*, 42–43, 47–48. A Shaf-

ter biographer has described the general as a man who did not know how to cooperate after having spent many years with an independent and unquestioned command in the West. It is possible that Shafter resented any attempt by Miles to foist upon him an officer over whom he had no direct control. As for his curt dismissal of Wagner, the same biographer has described Shafter, among other things, as "coarse and abrasive." See Carlson, *"Pecos Bill": A Military Biography of William R. Shafter*, xi, 172. After the Santiago campaign, which did not flatter Shafter's command abilities, the general complained that he had been hampered in Cuba because "there were no topographical maps of the country. . . . I had my engineering officers . . . out each day making maps . . . but it was simply a dense mass of brush, and you had to cut your way through. . . . It was impossible to move an army through there." Wagner, of course, had given Shafter all the information he had collected on the area around Santiago, including the maps of Cuba and Santiago that had been published that year by the MID. See "Testimony of General William R. Shafter," in U.S. Senate, *Report of the Commission Appointed by the President to Investigate the Conduct of the War Department in the War with Spain*, Serial 3865, 7:3200–1.

21. Wagner to J. C. Gilmore, Assistant Adjutant General, 21 July 1898, file 2908 ACP 1882, RG 94, NARA.

22. Wagner, *Santiago Campaign*, 57–60; Trask, *War with Spain*, 217–24.

23. Wagner, *Santiago Campaign*, 61–63; Wagner to Gilmore, 21 July 1898, file 2908 ACP 1882, RG 94, NARA. Although Derby's balloon did discover a trail that aided the advance against San Juan Hill, Wagner scornfully noted that the trail could easily have been found by "a single small patrol" and noted that the balloon's destruction by Spanish fire brought "the infinite satisfaction of everyone." He blamed the balloon's presence for the needless loss of between sixty and one hundred men and found it "hard to understand what fantastic conception of the art of war could have caused such a reconnaissance to be seriously contemplated in the first place." See Wagner, *Santiago Campaign*, 81–82, 93–94.

24. Wagner, *Santiago Campaign*, 64–69.

25. Wagner, *Santiago Campaign*, 69–74.

26. Wagner to Gilmore, 21 July 1898; Wagner to J. Franklin Bell, 28 April 1904, both in file 2908 ACP 1882, RG 94, NARA; Wagner, *Santiago Campaign*, 102, 104.

27. Wagner, *Santiago Campaign*, 22–24.

28. Shafter testimony in U.S. Senate, *Report of the Commission*, Serial 3865, 7:3200–1. Wagner, *Santiago Campaign*, 69, 96–97.

29. Wagner, *Santiago Campaign*, 68, 80.

30. See Wagner, "Artillery in Attack and Defense," in *Organization and Tactics* 343–52. Wagner, *Santiago Campaign*, 106, 116; Wagner, Schwan, and Carter, "Memorandum."

31. Wagner, *Santiago Campaign*, 116–18. See Wagner, "An Antiquated Artillery Organization," 41–57, and *Organization and Tactics*, 387–88.

32. Wagner, *Santiago Campaign*, 116–18.

33. Wagner, *Organization and Tactics*, 170; Wagner, *Santiago Campaign*, 112–15.

34. Wagner, *Organization and Tactics*, 105, 141; Wagner, *Santiago Campaign*, 70, 75, 106, 108–10.

35. Wagner, *Santiago Campaign*, 125. An excellent summation of the conservative reaction to individualism in battle is Chester, "Dispersed Order and Individual Initiative."

36. General Order No. 53, 29 December 1896, in Department of War, *General Orders*; Crane, *Experiences of a Colonel of Infantry*, 278–79; Carter, *From Yorktown to Santiago*, 297; Bigelow, *Reminiscences of the Santiago Campaign*, 125; Wagner, *Santiago Campaign*, 125–26.

37. Wagner to J. Franklin Bell, 28 April 1904, file 2908 ACP 1882, RG 94, NARA; Wagner, *Santiago Campaign*, 8.

38. Henry C. Corbin to Wagner, 28 October 1899; Wagner to Corbin, 30 October 1899, both in file 2908 ACP 1882, RG 94, NARA; Parker, *The Old Army*, 299–303.

39. J. Franklin Bell to Adjutant General, 18 June 1903, file 2908 ACP 1882, RG 94, NARA. Wagner was assigned, briefly, to detached service on the southern islands of Jolo, Mindinao, and Cebu, organizing the home battalion of the Twenty-fourth Infantry. See Wagner to Adjutant General, 30 June 1900, and Wagner's consolidated service record, both in file 2908 ACP 1882, RG 94, NARA. For his letter requesting a new carriage, see Wagner to Depot Quartermaster, Manila, P.I., 6 July 1900, Spanish-American War Miscellaneous Collection, USAMHI.

40. Crane, *Experiences of a Colonel of Infantry*, 328; Wagner, *Security and Information*, 9th ed. (1903), title page and 3; Wagner, *Organization and Tactics*, 7th ed. (1906), x.

41. Report of Arthur L. Wagner, Headquarters Department of North Philippines, Manila, P.I., 22 March 1902, file 7788/2635, RG 395, NARA.

42. James F. Wade, Efficiency Report of Arthur L. Wagner, noted in Wagner's "Summary of Efficiency Reports"; Henry C. Corbin to William H. Carter, 4 February 1902; Elihu Root to Henry C. Lodge, Chairman, Committee on the Philippines, 22 May 1902; Assistant Adjutant General to Wagner, 24 May 1902, all in file 2908 ACP 1882, RG 94, NARA.

43. Statement of Col. Arthur L. Wagner, Assistant Adjutant-General, U.S. Army, in U.S. Senate, *Affairs in the Philippine Islands*, Serial 4244, 2846–80, passim. An excerpt from Wagner's testimony is reprinted in Henry F. Graff, ed., *American Imperialism and the Philippine Insurrection: Testimony taken from Hearings on Affairs in the Philippine Islands before the Senate Committee on the Philippines—1902* (Boston: Little, Brown and Co., 1969), 128–32.

6. MASTER OF THE ART OF WAR

1. Chester, "Impending Changes," 84–85.

2. Arthur L. Wagner, "Comments and Criticism," review of of J. B. Babcock, "Field Exercises and the Necessity for an Authorized Manual of Field Duties," JMSI 12 (September 1891): 1035–36.

3. The "maneuvers" staged by Miles are briefly described in Smythe, *Guerilla*

Warrior, 16–19. Merritt's exercises are noted in Babcock, "Field Exercises," 938–51. See also McKenna, "Forgotten Reform," 19–21.

4. U.S. Senate, *Creation of the American General Staff*, Serial 8254, 2.

5. ARSW 1899, 1:46, 48–49.

6. Special Orders No. 125, September 1901, in Department of War, *General Orders*; Heistand, "Requirements of a Maneuver Site," 470; William C. Carter to J. C. Bates, 18 August 1902; Bates to Adjutant General, 6 September 1902; Bates to Adjutant General, 10 September 1902, in file 443886 AGO, RG 94, NARA. For a more detailed examination of the events leading to the first Fort Riley maneuvers, see McKenna, "Forgotten Reform," 39–46.

7. Special Orders No. 150, Department of the Lakes, 29 August 1902, RG 393, NARA; "Proceedings of a Board of Officers Convened by Special Orders No. 163, Current Series, Headquarters Department of the Missouri," file 443886 AGO, RG 94, NARA; Wagner, "Fort Riley Maneuvers," 71. The other members of the board were Colonel C. C. C. Carr, Major Edward McClernand, and Captain Horace M. Reeve; see Bates to Adjutant General, 23 August 1902, file 443886 AGO, RG 94, NARA.

8. Wagner, "Fort Riley Maneuvers," 73, 87, 90; block quotation, 92–93.

9. Rules for umpires at Fort Riley may be found in Circular No. 1, Headquarters, Maneuver Division, Fort Riley, Kansas, 20 September 1902, file 443886 AGO, RG 94, NARA. Wagner's additional suggestions are in his *Report of Colonel Arthur L. Wagner . . . Camp Root*, 49–71; Wagner, "Fort Riley Maneuvers," 74–75; Bates to Adjutant General, 6 September 1902, file 443886, RG 94, NARA; "Resolutions Adopted by Officers of the National Guard of Various States and Territories," in ARSW 1903, 1:207; see page 203 for Bates's comment. Wagner's lecture was later published under the title *Strategy*.

10. Wagner, "Fort Riley Maneuvers," 71–73; Wagner, *Report . . . Camp William Cary Sanger*, 1–2.

11. Report of Major J. P. Duvall, General Staff, on the Maneuvers at West Point, Kentucky, file 458458/S AGO, RG 94, NARA; Johnston, "A Military Chautauqua," 84, 86; Sharpe, "Our Autumn Maneuvers," 66; Wagner, *Report . . . Camp William Cary Sanger*, 71–72, 126, 135, 245. See also Third Division General Staff, Memorandum Report No. 131, 30 July 1904, file 512391 AGO, RG 94, NARA.

12. Wagner to Chief of Staff, 27 July 1904; Adna R. Chaffee to Wagner, 30 July 1904; "Extracts from Official Papers on File in the Office of the Military Secretary, Pertaining to the Record of Colonel Arthur L. Wagner," General Staff, U.S. Army, in file 2908 ACP 1882, RG 94, NARA.

13. "Justice," letter to the editor, ANJ (16 January 1904): 508.

14. Wagner to Bell, 28 April 1904, file 2908 ACP 1882, RG 94, NARA.

15. Bell to Chaffee, 10 June 1904, file 2908 ACP 1882, RG 94, NARA. Scott, *Some Memories of a Soldier*, 223.

16. General Order No. 155, 27 November 1901, in Department of War, *General Orders*; ARSW 1903, 1:94. A board of officers was convened in July 1902 to determine the course of instruction at the Staff College. The board evaded this respon-

sibility, recommending only that instruction should include "many subjects which should be eliminated from the [Staff College] course when . . . elementary instruction at Posts shall have been established." The board assumed that some sort of "theoretical and practical instruction" would take place, but it did not say what kind or how much, although it did precisely fix the number of hours, by department, required for graduation. The format and curriculum for classes was decided by the head of each department. See Smith S. Leach, "Proceedings of a Board of Officers," 21 July 1902, AGO 444632, RG 94, NARA.

17. General Service and Staff College, *Annual Report* 1903, 9; Dickman to the Secretary, General Service and Staff College, 26 May 1903, file 484448 AGO, RG 94, NARA; Nenninger, *Leavenworth Schools*, 60; "Report on the Semi-Annual Examination," 2 January 1903, file 469189 AGO, RG 94, NARA.

18. Bell to War College Board, 31 July 1903, file 525015 AGO, RG 94, NARA.

19. J. Franklin Bell, "Report Containing Suggestions for Future Development of the General Service and Staff College," 31 July 1903, file 525015 AGO, RG 393, NARA.

20. Wagner, "Memorandum for the Commandant," 28 December 1903, printed in appendix H, General Service and Staff College, *Annual Report* 1904, 86–95.

21. Wagner, "Memorandum for the Commandant," 3–4, 96–102.

22. Wagner to Swift, 4 November 1903, Eben Swift Papers, USMA Archives.

23. General Order No. 115, 27 June 1904, in Department of War, *General Orders*. See pages 48–61 for regulations governing both schools. Bell to Adjutant General, 9 March 1904; Bell to Chaffee, 24 March 1904; Bell to Chaffee, 25 March 1904; Adjutant General to Swift, 1 April 1904, all in 6144 ACP 1886, RG 94, NARA.

24. ARSW 1901, 1:20–25; Tasker H. Bliss to Adjutant General, 11 November 1903, Bliss Papers, USAMHI (a copy of this report is printed in ARSW 1903, 4:89–98); Bliss, Memorandum as to the Proper Line and Work of the Army War College, 3 August 1903, in Ahern, "A Chronicle of the Army War College," 17–20; Memorandum from Office of the Chief of Staff, 2 February 1904 (no file number listed) in RG 165/3, "General Staff Personnel and Duties," NARA. A detailed examination of this period in the development of the Army War College is Ball, *Of Responsible Command*, 57–104. Bliss's interpretation of the War College's function was not insubordinate, for the language Root used in describing it was quite straightforward: the War College "should acquire the information, devise the plans . . . [and] advise the Commander-in-Chief upon all questions of plans, armament, transportation, mobilization, military preparedness and movement." See ARSW 1899, 1:49.

25. U.S. Army War College, Memorandum 1, 26 September 1904, in Bliss Papers, USAMHI; General Order No. 155, 17 September 1904, in Department of War, *General Orders*; Memorandum from Office of the Chief of Staff, 2 February 1904, RG 165/3, NARA. Wagner was also responsible for the drafting and publication of technical manuals, oversight of post libraries, assignment of officers to colleges and universities, examinations for promotion, a Board of Ordnance and Fortification, and the nation's coast and submarine defenses.

26. Bell to Wagner, 11 February 1904, file 2908 ACP 1882, RG 94, NARA.

27. Bell, Memorandum for the School Staff, 15 March 1904, file 2327, RG 393/244, NARA; Wagner to Bliss, 28 March 1904, Bliss Papers, USAMHI.

28. Infantry and Cavalry School and Staff College, *Annual Report* 1905, 1–2, 7–8; General Service and Staff College, *Annual Report* 1903, 5; Wagner, Memorandum Report No. 73, "General Order Governing the System of Military Education in the Army," 12 March 1904, RG 165, NARA; *Annual Report* 1903, appendix K, Report of W. W. Wotherspoon, Department of Tactics, 113–23.

29. Wagner, Memorandum Report No. 73, 12 March 1904, RG 165, NARA; War Department General Order No. 115, 27 June 1904 (pages pertinent to the Infantry and Cavalry School, Staff College, and the Army War College are 48–64).

30. War Department General Order No. 115, 27 June 1904; Wagner to Bell, 2 March 1905; Koester to the Military Secretary (no date), both in file 537 AGO 1905, RG 393/221, NARA.

31. Koester to Wagner, 17 February 1905; Wagner to Bell, 21 February 1905; Memorandum Report No. 37, Third Division General Staff, file 975871 MSO; Wagner to Bell, 3 March 1905, all in file 537 AGO 1905, RG 393/244, NARA.

32. Wagner, "Military Necessities," 254, 259; Wagner, "An American War College," 301–3; War Department General Order No. 115, 27 June 1904, 64–67; a lengthy series of memoranda and letters relevant to guard details at Leavenworth are in file 2125, RG 165, NARA.

33. War Department General Order No. 65, 22 December 1903. Corbin's involvement in the Manassas maneuvers is comprehensively described in McKenna, "Forgotten Reform," 77–98; this section follows closely the material found in those pages.

34. Chaffee to Corbin, 2 June 1904; Corbin to Chaffee, 4 June 1904; Bliss, "Memorandum on Second Maneuver Problem (8–9 September 1904) at Manassas," 5 December 1904, all in McKenna, "Forgotten Reform," 84–85.

35. Memorandum Report No. 118, Third Division General Staff, 21 July 1904, file 901830 MSO, RG 165, NARA; Wagner to Bliss, 11 August 1904, Bliss Papers, USAMHI; Wagner to Chief of Staff, Atlantic Division, file 927584 AGO, RG 94, NARA; Wagner, "Report of Chief Umpire of the Maneuvers at Manassas, Virginia," 20 September 1904, file 927584 AGO, RG 94, NARA.

36. "The Manassas Maneuvers, September 5–10, 1904: Remarks by Umpires," JUSIA 1 (October 1904): 63.

37. Edwards, "Personal Impressions of Manassas Maneuvers," 53, 63, 66–69; Wagner, "Combined Maneuvers," 71–73, 85–86. For Corbin's views of the Manassas maneuvers, see his "The Third Battle of Bull Run."

38. Sharpe and Hake, "The Ohio State Maneuvers," 34, 37–38; Wagner, "Combined Maneuvers," 69.

39. Wagner, undated memorandum in Bliss Papers, USAMHI; for Congress and the army's appropriation request, see McKenna, "Forgotten Reform," 97; Wagner, "Combined Maneuvers," 86–87.

40. Wagner, *Strategy*, 3, 5, 7, 9.

41. Wagner, *Strategy*, 9, 12–27, 43–45.

42. Wagner, *Strategy*, 45–55; block extract at 54–55.

43. Wagner to Bell, 2 March 1905, file 537 AGO 1905, RG 393/221, NARA; Wagner to Bell, 14 March 1905, Army War College file 3932, RG 165, NARA; Wotherspoon to Bell, 3 April 1905 and 31 March 1905, in file 2908 ACP 1882, RG 94, NARA.

44. Wotherspoon to Bell, 1 April 1905; Guy L. Edie, M.D., Medical Certificate to Accompany Application for Leave of Absence, 1 May 1905; Wagner to Military Secretary, request for leave of absence, 11 May 1905; Edie to Military Secretary, 24 June 1905, all in 2908 ACP 1882, RG 94, NARA; ANJ, 24 June 1905, 327; "Funeral of Col. Wagner," *Washington Post*, 21 June 1905, p. 10.

7. AMONG THE GENERALS

1. Mrs. Anne H. Wagner to Franklin Hudson, 7 July 1905; J. Franklin Bell to Anne H. Wagner, 2 July 1905; J. Franklin Bell to Captain Malin Craig, 11 July 1905; Fred C. Ainsworth to Chief of Staff, 15 January 1907; J. Franklin Bell, Memorandum for the Secretary of War, 18 January 1907, all in file 2908 ACP 1882, RG 94, NARA.

2. J. Franklin Bell to Anne H. Wagner, 2 July 1905, file 2908 ACP 1882, RG 94, NARA; Bell, "Explanatory Note," in Wagner, *Organization and Tactics*, 6th rev. ed. (1907), x. For the army's nineteenth-century experience with unconventional war in the Philippines, see Linn, *The U.S. Army and Counterinsurgency*, and Gates, "Indians and Insurrectos." Albert Buddecke, *Tactical Decisions and Orders*, trans. Arthur L. Conger (Kansas City: Franklin Hudson Publishing Co., 1908); Otto F. Griepenkerl, *Letters on Applied Tactics: Problems Dealing with the Operations of Detachments of the Three Arms*, trans. Charles H. Barth (Kansas City: Franklin Hudson Publishing Co., 1906); Fritz Bronsart von Schellendorff, *The Duties of the General Staff*, trans. H. A. Bethell, J. H. V. Crowe, and F. B. Maurice (London: His Majesty's Stationary Office, 1907); Department of Military Art, *Studies in Minor Tactics* (Fort Leavenworth: Army Service Schools Press, 1908).

3. American Expeditionary Force, *Combat Instructions*, 1, 4–5, 7–8.

4. Wagner, "Hasty Intrenchments in the War of the Secession"; see also Wagner, *Organization and Tactics*, 1st ed. (1895), 156–60. Major General Robert L. Bullard, letter to Chief of Staff, American Expeditionary Force, 22 July 1918, in U.S. Army, Historical Division, *United States Army in the World War*, 3:341.

5. Colonel W. K. Naylor, "The Principles of War," Command Course No. 12, Army War College, 1922, in Bliss Papers, USAMHI.

6. Quotes are by Forrest C. Pogue and Charles D. Herron, in Nenninger, *Leavenworth Schools*, 89; Nenninger discusses Morrison's tactical ideas and his influence on Leavenworth on pages 87–94.

7. Ball, *Of Responsible Command*, 106–7.

8. Vetock, *Lessons Learned*, 49.

9. For comments on Swift's abilities, see his efficiency reports in file 6144 ACP 1886, RG 94, NARA. Henry E. Eames, *The Rifle in War* (Leavenworth, KS: United States Cavalry Association, 1909); Oliver L. Spaulding, Jr., *Notes on Field Artillery* (Leavenworth, KS: United States Cavalry Association, 1914); Harold B. Fiske,

Leroy Eltinge, and Augustus Bennett, *Notes on Infantry, Cavalry and Field Artillery* (Washington DC: Government Printing Office, 1917); Oliver L. Spaulding, Jr., Hoffman Nickerson, and John Womack Wright, *Warfare: A Study of Military Methods from the Earliest Times* (New York: Harcourt, Brace and Co., 1925).

10. Swift, "American Pioneer," 71; Hunt, *History of Fort Leavenworth*, 174, 182; Spaulding, *The United States Army in War and Peace*, 394; Naylor, *Principles of Strategy;* Ganoe, *The Army of the United States*, 363, 422.

11. Krause, "Arthur L. Wagner: Contributions from the Past," 10; Swift, "American Pioneer," 72.

12. Wagner, "An American War College," 288, 304.

Bibliography

PRIMARY SOURCES

Manuscript Materials

Library of Congress, Washington D C
  Tasker H. Bliss Papers
  John M. Schofield Papers
  William H. Taft Papers
National Archives and Records Administration, Washington D C
Record Group 94
  Adjutant General's Office Files
  Appointments, Commissions, and Personnel Files
Record Group 165
  War College Division Files
  War Department General and Special Staffs File
Record Group 393
  Army Service Schools Documentary File
Record Group 395
  Corps, Division, and Brigade Files, Santiago Campaign
Record Group 404
  United States Military Academy Files
U.S. Army Military History Institute, Carlisle Barracks, Pennsylvania
  Tasker H. Bliss Papers
  Henry C. Corbin Papers
  Matthew Forney Steele Papers
  Eben Swift Papers
  Spanish-American War Miscellaneous Collection
U.S. Military Academy, West Point, New York
  John Bigelow Papers
  George W. Cullum Papers
  Matthew Forney Steele Papers
  Eben Swift Papers

Published Materials

Alger, Russell A. *The Spanish-American War*. New York: Harper and Brothers, 1901.
American Expeditionary Force. *Combat Instructions*. Chaumont, France: General Headquarters, American Expeditionary Force, 1918.

Association of the Graduates of the United States Military Academy. *Thirty-Eighth Annual Reunion of the Association of the Graduates of the United States Military Academy, at West Point, New York, June 13th 1907.* Saginaw MI: Seemann and Peters, 1907.

Babcock, J. B. "Field Exercises and the Necessity for an Authorized Manual of Field Duties." JMSI 12 (September 1891): 938–51.

Barker, Albert Smith. *Everyday Life in the Navy: The Autobiography of Rear Admiral Albert S. Barker.* Boston: Badger Press, 1928.

Bigelow, John. *The Principles of Strategy: Illustrated Mainly from American Campaigns.* Philadelphia: Lippincott, 1894.

———. *Reminiscences of the Santiago Campaign.* New York: Harper and Brothers, 1899.

Birkheimer, William E. *Historical Sketch of the Organization, Administration, Materiél and Tactics of the Artillery, United States Army.* New York: James J. Chapman, 1884.

Carter, William H. "The Evolution of Army Reforms." USM 3, series 3 (May 1903): 1190–98.

———. *From Yorktown to Santiago.* Indianapolis: Bobbs-Merrill, 1915.

———. "A General Staff Corps." USM 3, series 3 (January 1903): 677–81.

———. "The Greater Leavenworth." JUSCA 25 (October 1914): 173–89.

———. "The Infantry and Cavalry School at Fort Leavenworth." JMSI 15 (July 1894): 752–59.

———. "One View of the Army Question." USM 2, series 2 (December 1889): 573–78.

———. "Post-Graduate Instruction in the Army." *Educational Review* 24 (December 1902): 433–39.

———. "Recent Army Reorganization." USM 2, series 3 (August 1902): 113–20.

———. "The Training of Army Officers." USM 2, series 3 (October 1902): 337–42.

Chester, James. "Dispersed Order and Individual Initiative in Line of Battle Work." JMSI 32 (May–June 1903): 356–63.

———. "Geniuses." JMSI 23 (December 1898): 427–37.

———. "Impending Changes in the Character of War." JMSI 19 (July 1896): 83–89.

———. "The Invisible Factor in Problems of War." JMSI 28 (May 1901): 352–64.

———. "Military Discipline: Its Character, Acquirement and Use." JMSI 23 (September 1898): 268–79.

———. "Military Misconceptions and Absurdities." JMSI 14 (June 1893): 502–18.

———. "Modern Bobadilism or the Marksman's Method of Defeating an Army." JMSI 12 (January 1891): 30–41.

Clausewitz, Carl von. *On War.* Ed. and trans. Michael Howard and Peter Paret. Princeton: Princeton University Press, 1976.

Corbin, Henry C. "The Third Battle of Bull Run." *Cosmopolitan* 38 (November 1904): 3–14.

Crane, Charles J. *The Experiences of a Colonel of Infantry.* New York: Knickerbocker Press, 1923.

Davis, Richard H. *The Cuban and Porto Rican Campaigns.* New York: Scribner, 1898.

DeForest, John William. "Our Military Past and Future." *Atlantic Monthly* 44 (November 1879).

Department of War. *Annual Report of the Secretary of War.* Washington DC: Government Printing Office, 1882–1905.

———. *Correspondence Relating to the War with Spain and Conditions Growing out of the Same, Including the Insurrection in the Philippine Islands and the China Relief Expedition, between the Adjutant-General of the Army and Military Commanders in the United States, Cuba, Porto Rico, China, and the Philippine Islands, from April 15, 1898, to July 30, 1902.* 2 vols. Washington DC: Government Printing Office, 1902.

———. *General Orders and Circulars of the Adjutant General's Office.* Washington DC: Government Printing Office, 1867, 1881, 1882, 1892, 1896, 1901, 1904.

———. *Index of General Court Martial Orders.* Adjutant General's Office, 1870. Washington DC: Government Printing Office, 1871.

———. *Infantry Drill Regulations.* Washington DC: Government Printing Office, 1891, 1895, 1911.

———. *Infantry Drill Regulations.* New York: D. Appleton, 1904.

Dickman, J. T. *Military Policy and Institutions: A Lecture Delivered before the Class of Officers at the United States Infantry and Cavalry School, Fort Leavenworth, Kansas, January 16th, 1896.* Fort Leavenworth: Infantry and Cavalry School, 1896.

Du Picq, Charles Ardant. *Battle Studies: Ancient and Modern Battle.* Trans. Col. John N. Greeley and Maj. Robert C. Cotton. Reprint, Harrisburg PA: Military Service Publishing Co., 1946.

Edwards, Clarence R. "Personal Impressions of Manassas Maneuvers." JUSIA 1 (October 1904): 51–69.

Funston, Frederick. *Memories of Two Wars: Cuban and Philippine Experiences.* New York: Charles Scribner's Sons, 1911.

Dudley, Sir Edward Bruce. *The Operations of War, Explained and Illustrated.* Edinburgh, Scotland: W. Blackwood, 1872.

Hardee, William J. *Rifle and Light Infantry Tactics for the Exercise and Maneuvers of Troops.* 2 vols. Philadelphia: Lippincott, 1861.

Heistand, H. O. S. "Requirements of a Maneuver Site and the Measures Necessary to Secure the Same." JMSI 35 (November–December 1904): 470–76.

Home, Robert. *A Précis of Modern Tactics.* London: Harrison and Sons, 1873.

Hubbard, Elbert. *A Message to Garcia: Being a Preachment by Elbert Hubbard.* East Aurora NY: Roycrofters, 1899.

Johnston, William H. "A Military Chautauqua." JMSI 34 (January–February 1904): 84, 86.

Kennan, George. *Campaigning in Cuba.* New York: Century, 1899.

King, Charles. "The Leavenworth School." *Harper's Monthly* 76 (April 1888): 777–92.

King, Ernest J. *Fleet Admiral King: A Naval Record.* New York: W. W. Norton, 1952.

Miles, Nelson A. "The War with Spain—III." *North American Review* 169 (July 1899): 125–37.

Mott, Thomas Bentley. *Twenty Years as Military Attaché.* New York: Oxford University Press, 1937.

Parker, James. *The Old Army: Memories, 1872–1918.* Philadelphia: Dorrance and Company, 1929.

Pettit, James S. "The New Infantry Drill Regulations and Our Next War." USM 10, series 2 (July 1893): 1–13.

———. "The Proper Military Instruction for Our Officers: The Method to be Employed, Its Scope and Full Development." JMSI 20 (January 1897): 29–31.

3M "Proper Military Instruction." JMSI 20 (May 1897): 631–34.

Powell, William H. "A New System of Drill Regulations for Infantry." USM 9, series 2 (May 1893): 403–23.

Reichman, Carl. "Infantry Action and Our New Drill Regulations." USM 8, series 2 (August 1892): 105–24; (September 1892): 218–27.

Richards, Captain W. V. "Is the Tendency of Modern Drill Regulations Salutary?" JMSI 13 (September 1892): 903–6.

Rowan, Andrew Summers. *How I Carried the Message to Garcia.* San Francisco: Walter D. Harney, n.d.

Rowan, Andrew S. "My Ride across Cuba." *McClure's Monthly* 11 (August 1898): 372–79.

Schofield, John M. *Forty-six Years in the Army.* New York: Century, 1897.

Scott, Hugh Lenox. *Some Memories of a Soldier.* New York: Century, 1928.

Senate. *Affairs in the Philippine Islands: Hearings before the Committee on the Philippines of the United States Senate.* Senate Document No. 331, 57th Cong., 1st sess., 1902. Serial 4242–43.

———. *Creation of the American General Staff: A Personal Narrative of the General Staff System of the American Army, by Maj. Gen. William Harding Carter.* Senate Document No. 119, 68th Cong., 1st sess., 1924. Serial 8254.

———. *Report of the Commission Appointed by the President to Investigate the Conduct of the War Department in the War with Spain.* 8 vols. Senate Document No. 221, 56th Cong., 1st Sess., 1900. Serial 3859–66.

Sharpe, Alfred C. "Our Autumn Maneuvers." JMSI 34 (January–February 1904): 66.

Sharpe, A. C., and Charles F. Hake Jr. "The Ohio State Maneuvers, August 16–23, 1904," JUSIA 1 (October 1904): 34–42.

Sherman, William T. *Address of General W. T. Sherman, to the Officers Composing the School of Application at Fort Leavenworth, Kansas, October 25, 1882.* Fort Leavenworth: School of Application, 1882.

Sumner, Edwin V. "American Practice and Foreign Theory," JUSCA 3 (June 1890): 141–50.

Swift, Eben. "An American Pioneer in the Cause of Military Education." JMSI 44 (January–February 1909): 67–72.

———. *Orders.* Fort Leavenworth: Department of Military Art, Infantry and Cavalry School and Staff College, 1905.

———. *Remarks, Introductory to the Course in Military Art, at the Infantry and Cavalry School and Staff College, Fort Leavenworth, Kansas, by Major Eben Swift, 12th Cavalry, Instructor, September, 1904.* Fort Leavenworth: Department of Military Art, Infantry and Cavalry School and Staff College, 1904.

Upton, Emory. *The Armies of Asia and Europe: Embracing Official Reports on the Armies of Japan, China, India, Persia, Italy, Russia, Austria, Germany, France, and England.* New York: D. Appleton, 1878.

———. *The Military Policy of the United States.* Washington DC: Government Printing Office, 1904.

———. *A New System of Infantry Tactics, Double and Single Rank, Adapted to American Topography and Improved Firearms.* Rev. ed. New York: D. Appleton, 1873.

U.S. Army. General Service and Staff College. *Annual Report of the Commandant of the U.S. Army General Service and Staff College.* Washington DC: Government Printing Office, 1902–4.

———. Historical Division. *United States Army in the World War, 1917–1919.* Vol. 3, *Training.* Washington DC: Government Printing Office, 1948.

———. Infantry and Cavalry School. *Annual Report of the Commandant, U.S. Infantry and Cavalry School.* Fort Leavenworth: U.S. Infantry and Cavalry School, 1882–97.

———. *Register of the Officers and Student-Officers and Regulations and Programme of Instruction of the U.S. Infantry and Cavalry School, Fort Leavenworth, Kansas.* Fort Leavenworth: U.S. Infantry and Cavalry School, 1888, 1890, 1895, 1897.

———. *Register of the Officers and Student-Officers of the U.S. Infantry and Cavalry School, Fort Leavenworth, Kansas.* Fort Leavenworth: U.S. Infantry and Cavalry School, 1887.

U.S. Army. Infantry and Cavalry School and Staff College. *Annual Report.* 1905.

Wagner, Arthur L. "American Practice and Foreign Theory." JUSCA 3 (June 1890): 150–55.

———. "An American War College." JMSI 10 (July 1889): 287–304.

———. "An Antiquated Artillery Organization." JMSI 17 (July 1895): 41–57.

———. *The Army of the United States: Being an Historical Sketch from the Earliest Period to the Present Time, with an Account of its Organization and Administration, a Synopsis of the Achievements of the Army in the Spanish War, and Some Remarks on Our Military Necessities.* Akron OH: Werner Publishing Co., 1899.

———. *Books for a Military Library.* Fort Leavenworth: Infantry and Cavalry School Press, 1895.

———. *The Campaign of Königgrätz: A Study of the Austro-Prussian Conflict in the Light of the American Civil War.* Leavenworth KS: C. J. Smith and Co., 1889.

———. *A Catechism of Outpost Duty: Including Reconnaissance, Independent Cavalry, Advance Guards, Rear Guards, Outposts, Etc.* Kansas City MO: Franklin Hudson Publishing Co., 1897.

———. "Cavalry in Attack and Defense." JUSCA 7 (March 1894): 3–40.

———. "Chapters from *Organization and Tactics*." JUSCA 6 (September 1893): 241–97.

———. "Combined Maneuvers of the Regular Army and Organized Militia." JMSI 36 (January 1905): 62–87.

———. "The Fort Riley Maneuvers." JMSI 32 (January 1903): 70–93.

———. "Hasty Intrenchments in the War of Secession." JMSI 22 (February 1898): 225–46.

———. "Historical Sketch of the Organization and Tactics of Modern Cavalry." JUSCA 6 (December 1893): 382–415.

———. "Is the Three-Battalion Organization Necessary for Us?" JMSI 15 (January 1894): 122–25; (May 1894): 567–70.

———. "The Military and Naval Policy of the United States." JMSI 7 (December 1886): 371–403.

———. *Military Geography: Being Lectures in the Department of Military Art, Delivered before the Class of Officers at the U.S. Infantry and Cavalry School, Fort Leavenworth, Kansas, 1893–1895.* Fort Leavenworth: Infantry and Cavalry School Press, 1895.

———. "The Military Necessities of the United States, and the Best Provisions for Meeting Them." JMSI 5 (September 1884): 237–71.

———. "The New German Drill Book and Some Deductions Therefrom." JUSCA 2 (March 1889): 43–60.

———. *Organization and Tactics.* Kansas City MO: Hudson-Kimberly Publishing Co., 1895.

———. "'Organization and Tactics': A Review Reviewed." JMSI 17 (May 1895): 559–64.

———. "Proper Military Instruction." JMSI 20 (March 1897): 421–29; 21 (July 1897): 205–8.

———. *Report of Colonel Arthur L. Wagner, Assistant Adjutant General, United States Army, Chief Umpire, Maneuver Division, Camp Root, Fort Riley, Kansas, 1902.* Kansas City MO: Hudson-Kimberly Publishing Co., 1902.

———. *Report of Colonel Arthur L. Wagner, Assistant Adjutant General, United States Army, Chief Umpire, Maneuver Division, Camp William Cary Sanger, Fort Riley, Kansas, 1903.* Kansas City MO: Hudson-Kimberly Publishing Co., 1903.

———. *Report of Colonel Arthur L. Wagner, Assistant Adjutant General, United States Army, Chief Umpire, Maneuver Division, Camp Young, West Point, Kentucky, 1903.* Kansas City MO: Hudson-Kimberly Publishing Co., 1903.

———. *Report of Colonel Arthur L. Wagner, General Staff, U.S. Army, Chief Umpire, Ohio Maneuvers, 1904.* Columbus OH: Adjutant General Department, Ohio National Guard, 1904.

————. *Report of the Santiago Campaign, 1898.* Kansas City MO: F. Hudson Publishing Co., 1908.

————. Review of Reginald Clare Hart, *Reflections on the Art of War*, JMSI 18 (January 1896): 228–31.

————. *The Service of Security and Information.* Kansas City MO: Hudson-Kimberly Publishing Co., 1893.

————. *Strategy: A Lecture Delivered by Colonel Arthur L. Wagner, Assistant Adjutant-General, U.S.A., to the Officers of the Regular Army and National Guard at the Maneuvers at West Point, Kentucky, and at Fort Riley, Kansas, 1903.* Kansas City MO: Hudson-Kimberly Publishing Co., 1904.

————. "The Value and Limitation of Field Exercises." JMSI 12 (September 1891): 1034–36.

Wagner, Arthur L., ed. *Cavalry Studies from Two Great Wars by Lt. Col. Bonie, Major Kaehler, and Lt. Col. George B. Davis.* Kansas City MO: Hudson-Kimberly Publishing Co., 1896.

————. *Cavalry vs. Infantry, and Other Essays by Captain F. N. Maude.* Kansas City MO: Hudson-Kimberly Publishing Co., 1895.

————. *Extracts from an Infantry Captain's Journal, or the Trial of a Method for Effectively Training a Company in Skirmishing and Outpost Duty, in a Limited Time, and under Unfavorable Circumstances, by General von Arnim.* Kansas City MO: Hudson-Kimberly Publishing Co., 1897.

————. *Military Letters and Essays by Captain F. N. Maude.* Kansas City MO: Hudson-Kimberly Publishing Co., 1894.

————. *Tactical Studies on the Battles Around Plevna by Thilo von Trotha.* Kansas City MO: Hudson-Kimberly Publishing Co., 1897.

Wagner, Arthur L., and Commander J. D. Jerrold Kelly. *Our Country's Defensive Forces in War and Peace: The U.S. Army and Navy, Their Histories, with Accounts of Their Organization, Administration, and Duties.* New York: Century, 1899.

Wagner, Arthur L., Eben Swift, J. T. Dickman, and A. L. Mills. *Strategical Operations, Illustrated by Great Campaigns in Europe and America.* Fort Leavenworth: United States Infantry and Cavalry School, 1897.

Wheeler, Joseph. *The Santiago Campaign, 1898.* New York, 1898; reprint, Port Washington NY: Kennikat Press, 1971.

SECONDARY SOURCES

Abrahamson, James L. *America Arms for a New Century: The Making of a Great Military Power.* New York: Free Press, 1981.

Ahern, George P. "A Chronicle of the Army War College, 1899–1919." Unpublished. Army War College, 24 June 1919. Copy in United States Army Military History Institute Library.

Ambrose, Stephen. *Upton and the Army.* Baton Rouge: Louisiana State University Press, 1964.

Andrews, Richard A. "Years of Frustration: William T. Sherman, the Army and Reform, 1869–1883." Ph.D. dissertation, Northwestern University, 1968.

Ball, Harry P. *Of Responsible Command: A History of the U.S. Army War College.* Carlisle Barracks PA: Alumni Association of the United States Army War College, 1983.

Bethel, Elizabeth. "The Military Information Division: Origin of the Intelligence Division." *Military Affairs* 11 (spring 1947): 17–24

Bidwell, Bruce W. *History of the Military Intelligence Division, Department of the Army General Staff: 1775–1941.* Frederick MD: University Publications of America, Inc., 1986.

Bland, Larry, and Sharon R. Ritenour, eds. *The Papers of George Catlett Marhall.* 3 vols. Baltimore: Johns Hopkins University Press, 1981.

Bland, Larry, Joellen K. Bland, and Sharon Ritenour Stevens, eds. *George C. Marshall Interviews and Reminiscences for Forrest C. Pogue.* Rev. ed. Lexington VA.: George C. Marshall Research Foundation, 1991.

Bradford, James C., ed. *Crucible of Empire: The Spanish-American War and Its Aftermath.* Annapolis MD.: Naval Institute Press, 1993.

Carlson, Paul H. *"Pecos Bill": A Military Biography of William R. Shafter.* College Station: Texas A&M University Press, 1989.

Chadwick, French Ensor. *The Relations of the United States and Spain: The Spanish-American War.* 2 vols. New York: Charles Scribner's Sons, 1911.

Coffmann, Edward M. *The Hilt of the Sword: The Career of Peyton C. March.* Madison: University of Wisconsin Press, 1966.

———. *The Old Army: A Portrait of the Army in Peacetime, 1784–1898.* New York: Oxford University Press, 1986.

Cooling, Benjamin Franklin. "To Preserve the Peace." *Washington History* 1 (spring 1989): 70–86.

Cooper, Jerry M. *The Army and Civil Disorder: Federal Military Intervention in American Labor Disputes, 1877–1900.* Westport CT: Greenwood Press, 1980.

———. "The Army as Strikebreaker: The Railroad Strikes of 1877 and 1894," *Labor History* 18 (spring 1977): 179–96.

Cosmas, Graham A. *An Army for Empire: The United States Army in the Spanish-American War.* Columbia: University of Missouri Press, 1971.

Crites, William Ralph. "The Development of Infantry Tactical Doctrine in the United States Army, 1865–1898." Master's thesis, Duke University, 1968.

Feuer, A. B. *The Santiago Campaign of 1898: A Soldier's View of the Spanish-American War.* Westport CT: Praeger Publishers, 1993.

Foner, Jack. *The United States Soldier between Two Wars: Army Life and Reforms, 1865–1898.* New York: Humanities Press, 1970.

Ganoe, William A. *The Army of the United States.* New York: D. Appleton–Century, 1924.

Gates, John M. "Indians and Insurrectos: The U.S. Army's Experience with Insurgency." *Parameters* 13 (March 1983): 59–68.

———. *Schoolbooks and Krags: The United States Army in the Philippines, 1898–1902.* Westport CT: Greenwood Press, 1973.

Griffith, Paddy. *Battle Tactics of the Civil War.* New Haven: Yale University Press, 1989.

Hacker, Barton C. "The United States Army as a National Police Force: The Federal Policing of Labor Disputes." *Military Affairs* 33 (April 1969): 255–64.

Hagan, Kenneth J., and William R. Roberts. *Against All Enemies: Interpretations of American Military History from Colonial Times to the Present.* Westport CT: Greenwood Press, 1986.

Hagemann, E. R., ed. *Fighting Rebels and Redskins: Experiences in the Army Life of Colonel George B. Sanford, 1861–1892.* Norman: University of Oklahoma Press, 1969.

Heller, Charles E., and William A. Stofft, eds. *America's First Battles, 1776–1965.* Lawrence: University Press of Kansas, 1986.

Hill, Michael D., and Ben Innis, eds. "The Fort Buford Diary of Private Sanford, 1876–1877." *North Dakota History* 52 (summer 1985): 2–40.

House, Jonathan M. *Toward Combined Arms Warfare: A Survey of 20th-Century Tactics, Doctrine, and Organization.* Washington DC: Government Printing Office, 1985.

Hunt, Elvid. *History of Fort Leavenworth, 1827–1927.* Fort Leavenworth KS: General Service Schools Press, 1926.

Hutton, Paul Andrew. *Phil Sheridan and His Army.* Lincoln: University of Nebraska Press, 1985.

Hutton, Paul Andrew, ed. *Soldiers West: Biographies from the Military Frontier.* Lincoln: University of Nebraska Press, 1987.

Jamieson, Perry. *Crossing the Deadly Ground: United States Infantry Tactics, 1865–98.* Lawrence: University Press of Kansas, 1995.

Karsten, Peter, ed. *The Military in America: From the Colonial Era to the Present.* New York: Free Press, 1986.

Kemble, C. Robert. *The Image of the Army Officer in America: Background for Current Views.* Westport CT: Greenwood Press, 1973.

Krause, Michael D. "Arthur L. Wagner: Contributions from the Past." Unpublished. Combat Studies Institute, United States Army Command and General Staff College Hall of Fame Files, Fort Leavenworth, Kansas, 5 May 1978.

———. "Arthur L. Wagner: Doctrine and Lessons from the Past." Military Review 58 (November 1978): 53–59.

Kreidberg, Marvin A., and Merton G. Henry. *History of Military Mobilization in the United States Army, 1775–1945.* Washington DC: Government Printing Office, 1955.

Lane, Jack C. *Armed Progressive: General Leonard Wood.* San Rafael CA: Presidio Press, 1978.

Linn, Brian McAllister. *The U.S. Army and Counterinsurgency in the Philippine War, 1899–1902.* Chapel Hill: University of North Carolina Press, 1989.

Luvaas, Jay. *The Military Legacy of the Civil War: The European Inheritance.* Chicago: University of Chicago Press, 1959.

Masland, John W., and Laurence I. Radway. *Soldiers and Scholars: Military Education and National Policy*. Princeton: Princeton University Press, 1957.

McKenna, Charles D. "The Forgotten Reform: Field Maneuvers in the Development of the United States Army, 1902–1920." Ph.D. dissertation, Duke University, 1981.

Michie, Peter S. *The Life and Letters of Emory Upton*. New York: D. Appleton and Co., 1885.

Miller, Stuart Creighton. *"Benevolent Assimilation": The American Conquest of the Philippines, 1899–1903*. New Haven CT: Yale University Press, 1982.

Millett, Alan R. *The General: Robert L. Bullard and Officership in the United States Army, 1881–1925*. Westport CT: Greenwood Press, 1975.

———. *Military Professionalism and Officership in America*. Mershon Center Briefing Paper No. 2. Columbus OH: Mershon Center, Ohio State University, 1977.

Naylor, William K. *Principles of Strategy, with Historical Illustrations*. Fort Leavenworth KS: General Service Schools Press, 1921.

Nenninger, Timothy. *The Leavenworth Schools and the Old Army: Education, Professionalism, and the Officer Corps of the United States Army, 1881–1918*. Westport CT: Greenwood Press, 1978.

Osterhoudt, Henry J. "Towards Organized Disorder: The Evolution of American Infantry Assault Tactics, 1778–1919." Master's thesis, Duke University, 1980.

Peake, Louis A. "Andrew Summers Rowan and the Message *from* Garcia." *West Virginia History* 44 (spring 1983): 226–40.

Palmer, Frederick. *Bliss, Peacemaker: The Life and Letters of General Tasker Howard Bliss*. New York: Dodd, Mead and Co., 1934.

Pappas, George S. *Prudens Futuri: The U.S. Army War College, 1901–1967*. Carlisle Barracks PA: Alumni Association, U.S. Army War College, 1967.

Paret, Peter, ed. *Makers of Modern Strategy from Machiavelli to the Nuclear Age*. Princeton: Princeton University Press, 1986.

Pogue, Forrest C. *George C. Marshall: Education of a General, 1880–1939*. New York: Viking Press, 1963.

Pohl, James W. "The General Staff and American Military Policy: The Formative Period, 1898–1917." Ph.D. dissertation, University of Texas, 1967.

Powe, Marc B. *The Emergence of the War Department Intelligence Agency: 1885–1918*. Manhattan KS: Military Affairs, 1975.

Raines, Edgar F., Jr. "The Early Career of Major General J. Franklin Bell, USA, 1856–1903." Master's thesis, Southern Illinois University, 1968.

Reardon, Carol A. *Soldiers and Scholars: The U.S. Army and the Uses of Military History, 1865–1920*. Lawrence: University Press of Kansas, 1990.

Reeves, Ira L. *Military Education in the United States*. Burlington VT: Free Press Printing, 1914.

Rodenbough, Theodore F., and William L. Haskin. *The Army of the United States: Historical Sketches of Staff and Line with Portraits of Generals-in-Chief*. New York: Maynard, Merrill and Co., 1896.

Roth, Russell. *Muddy Glory: America's "Indian Wars" in the Philippines, 1899–1935.* West Hanover, MA: Christopher Publishing House, 1981.

Shindler, Henry. *History of the Army Service Schools, Fort Leavenworth, Kansas.* Fort Leavenworth: Staff College Press, 1908.

Smythe, Donald. *Guerilla Warrior: The Early Life of John J. Pershing.* New York: Charles Scribner's Sons, 1973.

Spaulding, Oliver L. *The United States Army in War and Peace.* New York: Putnam, 1937.

Spiller, Roger J. "The Beginnings of the Kindergarten." *Military Review* 61 (May 1981): 2–12.

Steele, Matthew Forney. *American Campaigns.* Washington DC: B. S. Adams, 1909.

Trask, David F. *The War with Spain in 1898.* New York: Macmillan, 1981.

Utley, Robert M. *Frontier Regulars: The United States Army and the Indian, 1866–1891.* New York: Macmillan, 1973.

Vetock, Dennis J. *Lessons Learned: A History of U.S. Army Lesson-Learning.* Carlisle Barracks PA: U.S. Army Military History Institute, 1988.

Wainwright, John D. "Root vs. Bliss: The Shaping of the Army War College." *Parameters* 4 (spring 1974): 52–65.

Walton, George. *Sentinel of the Plains: Fort Leavenworth and the American West.* Englewood Cliffs NJ: Prentice-Hall, 1973.

Weigley, Russell F. *Towards an American Army: Military Thought from Washington to Marshall.* New York: Columbia University Press, 1962.

Wooster, Robert. *The Military and United States Indian Policy, 1865–1903.* New Haven CT: Yale University Press, 1980.

———. *Nelson A. Miles and the Twilight of the Frontier Army.* Lincoln: University of Nebraska Press, 1993.

Index